MW01482661

The Outsourcing Enterprise

Advanced praise for *The Outsourcing Enterprise*

'Leslie Willcocks has been a reliable guide to the latest outsourcing fashions for years. Here he and his colleagues are once again ahead of the curve in showing how sophisticated outsourcers are building collaborations and adding value, not just cutting costs. With examples from Machiavelli to leading-edge IT businesses, *The Outsourcing Enterprise* is an entertaining and practical guide to best practices.' – **Sir Howard Davies**, *Director, London School of Economics and Political Science*

'An invaluable guide to professional practice. This book is carefully thought through and well illustrated with myriad examples from the USA, Europe and Asia Pacific. As a CIO who has been and is still working in multiple industries and countries, I know too well precisely what the authors are describing and recognize from my own experience the value of their work in systematizing and distilling the practices that make the difference. This book should be on every outsourcing professional's desk.' – **Peter Mahler**, *CIO, Axa Australia, and formerly Coles Myer and Belgacom*

'Frustrated by the sense that you're failing to cash in on the opportunities that outsourcing presents? This book's for you! It's directive, insightful, and easy to read: the authors have leveraged their enormous research base to explain how smart companies can create real business advantage from strategic outsourcing.' – **Dr Jeanne W. Ross**, *Director, MIT Center for Information Systems Research, MIT Sloan School of Management*

'With two thirds of our members telling us that senior executives are more involved in outsourcing decisions than ever before, the timing of this book could not be better. Here Leslie Willcocks and colleagues ... show how outsourcing can produce great results, but only when outsourcing professionals ensure great execution.' – **Michael F. Corbett**, *Chairman, International Association of Outsourcing Professionals*

'Based on the learning from some 2500 practitioners, this book is an excellent source for CEOs, strategists, or anyone needing to understand the drivers and issues of outsourcing, especially global outsourcing, and how to use these opportunities to propel their business forward. The UK's National Outsourcing Association (part of the European Outsourcing Association) fully endorses this book's central theme that outsourcing has now moved firmly to the strategic corporate agenda.... It would be very useful to those considering or taking qualifications in outsourcing, such as the NOA's degree or Masters Pathway courses.' – **Martyn Hart**, *Chairman, National Outsourcing Association*

'If you are looking for a blueprint for understanding how to leverage external services, this book is required reading. IT and business executives, consultants, and academics alike, will find it invaluable .... Fundamental to attaining your strategic external services objectives is active engagement by the appropriate senior business executives. Demonstrating why and exactly how they should care is the decisive contribution made by this book.' – **Jerry Luftman**, *Executive Director & Distinguished Professor, Stevens Institute of Technology, New Jersey, USA*

Technology, Work, and Globalization

The Technology, Work, and Globalization series was developed to provide policy makers, workers, managers, academics, and students with a deeper understanding of the complex interlinks and influences between technological developments, including information and communication technologies, work organizations, and patterns of globalization. The mission of the series is to disseminate rich knowledge based on deep research about relevant issues surrounding the globalization of work that is spawned by technology.

Also in the series:

GLOBAL SOURCING OF BUSINESS AND IT SERVICES
Leslie P. Willcocks and Mary C. Lacity

ICT AND INNOVATION IN THE PUBLIC SECTOR
Francesco Contini and Giovan Francesco Lanzara

EXPLORING VIRTUALITY WITHIN AND BEYOND ORGANIZATIONS
Niki Panteli and Mike Chaisson

KNOWLEDGE PROCESSES IN GLOBALLY DISTRIBUTED CONTEXTS
Julia Kotlarsky, Ilan Oshri, and Paul C. van Fenema

GLOBAL CHALLENGES FOR IDENTITY POLICIES
Edgar Whitley and Ian Hosein

E-GOVERNANCE FOR DEVELOPMENT
A Focus on India
Shirin Madon

OFFSHORE OUTSOURCING OF IT WORK
Mary C. Lacity and Joseph W. Rottman

OUTSOURCING GLOBAL SERVICES
Ilan Oshri, Julia Kotlarsky, and Leslie P. Willcocks

BRICOLAGE, CARE, AND INFORMATION
Chrisanthi Avgerou, Giovan Francesco Lanzara, and Leslie P. Willcocks

CHINA'S EMERGING OUTSOURCING CAPABILITIES
Mary Lacity, Leslie Willcocks and Yingqin Zheng

The Outsourcing Enterprise

From Cost Management to Collaborative Innovation

Leslie P. Willcocks

Professor of Information Systems,
London School of Economics and Political Science,
London, UK

Sara Cullen

The Cullen Group
Melbourne, Australia

Andrew Craig

Carig Ltd.
London, UK

First published 2011 by
PALGRAVE MACMILLAN

Palgrave Macmillan in the UK is an imprint of Macmillan Publishers Limited, registered in England, company number 785998, of Houndmills, Basingstoke, Hampshire RG21 6XS.

Palgrave Macmillan in the US is a division of St Martin's Press LLC, 175 Fifth Avenue, New York, NY 10010.

Palgrave Macmillan is the global academic imprint of the above companies and has companies and representatives throughout the world.

Palgrave® and Macmillan® are registered trademarks in the United States, the United Kingdom, Europe and other countries.

ISBN: 978–0–230–23191–7

This book is printed on paper suitable for recycling and made from fully managed and sustained forest sources. Logging, pulping and manufacturing processes are expected to conform to the environmental regulations of the country of origin.

A catalogue record for this book is available from the British Library.

A catalog record for this book is available from the Library of Congress.

10 9 8 7 6 5 4 3 2 1
20 19 18 17 16 15 14 13 12 11

Printed and bound in Great Britain by
CPI Antony Rowe, Chippenham and Eastbourne

CONTENTS

Foundations

Key Practices

Outsourcing into the Future

FIGURES

TABLES

Acknowledgements

First and foremost, as with all our work on global sourcing over the last 20 years we sincerely thank the now over 2600 executives across the globe, from clients, advisers, legal firms, and suppliers, who have participated in our research. Without them our work just would not have been possible. Due to the often sensitive nature of outsourcing, many participants requested anonymity and cannot be individually acknowledged. Participants who did not request anonymity are acknowledged in the appropriate places throughout this book. We would also like to thank all at Logica for giving us the impetus to develop the concept of the outsourcing enterprise and distil our academic research into more accessible form as white papers over the years. Many thanks also for sponsoring part of the new research that went into Chapter 5 on collaborative innovation.

We also wish to acknowledge the supportive research environment that the London School of Economics and Political Science has provided over the last four years during which this book was conceived, additionally researched, and written. Leslie is very grateful to all his colleagues at Oxford and Warwick Universities and now LSE for their tolerance and support over the years. Very special thanks to Mary Lacity, not just a wonderful friend but an intellectual and research gold-miner of the first rank. Also thanks to Julia Kotlarsky and Ilan Oshri for rescuing him from ultimate busyness and making sure the important work got done – it so easily could have been otherwise. Much gratitude to Sara who co-authors this book, and who, with Peter Reynolds and Peter Seddon provided the happiest of Australian work climates year in year out as the research progressed.

Obviously research work of this scope over such a long period is not just a three-person effort. Several other colleagues who became friends made significant contributions and published with us in the earlier period, in particular Rudy Hirschheim, Wendy Currie, and Guy Fitzgerald. Latterly we have thoroughly enjoyed researching, conferencing, digesting, and writing with David Feeny, Thomas Kern, Joseph Rottman, Eric van Heck, Eleni Lioliou, Jae-Yong Lee, and John Hindle. They provided intelligence, inspiration and hard work in equal measure and have been a joy to be with. Thanks also to all the attendees of the Global Sourcing workshop, now in its fifth year, for your intellectual stimulation and friendship, and for working so hard, with us, to raise academic standards in, among other things, skiing.

We would like to thank our circles of family and friends for their forbearance and humor. Leslie would like to thank Chrisanthi, Catherine, and George for nights at the opera, ballet and all the sustaining things, and Damaris for making life anew, and what it should be. Sara thanks Joe, Gianni and Dante for their encouragement and tolerance, and Andrew would like to thank Christine for her unstinting support and yet also for being his sternest critic.

As a further testimony to the value of global sourcing, we are delighted to acknowledge the great contribution of our global publishing team, and in particular at Palgrave Macmillan Stephen Rutt, and Newgen Imaging Systems for their editorial and production services our copy editor and coordinator.

SERIES PREFACE

Series Editors: Leslie P. Willcocks and Mary C. Lacity

We launched this series in 2006 to provide policy makers, workers, managers, academics, and students with a deeper understanding of the complex interlinks and influences among technological developments, including in information and communication technologies (ICT), work, organizations, and globalization. We have always felt that technology is all too often positioned as the welcome driver of globalization. The popular press neatly packages technology's influence on globalization with snappy sound bites, such as 'any work that can be digitized will be globally sourced'. Cover stories report Indians doing US tax returns, Moroccans developing software for the French, Filipinos answering UK customer service calls, and the Chinese doing everything for everybody. Most glossy cover stories assume that all globalization is progressive, seamless, intractable, and leads to unmitigated good. But what we are experiencing in the twenty-first century in terms of the interrelationships between technology, work, and globalization is both profound and highly complex.

The mission of this series is to disseminate rich knowledge based on deep research about relevant issues surrounding the globalization of work that is spawned by technology. To us, substantial research on globalization considers multiple perspectives and levels of analyses. We seek to publish research based on in-depth study of developments in technology, work, and globalization and their impacts on and relationships with individuals, organizations, industries, and countries. We welcome perspectives from business, economics, sociology, public policy, cultural studies, law, and other disciplines that contemplate both larger trends and micro-developments from Asian, African, Australia, and Latin American, as well as North American and European viewpoints.

As of this writing, we have reached a critical milestone in the series in that we have eleven books published and several additional books under contract. The eleven completed books are introduced below.

1. *Global Sourcing of Business and IT Services* by Leslie P. Willcocks and Mary C. Lacity is the first book in the series. The book is based on over 1000 interviews with clients, suppliers, and advisors and fifteen years of study. The specific focus is on developments in outsourcing, offshoring,

and mixed sourcing practices from client and supplier perspectives in a globalizing world. We found many organizations struggling. We also found some organizations adeptly creating global sourcing networks that are agile, effective, and cost efficient. But they did so only after a tremendous amount of trial-and-error and close attention to details. All our participant organizations acted in a context of fast moving technology, rapid development of supply side offerings, and ever changing economic conditions.

2. *Knowledge Processes in Globally Distributed Contexts* by Julia Kotlarsky, Ilan Oshri, and Paul van Fenema, examines the management of knowledge processes of global knowledge workers. Based on substantial case studies and interviews, the authors – along with their network of co-authors – provide frameworks, practices, and tools that consider how to develop, coordinate, and manage knowledge processes in order to create synergetic value in globally distributed contexts. Chapters address knowledge sharing, social ties, transactive memory, imperative learning, work division, and many other social and organizational practices to ensure successful collaboration in globally distributed teams.

3. *Offshore Outsourcing of IT Work* by Mary C. Lacity and Joseph W. Rottman explores the practices for successfully outsourcing IT work from Western clients to offshore suppliers. Based on over 200 interviews with 26 Western clients and their offshore suppliers in India, China, and Canada, the book details client-side roles of chief information officers, program management officers, and project managers and identifies project characteristics that differentiated successful from unsuccessful projects. The authors examine ten engagement models for moving IT work offshore and describe proven practices to ensure that offshore outsourcing is successful for both client and supplier organizations.

4. *Exploring Virtuality within and Beyond Organizations* by Niki Panteli and Mike Chiasson argues that there has been a limited conceptualization of virtuality and its implications on the management of organizations. Based on illustrative cases, empirical studies and theorizing on virtuality, this book goes beyond the simple comparison between the virtual and the traditional to explore the different types, dimensions, and perspectives of virtuality. Almost all organizations are virtual, but they differ theoretically and substantively in their virtuality. By exploring and understanding these differences, researchers and practitioners gain a deeper understanding of the past, present, and future possibilities of virtuality. The collection is designed to be indicative of current thinking and approaches, and provides a rich basis for further research and reflection in this important area of management and information systems research and practice.

5. *ICT and Innovation in the Public Sector* by Francesco Contini and Giovan Franceso Lanzara examines the theoretical and practical issues of implementing innovative ICT solutions in the public sector. The book

is based on a major research project sponsored and funded by the Italian government (Ministry of University and Research) and coordinated by Italy's National Research Council and the University of Bologna during the years 2002–06. The authors, along with a number of co-authors, explore the complex interplay between technology and institutions, drawing on multiple theoretical traditions such as institutional analysis, actor network theory, social systems theory, organization theory, and transaction costs economics. Detailed case studies offer realistic and rich lessons. These cases studies include e-justice in Italy and Finland, e-bureaucracy in Austria, and Money Claim On-Line in England and Wales.

6. *Outsourcing Global Services: Knowledge, Innovation, and Social Capital* edited by Ilan Oshri, Julia Kotlarsky, and Leslie P. Willcocks assembles the best work from the active participants in the *Information Systems Workshop on Global Sourcing* which began in 2007 in Val d'Isere France. Because the quality of the contributions was exceptional, we invited the program chairs to edit a book based on the best papers at the conference. The collection provides in-depth insights into the practices that lead to success in outsourcing global services. Written by internationally acclaimed academics, it covers best practices on IT outsourcing, business process outsourcing and netsourcing.

7. *Global Challenges for Identity Policies* by Edgar Whitley and Ian Hosein provides a perfect fit for the series in that the authors examine identity policies for modern societies in terms of the political, technical, and managerial issues needed to prevent identity fraud and theft. The scale of the problem exceeds political boundaries and the authors cover national identity policies in Europe and the rest of the world. Much of the book provides in-depth discussion and analysis of the United Kingdom's National Identity Scheme. The authors provide recommendations for identity and technical policies.

8. *E-Governance for Development* by Shirin Madon examines the rapid proliferation of e-Governance projects aimed at introducing ICTs to improve systems of governance and thereby to promote development. In this book, the author unpacks the theoretical concepts of development and governance in order to propose an alternative conceptual framework which encourages a deeper understanding of macro and micro-level political, social, and administrative processes within which e-Governance projects are implemented. The book draws on over fifteen years of research in India during which time many changes have occurred in terms of the country's development ideology, governance reform strategy, and ICT deployment.

9. *Bricolage, Care, and Information Systems,* edited by Chrisanthi Avgerou, Giovan Francesco Lanzara and Leslie P. Willcocks, celebrates Claudio Ciborra's Legacy in information systems research. Claudio Ciborra was one of the most innovative thinkers in the field of information systems.

He was one of the first scholars who introduced institutional economics in the study of IS; he elaborated new concepts, such as 'the platform organization', 'formative contexts'; and he contributed to the development of a new perspective altogether through Heideggerian phenomenology. This book contains the most seminal work of Claudio Ciborra and work of other authors who were inspired by his work and built upon it.

10. *China's Emerging Outsourcing Capabilities* edited by Mary C. Lacity, Leslie P. Willcocks, and Yingqin Zheng, marks the tenth book in the series. The Chinese government has assigned a high priority to science and technology as its future growth sectors. China has a national plan to expand the information technology outsourcing (ITO) and business process outsourcing (BPO) sectors. Beyond the hopes of its leaders, is China ready to compete in the global ITO and BPO markets? Western companies are increasingly interested in extending their global network of ITO and BPO services beyond India and want to learn more about China's ITO and BPO capabilities. In this book, we accumulate the findings of the best research on China's ITO and BPO sector by the top scholars in the field of information systems.

11. *The Outsourcing Enterprise: From Cost Management to Collaborative Innovation* by Leslie Willcocks, Sara Cullen, and Andrew Craig. The central question answered in this book is 'How does an organization leverage the ever growing external services market to gain operational, business, and strategic advantage?' The book covers the foundations of mature outsourcing enterprises that have moved outsourcing to the strategic agenda by building the relationship advantage, selecting and levering suppliers, keeping control through core retained capabilities, and collaborating to innovate. The book provides proven practices used by mature outsourcing enterprises to govern, design, and measure outsourcing. The final chapter presents practices on how mature outsourcing enterprises prepare for the next generation of outsourcing.

In addition to the books already published or under contract, we encourage other researchers to submit proposals to the series, as we envision a protracted need for scholars to deeply and richly analyze and conceptualize the complex relationships among technology, work, and globalization. Please follow the submissions guidelines on the Palgrave Macmillan website (http://www.palgrave.com/authors/publishing.asp). Stephen Rutt (email: s.rutt@palgrave.com) is the publishing director for the series.

Leslie P. Willcocks
Mary C. Lacity
March 2010

FOREWORD

Over the past 20 years outsourcing has become established as a key strategy, by both commercial and public sector organizations, to help maximize their efficiency and effectiveness. However the key challenge, for client and supplier organizations alike, remains the establishment of the right sort of outsourcing relationship that is mutually beneficial. Leslie Willcocks and his colleagues have been carrying out in-depth global research into outsourcing since the early 1990s. Over this period they have published findings and advice on outsourcing best practice, which has been much valued both because of the rigorous research on which it is based and its objectivity.

Seeing the practical value of their work, Logica has collaborated with Leslie Willcocks and his colleagues since 2005 on a series of major research projects. Our partnership has resulted in a series of papers that outline insightful and leading-edge thinking on the outsourcing market. The present volume is a fine and well-thought-through distillation of their work. It covers not just IT outsourcing, but also business process outsourcing and offshoring.

The book includes a succinct and knowledgeable review of the evolution of outsourcing globally. It takes the reader on a clearly described and well-illustrated journey through the key topics that really need to be addressed if outsourcing is to be successful. The authors suggest, correctly I believe, that outsourcing is now well above the parapet in terms of its implications for the strategy and economics of most commercial and public sector organizations. As such *The Outsourcing Enterprise* will repay the attention of CEOs, senior executives and others involved in the implementation of outsourcing within their organizations.

The book describes the leadership that senior executives need to take when engaged in an outsourcing programme, how to shape strategy, build relationships and select suppliers. It also describes how to build internal capabilities to keep control while maintaining flexibility and responsiveness in the face of changing business conditions and requirements. The focus on innovation – relating to the mode of collaboration as well as to technologies and services – is particularly prescient and complements our own experiences and strategy. The stress on establishing suitable management processes and a long-term collaborative approach to enable an outsourcing relationship to evolve and thrive, also very much accords with our view.

A great strength of the book is the multiple lessons and concrete pieces of advice that are provided, all illustrated and based on strong evidence. They ask the right questions and provide detailed answers that will help the reader determine the right outsourcing strategy for their organization.

The content of the book, of course, reflects the research and opinions of the authors. However, much of it accords with our strategy for outsourcing, and our "Client Value Proposition". This includes building strong client relationships which are tailored to the particular culture and structure of the client organisation. The processes and governance models we follow are based on the business needs of the client. In line with the research and findings, our strategy has always been to make innovation a cornerstone of the way we work with clients. This means adapting the services we provide to respond to changes in our client's business as well as developments in technology, in order to provide the most business aligned, cost effective and green outsourcing solutions.

Over the past five years, we have promoted the series of "Outsourcing Enterprise" publications, written by Leslie Willcocks and his team. Many clients have found this a valuable source of advice. It is therefore very welcome that much of this advice, and more besides, is distilled into this book, which I commend to the reader.

Joe Hemming
Logica CEO for Outsourcing Services

About the Authors

Leslie P. Willcocks is Professor of Technology Work and Globalization and Director of the Outsourcing Unit in the Information Systems and Innovation group, Department of Management at the London School of Economics and Political Science. He is recognized as one of the world's foremost authorities on outsourcing and has an international reputation for his research and advisory work on the management of information and communications technologies and organizational change. He is co-author of 33 books and over 180 papers in journals such as *Harvard Business Review, Sloan Management Review, California Management Review, MIS Quarterly, MISQ Executive,* and *Journal of Management Studies.* In February 2001 he won the PriceWaterhouseCoopers/Michael Corbett Associates World Outsourcing Achievement Award for his contribution to this field. He is a regular keynote speaker at international practitioner and academic conferences, and is regularly retained as adviser by major corporations and government institutions.

Sara Cullen is the Managing Director of The Cullen Group (www.cullengroup.com.au), an Honorary Research Fellow at the University of Melbourne, and a former National Partner at Deloitte (Australia). She has a leading international profile in contracting and is one of Asia Pacific's most experienced sourcing advisors. She has consulted to over 125 organizations, spanning 51 countries, in over 150 projects with contract values up to $1.5B p.a. Sara is a widely published, internationally recognized author having written over 110 publications, conducted 7 government reviews, and presented in over 300 major conferences. Her recent books include: *Toward Reframing Outsourcing, The Contract Scorecard, Contracting for the Outsourcing Lifecycle: A Practical Guide,* and *Intelligent IT Outsourcing* (with Leslie Willcocks). She holds a PhD (Outsourcing), Masters (Technology), and BSc (Accounting) in addition to being a Chartered Accountant, Certified Mediator, and Certified Trainer and Teacher.

Andrew Craig heads the IT leadership and governance stream of Carig Ltd and is also a director of Board Coaching Ltd. He is a visiting Senior Research Fellow at the LSE working in the Outsourcing Unit. He has coached executives, teams, and boards in the Defence Procurement

Agency, the UK Border Agency, the leisure industry, Balfour Beatty, HSBC and finance and fund management companies. In his professional Army career, as Brigadier, he directed the recruiting operation – an annual requirement of 16,000 people – and was responsible for Human Resource planning for a workforce of 120,000. He commanded engineering operations worldwide, including in the first Gulf War and Bosnia, and led the UK's planned military response to nuclear, biological, and chemical terrorism. He was awarded an OBE in 1998.

In the fifteenth and sixteenth centuries the Italian states made widespread use of mercenaries. A condottiero was a military chief offering his troops as paid professionals (condottieri) to city-states. In his masterpiece *The Prince* (Italian: Il Principe – written in 1513, but finally published in 1532), Niccolo Machiavelli called this medieval form of outsourcing *'the custom of Italy'*. It was once fashionable, probably misleadingly, to recommend *The Prince*, which is after all a handbook of political philosophy, to modern senior executives looking to manage contemporary organizations.[1] Those going down this line of thinking will be disappointed to find that Machiavelli's advice to his prince cuts right across the modern rise of outsourcing. In times of political and economic turmoil, with state against state: *'no principality is secure without having its own forces…. Nothing can be so uncertain or unstable as fame or power not founded on its own strength'*.

Machiavelli was sufficiently convinced that mercenaries and auxiliaries (allied troops) were *'dangerous and useless'* that he devoted two whole chapters of his book, replete with many examples, to the subject of exactly how. He saw mercenaries as undisciplined, cowardly and without loyalty: *'in peace one is robbed by them, in war by the enemy. The fact is that they have no reason for keeping the field than a trifle or stipend, which is not sufficient to make them die for you.'* He also uses examples of what modern transaction cost economics would call opportunistic behavior by the supplier, whereby work, campaigning, attacking towns by night, maintaining sufficient soldiery, fatigue and danger were avoided according to military rules or custom and practice. Yet at much the same time condottieri were being glorified. In 1480 Leonardo da Vinci was drawing (beautifully) the resplendent Il Condottiero, while Piero Della Francesca, in 1451, was painting (wonderfully) Sigismondo Pandolfo Malatesta, condottiero and ruler of Rimini. Clearly there was more to the hiring and use of external third parties than can be found in Machiavelli's short text.

History is of course replete with the use of mercenaries, mainly for military purposes, going back to ancient Egypt, through the early classical era, the Roman imperial era, in Asia and Africa, right up to modern wars of the twenty-first century. The following example illustrates the level of sophistication now reached. According to a report in the *Times* in February 2010 QinetQ, the privatized British defence technology company, had operators working with the Royal Netherlands Army in central Afghanistan, providing a system of unmanned aerial vehicles (UAVs) that could be called upon at any time by the Dutch forces. The *Times* commented that, as military chiefs looked at where spending cuts may fall: *'turnkey systems provided by private companies – that is systems supplied and/or installed for immediate use, sometimes including providing the necessary operators – could help the Ministry of Defence to make difficult choices on what can be afforded.'*

With some echoes of Machiavelli's points, the article pointed to outsourcing being controversial in conflict zones because it requires qualities such as flexibility, trust, and mutual understanding that are difficult to write into a standard contract. It also raises ethical questions, since defence companies are developing combat UAVs to replace fighter aircraft. In future the decision to pull the trigger could be part of a commercial contract.

All this helps to frame the present book and its purpose. The central question we address is the one implied in all the above, namely: how does an organization leverage the ever growing external services market to gain operational, business, even strategic advantage. Machiavelli's view in *The Prince* is at one end of the polarity, while endorsement of UAVs and the privatization of war are at quite the other. The outsourcing of business and IT services, which is the focus of the present book, began in earnest around 1989, and ever since every view between these end points has been expressed, based on convincing, and sometimes more scanty, experiences and evidence. In writing this book our purpose has been to nail the fundamental lessons and practices learned from studying and participating in the twenty-year plus evolution of outsourcing from $US10 billion a year revenues in 1989 to what by 2010 was a $US 450 billion a year global industry.

And despite today's managerial tendency to rush to prescription and the tool-box, the truth is that a little history *is* in order. Not only can one learn lessons from past examples – what works, and what does not; one can also unpack why the present takes the form it does, and whether today's practices were developed for other contexts and problems, and so need to be changed in new contexts, in order to address new requirements. Let us look first, then, at the development of the market, and how we got here. Then we review how clients have been climbing up the outsourcing learning curve.

The beginning date of modern outsourcing of IT and business services is usually attributed to 1989 and the landmark Eastman Kodak large-scale outsourcing arrangement with three suppliers. From then information technology (IT) outsourcing accelerated reaching about $50 billion revenues in 1994, $US 152 billion in 2000, to, on most forecasts, over $US340 billion by 2014. Within a wider early 1990s debate about the core competence of the corporation, organizations increasingly looked to outsource 'commodity' IT to reduce costs, access expertise, and/or catalyse performance. Interestingly, the period 1989–97 saw some high profile large-scale, sometimes single supplier, IT outsourcing deals – examples are BP, General Dynamics, DuPont, Xerox, Commonwealth Bank, UK Inland Revenue – but these represented a minority practice. By 1999 there were globally just over 120 such deals. The dominant practice was multiple supplier outsourcing with shorter term (3–7 years) contracts, that focused on outsourcing stable, discrete activities. IT outsourcing has continued apace in the first decade of the new century, with, from mid-decade, a renewed more strategic interest in multi-sourcing – in this respect the ABNAmro bank deal with four suppliers in 2005 was seen as the way strategic sourcing would go. At the same time the period 2005–10 has seen more, smaller, shorter term contracts driving market growth. With the economic downturn, an interest in consolidating supplier numbers took place. On the back of this the economic and management advantages of 'bundled' outsourcing – going with one supplier for several different IT and also business process services – grew.[2]

Mainstream business process outsourcing (BPO) and offshoring/offshore outsourcing have been latecomers to this essentially IT trajectory. There were pioneering developments in both areas during the 1990s. For example, as early as 1991 oil major BP Exploration outsourced all of its European accounting operations to one supplier, consolidating them in a single site at Aberdeen, Scotland. Likewise in 1996 BP did the same for its US upstream, downstream, and chemical businesses, moving to two outsourcing suppliers in 1999. The Aberdeen shared services centre also attracted additional oil industry clients, for example Britannia Operator and Conoco. On offshoring, a number of American and West European firms developed captive centers and outsourced some IT work in India and elsewhere, for example, Baan, GE, while Indian suppliers began to develop their capabilities and markets, for example, Infosys, TCS, Wipro. But it was the increasing, and successful, use by North American and European companies of Indian suppliers and locations to deal with the Y2K problem that really began to put offshore models on the map from around 2000.

Both BPO and offshoring genuinely opened up the global outsourcing market in the new decade, offering real routes to cost savings, and greater value from outsourcing. BP were again pioneers – this time in human resource outsourcing in their 1999 deal with Exult. Another new BPO 'pure play' – Xchanging – signed a similar deal, though on a joint venture basis, with British Aerospace in May 2001, while Bank of America contracted with Accenture. From the turn of the century the BPO market picked up considerably. The issue for BPO generally was whether clients had the confidence to outsource, even transform, their back-offices – HR, procurement, legal, accounting, finance, asset management – against a background of a global supplier market still developing its capabilities. The outcome by 2010 was that there had been rapid BPO expansion, but that there remained still massive untapped potential growth for the BPO market.

Of all the outsourcing variants offshore outsourcing saw much the fastest growth in the first decade of the new century. With its head start, scale and group of major suppliers, by 2010 India continued to dominate the global market, but at the same time, many other countries have been actively offering services, and developing their outsourcing services industries dynamically, most successfully with government backing.[3] One small market – that for Application Service Provision (ASP) – is also worth commenting on here. Concerned with delivering applications, infrastructure, and services on a rental basis over the internet, this phenomenon, which we dubbed 'netsourcing', grew in the 1997–2001 period, but then fell away with the bursting of the Internet bubble, only seemingly now being resurrected in newer forms with the growing interest from 2008 in 'cloud computing' – including among big product as well as service suppliers.[4]

In retrospect this rapid growth has had several impacts. One is that clients and suppliers alike have had to run very fast to catch up with the latest twists in the market and new sources of competition and value. Senior executives have been short on time to think through long-term issues and requirements, even though that is precisely what sourcing strategy requires. Relatedly, finding out what works and what does not has been, perhaps too often, a 'suck-it-and-see' experience. When one is committing to what can be ten-year large-scale contracts, this is not necessarily the optimal way to proceed. Thirdly, creating a body of knowledge about outsourcing, in terms of governance, contracting, measurement, processes, relationship practices, is still very much work in progress, though we would like to believe we have made, in our previous work, and in this book substantive contributions in this area. Fourthly, and another reason why the present book has been written, the outsourcing industry is still at the early stages of professionalizing itself. The benefits of professionalization in terms of, for example, standard practices, codes of conduct, minimum standards of competence, an understanding of roles required and what it takes to fill them are not really with us yet. We hope we make here a contribution to these developments.

Throughout this short history there has been much learning and evolution by clients and suppliers alike. We capture the main parameters in Figure 0.1., developed originally by our colleagues Mary Lacity and Joe Rottman. It is this learning that we endeavor to distill in the first five chapters of this book. In Figure 0.1 we capture the voyage of discovery that client organizations have been on. An organization contemplating its first generation outsourcing arrangement will typically be at Phase 1. In our research we have seen such clients either far too believing of what they read in marketing brochures and hear from suppliers pitching for work, or

Figure 0.1 The Outsourcing Learning Curve

far too disbelieving and skeptical of what to expect. Either approach has not proven to be a sound basis for entering into an outsourcing relationship. In Phase 2 clients tend to focus mainly on cost, and usually pass through a baptism of hard learning. In all outsourcing arrangements, at any time in a client's evolution, risk mitigation is central. Interestingly we found what seemed at first a surprising number of the 1990s deals had been relatively, if quietly, successful. The characteristics of these? They had limited objectives, usually related to cost and service. They outsourced typically 20–30 percent of the IT budget only, thus retaining quite a lot of in-house capability; they outsourced stable, discrete activities they could write complete contracts for, on 3–5 year contracts to multiple suppliers. This remains a good starting point for clients wishing to build their learning incrementally through the actual experience of outsourcing. Once requisite organizational capability has been built, much more scale, complexity, and sophistication becomes possible, as this book will document.

A client will learn much from its first generation outsourcing deal, and this can be put to good use for the second generation. We have found most clients sticking with incumbent suppliers (though sometimes bringing some work back in-house), building up more retained capability, getting smarter on contracts, and about what was realistically attainable through outsourcing. Ironically, some clients did not build on their learning, though, but, scarred by their first outsourcing encounter, have done something completely different in their second, and sometimes different again in their third generation deals. Clients that have reached Phase 3 are older and wiser, and are able to get the balance of contract and relationship management right, have secured the right internal capabilities to keep control of their IT/back-office destiny, and focus on leveraging the relationship with their supplier(s). By 2010 we found very few organizations had reached Phase 4 of their journey. An extended set of practices needs to be adopted to get there, and we detail these in Chapter 5. How does being in these different phases *feel* to clients? They report to us the following growth path:

- Phase 1 – Undue optimism or panic
- Phase 2 – Learning
- Phase 3 – Maturing relationship
- Phase 4 – Collaborative leadership

There are multiple reasons why so many organizations have progressed quite slowly, often painfully up the learning curve. Key people learn, then leave. Organizational learning is not institutionalized. Nor is learning on one type of outsourcing routinely transferred and applied to another. Thus in Figure 0.1 we show client's IT outsourcing learning higher up the curve than it is for BPO and offshoring. Objectives change and new forms of outsourcing and contracts are entered into, with new suppliers, and a client moves down the learning curve once more. Moreover, organizations seem to have a preference for what we call 'hard learning'. Unless they have experienced it themselves, they never quite believe, let alone enact, the advice given to them or is available.

This brief history indicates that each client organization will, at any one moment in time inhabit its own distinctive place on the learning curve, and within each client that learning will tend to be more advanced on ITO, than for BPO and offshore outsourcing. This book aims at getting a client organization to an advanced stage of Phase 3 as shown in Figure 0.1., and prepare to move to Phase 4. To achieve this, the book distills the key learnings and lessons from the comprehensive longitudinal case research we have carried out on over 1600 outsourcing arrangements on a global basis over the 1989–2010 period.[5] Studying cases over time – some outsourcing arrangements we have researched over three generations of deals – gives us distinctive, perhaps unique insight into what works, what does not, what outcomes are achieved, under what conditions, what people and capabilities are needed, timing issues, and how productive relationships can be constructed over several years. Moreover, combined, this research base covers all major economic and government sectors, including financial services, energy and utilities, defense/aerospace, retail, telecoms and IT, oil, transportation, central, state and local government, health care, industrial products and chemicals, and is drawn from medium, large and multinational organizations based in Europe, USA, and Asia Pacific. The key lessons and emerging practices from this research are presented in Chapters 1 to 4 and Chapters 6–9 as the fundamental building blocks needed for effective outsourcing experiences for clients and suppliers alike. In Chapters 5 and 10, we extend that learning into how to prepare for the next five years.

Sometimes we are asked: are you for or against outsourcing? The question ignores the essential situatedness of all outsourcing practice. Also the fact that generally we are more interested in bigger sourcing questions rather than just outsourcing ones. The real managerial question we have asked ourselves for the present book, as researchers and advisers, is: *under what conditions does outsourcing become an effective approach to achieving organizational objectives?* The answers, for us, have to be evidence-based. Clearly, Machiavelli himself drew upon evidence of past examples when advising his prince, but his book Il Principe was always a highly selective document designed primarily to achieve princely favor. It also embodies what we call in Chapter 2 a power-based approach to management and relationships. Trust and power represent alternative ways to minimize risk and secure cooperation. Power-based relationships are based on the negative threat of sanctions that might be applied to gain compliance. In Il Principe, the assumptions founding relationships are distrust, opportunism, competition, short term, material motivation. These may be quite good assumptions to make in sixteenth century Florence. However, as we show in Chapters 2 and 5, in modern outsourcing power is a poor substitute for governance structures and building trust, given the high costs involved in monitoring and imposing sanctions, the negative orientations and behaviors adopted, and the limited goals that can be pursued by the parties.

Moreover, notoriously, Machiavelli's messages in Il Principe were also at odds with what he considered his major work – The Discourses (Il Discorsi published 1531). There he provides detailed lessons on how to start and structure a republic with a system of checks and balances among executive, judicial, and legislative arms. For him, this governance structure is much superior as a form of government when compared with a principality. Moreover: *'in a well-ordered republic it should never be necessary to resort to extra-constitutional means* (Book 1, ch 34). These may be more sober, but are certainly more central, founding, more complete lessons to take from reading Machiavelli. But the real message worth taking away from all his work is the major inherent danger in outsourcing, namely the risk of losing control of fortune and destiny unless there is strategy, a governance structure, a rigorous process, and a retained, mature capability able to deal with the scale of outsourcing undertaken, and much more besides. Within such a framework selecting and working with the right third party service provider to build a productive relationship that delivers are then key components. It is a message that guides this book. In that way we steer outsourcing away from becoming – to update Machiavelli – *'the custom of globalization,'* and the pejorative sense in which he would have used such a term.

References

(1) See for example Jay, A. (1968) *Management and Machiavelli*. Holt, Rinehart & Winston, New York, NY; Griffin, G.R. (1991) *Machiavelli on Management: Playing and Winning the Corporate Power Game*, Praeger, New York, NY; Mansfield, H. (1989), *Taming the Prince: The Ambivalence of Modern Executive Power*. The Free Press, New York, NY. There is in fact a very large literature on management and Machiavelli that stretches over the last 40 years.

(2) Detailed histories of IT and business process outsourcing can be found in Lacity, M., Willcocks, L. and Rottman, J. (2008) 'Global Outsourcing of Back Office Services: Lessons, Trends and Enduring Challenges', *Strategic Outsourcing*, 1, 1, 13–34; Willcocks, L. and Lacity, M. (2009) *The Practice of Outsourcing: From Information Systems to BPO and Offshoring*. Palgrave Macmillan, London; Campbell, K. (2010) *Outsourcing: A New Value Proposition*. Accenture, London. Our research on bundled outsourcing appears in Willcocks, L., Oshri, I. and Hindle, J. (2009) To Bundle or Not To Bundle? Effective Decision-Making for Business and IT Services. LSE/Accenture, London.

(3) See Willcocks, L., Griffiths, C. and Kotlarsky, J. (2009) *Beyond BRIC: Offshoring in Non-BRIC Countries – Egypt as a Growth Market*. ELSE, London. Also Lacity, M. Willcocks, L. and Zheng, Y. (2010) *China's Emerging Outsourcing Capabilities*. Palgrave Macmillan, London.

(4) See Kern, T., Lacity, M. and Willcocks, L. (2002) *Netsourcing: Renting Applications, Services and Infastructure over Networks*. Prentice Hall, New York.

(5) The first research base consists of 112 sourcing case histories (mainly in the area of IT) studied longitudinally from 1990 to 2001. These are described in Lacity, M. and Willcocks, L. (2001) *Global IT Outsourcing: In Search Of Business Advantage* (Wiley). The second is a study of relationships through seven case histories. This appears in Kern, T. and Willcocks, L. (2001) *The Relationship Advantage*. OUP, Oxford. The third is a 2001–05 longitudinal study of business process outsourcing practices, with a particular focus on four cases in aerospace and insurance. See Willcocks, L. and Lacity M. (2006) *Global Sourcing of Business and IT Services*. Palgrave Macmillan, London. We also draw upon a fourth research stream consisting of ten cases of application service provision, published in Kern, T., Lacity, M. and Willcocks, L. (2002) *Netsourcing*. Prentice Hall, New York. A further research stream analysed vendor capabilities, including innovation, and is represented in Feeny, D., Lacity, M. and Willcocks, L. (2005) 'Taking the measure of outsourcing providers', *Sloan Management Review*, 46, 3. We also draw upon five outsourcing surveys carried out in USA, Europe, and Australasia in 1993, 1997, 2000, 2001 and 2002 covering multiple sectors and over 900 organizations. A further research stream, by Sara Cullen, assessed 100 ITO/BPO initiatives of a variety of business functions during the decade from 1994 to 2003 to determine what worked and what did not work, what

drove the various degrees of success and failure, and the emerging lessons. The research is represented in Cullen, S. and Willcocks, L. (2004) *Intelligent IT Outsourcing* (Butterworth) and Cullen, S., Seddon, P. and Willcocks, L. (2005) 'Managing outsourcing: the lifecycle imperative', *MISQ Executive,* 4, 1. We also draw upon 2006–10 research into innovation in the contexts of offshoring and business process outsourcing. This covers ten case studies and is represented in Lacity, M. and Willcocks, L. (2009) *Information Systems and Outsourcing: Studies in Theory and Practice.* Palgrave Macmillan; Oshri, I. et al. (2008) *Outsourcing Global Services.* Palgrave Macmillan; and Willcocks, l. and Lacity, M. (2009) *The Practice of Outsourcing: From ITO to BPO and Offshoring.* Palgrave Macmillan, London.

Foundations

CHAPTER 1

Moving to the strategic agenda

Looking for value shifts is perhaps the most important dimension of leadership.

– Michael Dell

The customer from hell is the naïve buyer.

– Supplier CEO

The major lesson? Getting sufficient granularity in plans, processes, and actions to give us transparency, then control.
– Bank senior executive, in the sixth year of a multi-billion dollar ten-year outsourcing arrangement

Introduction

Why should hard-pressed CEOs devote attention to the outsourcing of IT-enabled services? Because a substantial, and rapidly rising, amount of most large organizations' cost base is already with outsourcing service providers. Because getting large-scale outsourcing wrong can seriously damage the business. Because, from now, outsourcing is part of any future strategy. In our experience, the announcement of a large-scale outsourcing deal regularly has a positive effect on share price. That said, the opposite can occur if the market perceives outsourcing to be an inadequate measure, or details subsequently emerge leading to a price correction. More positively, the evidence from our LSE Outsourcing Unit research shows clearly that outsourcing – properly planned, resourced, and managed – can deliver significant competitive advantage to companies and organizations in all sectors. But only when the CEO plays a key role – taking crucial strategic decisions, creating vital capabilities, putting in place integrated management processes, and applying effective monitoring and evaluating mechanisms. Let us look at these issues in more detail. The Outsourcing Unit's research points to five main reasons why outsourcing must now move up the CEO agenda.[1]

Reason one: Outsourcing impacts on market value

Share price is a fundamental barometer of corporate performance. Previous research, as well as our own case histories, have identified a significant correlation between firms outsourcing their IT infrastructure or back offices and a positive stock market response. Investors consider movement toward outsourcing as an important and generally favorable variable when assessing a firm's worth. In the Outsourcing Unit's experience, the announcement of a large-scale outsourcing deal regularly has a positive effect on share price that can last between three and ten months. Outsourcing is seen as a sign of active investment and management on the part of the firm.

That said, the opposite can occur if the market perceives outsourcing to be an inadequate measure given the scale of difficulties involved, or where the deal seems to be flawed or hastily contrived, or where the CEO and organizations ultimately fail to deliver the financial results stated or implied in the initial announcement. The danger for the CEO is being swayed by short-term share price concerns and signing a large, long-term deal in order to try to shift the share price substantially upwards or perhaps to buy time rather than focusing on the fundamental business logic of the outsourcing deal. Long-term outsourcing contracts signed for short-term reasons invariably bring about major disappointments for CEOs and their organizations.

Reason two: Outsourcing is pervasive and growing – the spending alone needs attention

Outsourcing makes up a substantial and rapidly increasing proportion of expenditure in corporations and government agencies alike. On our figures global IT outsourcing revenues exceeded $US270 billion by end of 2010 and were scheduled to rise at 5–8 percent per annum over the next five years. Global business process outsourcing revenues, in areas such as the human resource function, procurement, back office administration, call centers, finance and accounting, were over $US165 billion by 2010 and likely to rise by 8–12 percent per annum through 2011–14.[2] Meanwhile, as part of this, offshore outsourcing exceeded $US60 billion revenues in 2010, and was set to grow at a faster rate over the next five years. Organizations are choosing to outsource more and more and for a variety of reasons: for example, to get more quickly to market, to cut internal costs, or to leverage the increasing capabilities of external services providers. For many organizations, outsourcing is well above the parapet in sheer expenditure terms. Outsourcing is not a fad, but a substantial part of corporate and government expenditure, needing top team oversight and management.

However, in practice, too often, this process is happening incrementally, as a response to immediate market conditions and specific opportunities to cut costs, rather than on the basis of long-term strategic thinking. CEOs, if they have not already done so, need to put such large spending on to a much more strategic footing.

Reason three: Outsourcing bears many risks – it can enable or disable business strategy

The outsourcing highway is littered with casualties. We have seen even experienced organizations repeatedly running into massive problems, suffering from slow organizational learning, and working in a reactive rather than an anticipatory mode.[3] Here are some twenty-first century examples:

- In 2000, UK retailer Sainsburys signed a 7-year $US3.25 billion deal with Accenture to outsource its IT operations. By late 2004, the deal had been renegotiated twice, and Sainsbury had announced a 2004–05 write-off of $254 million of IT assets, and a further $218 million write-off of automated depot and supply chain IT. The way forward was to reduce costs and simplify systems.[4]
- In the face of poor financial results, the CEO of one of our cases signed a 10-year $520 million IT outsourcing deal with a single supplier. Within 17 months, he had been removed and the contract was then terminated prematurely. As well as paying supplier fees, the company incurred $50 million implementation and $30 million termination costs. More money was swallowed up in then rebuilding in-house capability and shifting to a multi-supplier model.
- A 2003 report into 182 outsourcing deals found that more than a fifth had ended prematurely.[5]
- In 2004, JP Morgan and Chase scrapped its $5 billion contract with IBM two years into a 7-year deal, concluding that much of the work could be better handled in-house (see also Chapter 9).[6] Also in 2004, DuPont was reported to have discovered $150 million in over-charges relating to outsourcing services with its supplier.[7]
- In autumn 2004, the Child Support Agency-EDS deal surfaced as the latest in a long catalogue of outsourcing failures in the UK public sector. The pattern continued across the rest of the decade as revealed by a series of House of Commons Public Accounts Committee reports.[8]
- In January 2010 media company Sky won a judgment against EDS, a supplier contracted as software supplier and integrator for a £50 million customer relationship management system at its contact centers in Scotland. Two years in, the supplier was removed for poor performance

and the system was finally completed by Sky in March 2006 at an estimated cost of £265 million. On the basis of this judgment the supplier could be liable to damages of up to £200 million.[9]

While it appears that clients have a history of outsourcing experiences to draw upon, the problem is change. First generation clients often change what and how they outsource the second and third time around. Each time they find themselves in a relatively new situation, having to learn anew. Moreover, if their knowledgeable people had left and not been replaced, organizational learning may not occur until the fourth or fifth generation deal.

Why should the CEO be involved? Because in outsourcing, strategic risk mitigation is fundamental. Furthermore, pursuing an operational, cost-reducing outsourcing strategy can drive costs down but often at the expense of other expected benefits. Strategic and even operational inflexibilities can result.[10] As one example, while the Xerox-EDS 1994–2004 IT outsourcing deal successfully achieved cost reductions, at one point it damaged Xerox's ability to respond effectively to a major change in market structure. In late 1999 Xerox lost control of its billing and sales commission systems, and this had major consequences for profitability. By the following year Xerox's market share value had dropped from above $90 to below $20.[11]

The CEO must also care because, as the examples above show, strategic decisions to merge, acquire, or enter new markets can incur substantial unforeseen damage, delays and costs, if existing outsourcing arrangements need to be refocused.

Reason four: Outsourcing can play a positive, strategic role

However we are increasingly seeing leading organizations utilize forms of outsourcing and partnering in order to:

- penetrate new markets quickly
- operate in new regions (for instance, Boeing sourcing IT to Malaysia to sell core products there or Dell looking to sell into China)
- achieve strategic agility (for instance, adjusting volumes in response to business cycles or to provide business continuity in times of crisis)
- achieve strategic sourcing (for instance, offshoring; using offshore competition to get better prices and service; best-of-breed sourcing)
- enhance strategic capabilities by partnering with a complementary supplier.

In our latest research, discussed in Chapter 5, we have also seen CEOs using outsourcing to pursue the following strategies:[12]

- financial restructuring – 'improving the business's financial position while reducing or at least containing costs'
- core competence – 'redirecting the business and IT into core competencies'
- technology or business process catalyst – strengthening resources, services and flexibility in technologies and/or business processes to underpin business's strategic direction
- business transition – 'facilitating and supporting major organizational change'
- business innovation – 'using outsourcing to innovate processes, skills and technology, while mediating financial risk to achieve competitive advantage'
- new market – direct profit generation through joint venturing with vendor partner'.

All of these need meticulous CEO attention. In fact, for these moves to any way pay off, the CEO needs to shift from a tactical hands-off view, to a strategic and much more personally involved approach to outsourcing. If one becomes increasingly reliant as a business on an array of suppliers and partners, the practices described in this book become the only secure foundation for the CEO to ensure future business strategy is leveraged, rather than crippled.

Reason five: CEOs alone possess the crucial bargaining power

There is one element in outsourcing which the CEO alone can bring to bear on the massive scale that is required – bargaining power. Organizationally and strategically the CEO is the ultimate pivot of bargaining power. As a management process, the constant aim during the outsourcing lifecycle is to build and manage relative bargaining power. Enter that lifecycle without having first amassed the best possible bargaining power prior to negotiation, and you will find it almost impossible thereafter to improve your position. A key CEO role, therefore, is to ensure that their organization's bargaining power is sustained – both through their personal influence with the supplier's power brokers and by putting in place the strategies, processes, and people needed to keep the relationship with the supplier sharply competitive and productively leveraged.

What the CEO and senior executives need to know

In the first five chapters of this book we distill the fundamental architecture a CEO must ensure is in place, if the outsourcing enterprise is to succeed. This present chapter focuses on how to make strategic choices, and the process by which sourcing strategy is delivered. On the subject of process we will refer throughout the book to an outsourcing lifecycle of four phases and nine building blocks (see Figure 1.1):

- *The Architect Phase* is where the foundation for outsourcing is laid. It consists of the first four building blocks – investigate, target, strategize, design. At the end of this phase, the organization knows itself well enough to confidently publicize its needs.
- *The Engage Phase* is where one or more suppliers are selected and the deal is negotiated. It consists of the fifth and sixth building blocks – select and negotiate.
- *The Operate Phase* is where the deal is put in place, operationalized, and managed through its term. It comprises the seventh and eighth building blocks – transition and manage.
- *The Regenerate Phase* is where next-generation options are assessed. It consists of one building block: refresh. Following this phase, the lifecycle begins anew, returning to the Architect Phase, where the organization prepares for its next-generation deal(s).

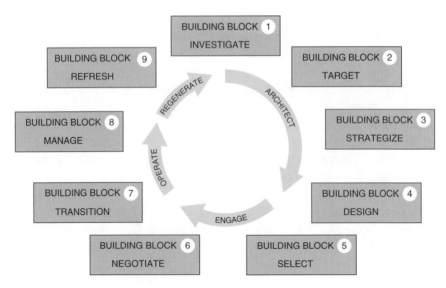

Figure 1.1 The outsourcing lifecycle

We have referred already to why the CEO, as the ultimate organizational guarantor of bargaining power, should be involved in this process. Should an organization enter the lifecycle without having built the best possible bargaining power prior to negotiation, it will rarely ever be able to improve that power. Figure 1.2 shows how bargaining power can operate under the lifecycle.

Before the commencement of about any type of outsourcing initiative, the CEO and top team may well have little knowledge on how these deals have been conducted before, what works and does not work, even what exactly it is that the organization will end up outsourcing. Building blocks 1–5 of the lifecycle help to build power through knowledge, expertise, and purpose. In building blocks 1–5, you also have optimal influence over the deal and getting what you want. Once the preferred service provider has been notified, and negotiation begins (building block 6), the power curve begins its downward tilt in favor of the service provider. Other competitors have been eliminated; and in terms of service, the client enters a more or less monopolistic situation.

This is the case even if the other bidders are 'on call' in case the negotiation falls through, as an organization will rarely be in a position to remove the preferred service provider and start negotiating with the second place bidder – even if it has retained the right to do so. From now on switching costs can be very prohibitive. By this time, the client will probably be under time and cost constraints to execute and transition-in/set-up, and the outsourcing arrangement itself, which further lessens client power. Service providers know this, and most organizations have experienced their preferred service providers beginning to change tack once negotiations begin.

It is the end of the courtship and the beginning of the actual outsourcing arrangement. You will no longer hear the unconditional promises made during the bidding process; promises will now be conditional. You will start to hear things like, 'what we meant in the bid was not quite how you've interpreted it'; 'our lawyers can't really accept what you have put in the contract', and so on.

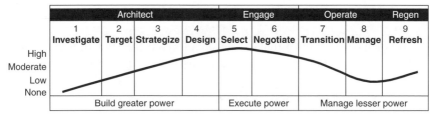

Figure 1.2 Bargaining power, the CEO and outsourcing

Client bargaining power erodes even further once the contract has been signed and you enter building block 7 (transition). Though we have seen a few deals terminate at this stage – for example Sears Holding Corporation and CSC terminated their 2004 ten-year agreement in the first year (the resulting legal dispute was settled in 2007 for an undisclosed sum paid to CSC) – there is no real feasible alternative for most clients but to continue with the deal with the chosen provider. In the Operate Phase, lesser power can be managed, provided the CEO and senior team have ensured that appropriate strategies, processes, and relationship management were designed into the earlier stages.

Lastly, once an agreement has been transitioned and is in place (building block 8 – manage), a monopolistic situation is now in full effect. The client will rarely have any economic and/or politically feasible choice other than to continue with the service provider if the deal is not working, as outsourcing deals can be prohibitively expensive to renegotiate, terminate, and either backsource (bring back in-house), or transfer to another service provider. This is when client power is at the lowest point in the lifecycle, and the work done (or not done) in the previous building blocks reveals its effects. As one canny senior executive told us: 'Bargaining power was something we planned for from the beginning. We always saw ourselves in competition for the supplier's attention and resources against all its other customers.'

Client power begins to build back up during building block 9: refresh. This is because the contract is nearing its end and the service provider wishes to gain an extension or renew the contract. The client has a very powerful bargaining tool – the next contract. As one CEO told us: 'It is amazing the level of attention and service you get when contract renewal is close.'

The role of the CEO? To ensure that bargaining power is maintained – through personal influence with the supplier's power brokers, and through putting in place the necessary strategy, processes and people to keep the relationship with the supplier keen and leveraged.

Strategy and outsourcing

According to the CEO of Capital One, the US Credit Card Group (in 2001):

> If you have a business that churns out products then outsourcing makes sense. But in the case of IT, it's actually our central nervous system. If I outsourced tomorrow, I might save a dollar or two on each account, but I would lose flexibility, and value and service levels.

Contrast this with Cisco Systems at much the same time. It had outsourced much of its production to 37 factories. Suppliers made all components and carried out 55 percent of sub-assembly and final assembly work. According to one senior executive, 'We can go from quote to cash without ever touching a physical asset or piece of paper. You've heard of JIT manufacturing, well this is not-at-all manufacturing'.

Two different businesses – both successful – each with a completely different philosophy on outsourcing. What explains this? Are there then no obviously adoptable outsourcing strategies? For the CEO, there is work to do in arriving at strategic sourcing decisions, configuring outsourcing deals, and ensuring these continue to underpin strategic direction of the business.

There are CEOs who outsource because they are not willing to invest in, or have given up on the ability of a particular business function or process – for example IT, human resources, procurement, legal – to keep costs down, deliver required service, or significantly improve. As we will detail, there are ways of making such outsourcing work. Nevertheless, even if such outsourcing is successful it can only achieve so much. This is because fundamental strategic flaws in the organization cannot be sold off – they must be understood and addressed. Applying outsourcing to an extant, flawed business model can, at best, only result in a more efficient version of that flawed model. As one vice-president commented to us, 'The belief is if you give the problem away, the third party will make it magically disappear. This tactic doesn't succeed because the client has not invested the time to address the underlying business processes or model.' Management must be able to provide the answers to these perennial questions: where are we now, where do we want to be, and how do we get there? Outsourcing is then a management tool that can be used to leverage the resulting answers. Without such an analysis, and without integrating the outsourcing strategy with business strategy, outsourcing becomes at best a tactical device for achieving lower level goals. The Dell case below provides an example of a company that has done the thinking.

Here we suggest three ways in which the CEO can align strategic business intent with a viable sourcing strategy. Using two matrices, we describe how to make strategic sourcing decisions. We point to the issue of getting the seven attributes of Configuration right. We describe a process and related activities therein that keep an outsourcing arrangement managed and on track.

Making strategic sourcing decisions

In 1994 John Browne, CEO of oil major BP stated: 'Failure to outsource our commodity IT will permanently impair the future competitiveness of our business.' From 1993, when BP Exploration signed five-year total outsourcing contracts with three suppliers, BP itself has risen to be consistently one of the top three oil companies in the world. Our own analysis shows how BP made strategic sourcing decisions that underpinned business strategy over many years into the new century.[13] How can this be achieved?

Our 'root cause' research regarding outsourcing failures suggests strongly that you can easily fail if you:

- see the outsourcing candidate area (e.g., IT, HR, procurement) as an undifferentiated commodity that can be outsourced in its entirety;
- outsource for dramatic cost reductions and because you have given up on the in-house ability to deliver;
- buy what is on offer rather than what you need;
- sign long-term contracts for short-term, tactical reasons
- draw up adversarial contracts; and/or
- do not put in place the necessary management capability throughout the lifecycle to keep control and leverage supplier performance.

There is another way ...

It is important to acknowledge different outsourcing models and choose the right mix to deliver on the strategic goals sought through outsourcing. There are many forms of outsourcing, and many ways to employ it strategically as a management tool. Below we present high-level decision frameworks successfully employed by numerous organizations to determine the nature of the services best retained, and those that should be investigated for outsourcing. Once this fundamental thinking has been achieved, CEOs open up for themselves a number of alternative strategic sourcing approaches. One company, Dell, a top performer from the early 1990s for a decade, is worth using as an example. From 2004 Dell did run into more business problems which are not the focus here, though one component is that subsequent to the case detailed below, they changed, and lost their way somewhat, on their sourcing strategy.[14]

Case example: Dell as a virtual integrator

From the late 1990s, Dell explicitly described its strategy as virtual integration. Its success was invariably put down to customer focus and attention to detail. However, an underlying vital component was sourcing strategy and management. Commenting on the company's growth through the 1990s into the new century Michael Dell said: 'I don't think we could have created a $12 billion business if we had tried to be vertically integrated.' With fewer physical assets and people, there were fewer things to manage and fewer barriers to change.

Through IT-enabled coordination of its value network of suppliers and partners, Dell could operate with a 20,000 rather than an 80,000 workforce. In the supply arena, it focused on making long-term deals with as few leading suppliers as possible. Datalinks measured and fed back supplier performance in real time. Close ties with suppliers (*'their engineers are part of our design and implementation teams'*) meant that Dell bought in innovation from its suppliers. Information technologies allowed speed and information sharing and much more intense forms of collaboration. It also meant that suppliers could be notified precisely of Dell's product requirements. This also allowed Dell to focus on inventory velocity and keep inventory levels low.

Dell also, throughout its short history, sought strong partnering relationships with key customers. Seen as 'complementors', customers are often involved in research and development, where Dell's focus is on relevant, easy-to-use technology, improvements in the customer buying process, keeping costs down, and superior quality in manufacturing. Dell also offered service centers in large organizations to be close to the customer. Thus, in the early 2000s Boeing had over 100,000 Dell PCs and over 30 dedicated Dell staff on the premises.

How are such effective sourcing decisions made? In Figures 1.3 and 1.4, we provide two matrices, born of experience and research, to facilitate decision-making. Sourcing must start with the business imperative.

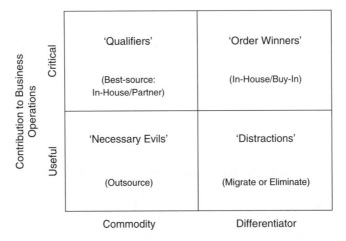

Figure 1.3 Strategic sourcing by business activity

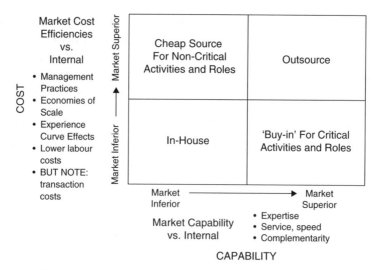

Figure 1.4 Strategic sourcing by market comparison

Strategic sourcing by business activity

Figure 1.3 indicates two ways of defining activities. The first is in terms of a business activity's contribution to business positioning. Some activities are frequently categorized as 'commodities' – for example in IT payroll and mainframe processing, in HR, administration. These need to be done, but do not differentiate the organization competitively. On the other hand, British Airways' yield management system for many years gave the company a competitive edge in ticket pricing and has been regarded as a 'differentiator'. The vertical axis allows us to assess whether a business activity critically underpins strategic direction and its delivery, or merely makes incremental contributions to the bottom line. This creates four quadrants.

Let us use the well-known history of Dell to illustrate the thinking here. 'Order Winners' are those business activities that critically and advantageously differentiate a firm from its competitors. Looking at Dell around 2002, Dell had six such 'order winners' or 'critical differentiators':

1. Dell focused its attention on all activities that create value for the customer. This included R&D involving over 1500 people and a $250 million plus budget that focused on customer-facing activity and the identification of 'relevant' technology. It tended to outsource as much as possible all other activities that needed to be done.
2. At the time Dell defined its core capability as a solutions provider and technology navigator. It used partners as much as possible to deal with such matters as products, components technology development, and assembly.

3. A key task was coordination, as against 'doing' tasks such as manufacturing and delivery.

4. A core capability was control of the network through financial and informational means to ensure requisite speed, cost, and quality. The company appointed and monitored reliable, responsive, leading edge supplies of technology and quality.

5. Dell took responsibility for seeking and improving all arrangements that gave it speed and focus in the marketplace and in its organizational arrangements.

6. Dell treated (and still does) information management and orchestration as a critical differentiator. This is an outcome of two strategic moves on its part. The first is to convert as much of the physical assets it manages into digital form. The second is to outsource as much as possible of the remaining physical assets and tasks, while rendering management of the digital world a core set of tasks.

One secret of Dell's success, we would suggest, was its massive clarity about what is core, and what is not. It also recognized that this may change dynamically with circumstances. This enabled it to authoritatively place 'non-core' activities as candidates for external sourcing, and make decisions on the best types of external sourcing, and on suitable candidates. The strong steer is to carry out these core activities in-house, buying in resources to work under internal control where expertise is lacking, and a build-up of learning is required.

'Qualifiers' are business activities that must be carried out as a necessary minimum entry requirement to compete in a specific sector. For airlines, aircraft maintenance systems are such a minimum requirement, but do not differentiate the airlines from each other. One can see in Dell's strategy their preference to outsource as many critical commodities as possible. Often critical differentiators can become commodities and move to this quadrant. One task of the CEO is to monitor and act upon such value migration. During 2003, Dell defined assembly, manufacturing, and delivery as 'Qualifiers'. These should be best sourced and can be done by third parties where they meet the right cost and competence criteria (see below).

'Necessary Evils' (as one executive called them) are tasks that have to be done but are not core activity and gain no strategic leverage from their fulfillment. Dell has tended to cut down on administration, payroll, and inventory tasks for example, but would seek to outsource as much of these activities as possible. 'Distractions' are failed or failing attempts to differentiate the organization from its competitors. The goal here must be to eliminate the activity, or migrate it to another quadrant. Thus in 1989, Dell opened retail outlets but soon discovered this development was not going to be successful, and fell back on its direct business model. A more profound mistake is not to notice until too late the value shifts in a specific competitive arena, for example IBM against Microsoft and Intel in the late 1980s/early 1990s. Dell had made few such mistakes in its rise to being one of the best global performers in the 1990–2003 period. Perhaps this resulted from its CEO's explicit recognition that 'looking for value shifts is perhaps the most important dimension of leadership'.

Strategic sourcing by market comparison

It is not enough, however, to identify a potential use for service providers or business allies. What is available on what, in Figure 1.4, we define as 'the market' also requires detailed analysis. If the market is not cheap, capable, or mature enough then the organization will need to seek a largely in-house solution. A second matrix is needed to capture fully the major elements for consideration.

In Figure 1.4, we plot the cost efficiencies and capabilities the market can offer against carrying out tasks and functions internally. Where the market is cheaper and better, then outsourcing is the obvious decision, but only for 'Qualifiers' and 'Necessary Evils'. An example is Federal Express providing customer delivery for Dell. In the London Insurance Market, across the 2001–10 period, an ongoing, Xchanging provided back-office processing and services for policy and claims settlement. Major US and European companies offshore software development and call centers for similar reasons. Where the market offers an inferior cost and capability, then in-house sourcing will be the best alternative (assuming 'Distractions' are best not sourced at all). Where the market offers a better cost deal then this should be taken, but only for non-key activities ('Necessary Evils'). Where the market offers superior capability, but at a premium price above what the in-house cost might be, then there still may be good reasons for buying-in or close partnering with the third party, not least to leverage and learn from their expertise, and apply it to 'Qualifying' and 'Order Winning' activities.

Thus, the two figures help to summarize the main criteria for making sourcing decisions. Use of the matrices requires decisions on trade-offs in order to establish the least risky ways external parties can be leveraged to organizational advantage. We will deal with this in the following section. However, making the right sourcing decisions does not guarantee their successful implementation. Chapter 4 will detail the internal capabilities that must be developed to manage the risks, relationships, and performance issues inherent in the extensive use of external service providers and business allies.

Configuration as a key task

Configuration is central to any decisions about outsourcing. Simple discussions about selective versus total outsourcing just do not cut it. Why should the CEO be involved? A vendor CEO put it succinctly: 'The customer from hell is the naïve buyer.' He was referring to senior client executives who did not know what they wanted, kept changing their minds, had disputes among themselves, did not do the detailed work up front, but having created a poor context and framework, nevertheless subsequently consistently blamed the supplier when things went wrong.

The CEO and senior team make key decisions when arriving at sourcing strategy. Where outsourcing is likely, the CEO needs to be further involved in what we call 'Configuration', that is making decisions about outsourcing scope; to whom; on what financial scale; how it is charged; the duration of the deal; resource ownership; and type of commercial relationship. The resulting portfolio of sourcing decisions in fact makes each organization's approach to outsourcing very different. This is one reason why management consultancy templates for outsourcing often run into problems.

Case example: Configuration

Consider the configuration differences between the following two examples. One is an insurer, the other a logistics provider. Both operate nationally with annual revenues of between $US2–5 billion. Both started outsourcing over nine years ago for similar reasons – cost savings – but their portfolios are very different.

The insurer entered into a facilities management arrangement with a sole supplier in a 3+2 term and $10 million yearly fixed-price. It sold its IT assets and data center at a high price, agreeing in return to pay high rates for services, and transferred its staff to the supplier. By contrast, the logistics provider entered into labor contracts with various suppliers that provided programmers to develop applications under the client's supervision. Its contracts were five-year fixed-term with a combined value of $30 million a year, unit-priced at per hour rates.

The main issue for the logistics company revolved around the extent to which its suppliers were expected to provide project management and methodology. The main issues the insurer had were the datacenter sale, staff transfers, and contracted costs greater than market price. Although both described their arrangements as 'outsourcing', the nature of the services they purchased, their contractual arrangements, their suppliers, and the issues faced were very different. If the CEOs of the two organizations met to share lessons, they could talk in general terms, but neither would have much to say of distinct benefit to the other.

Attributes of configuration

To provide a framework for understanding and crafting outsourcing solutions within and between organizations, we introduce the concept of 'configuration' – defined as *a high-level description of the set of choices the client has made in crafting its outsourcing portfolio and deals therein*. Reviewing an organization's outsourcing configuration is like looking out from a high vantage point over the buildings of a city and saying, 'We have one deal over here, the tall, thin, brown one. We have another deal over there, the short, fat, blue one', and so on. Each building is like an individual deal. Zooming in on any one building, the deal can be described in enormous detail: by the contract; service level agreements; and many other parameters. Configuration takes a 'zoomed out' view.

The configuration attributes show the choices available to management to structure deals that work for them (see Figure 1.5). The three attributes at the *portfolio* level are: (1) scope grouping, (2) supplier grouping, and (3) financial scale. The four attributes at the *specific* deal level are: (4) pricing framework; (5) duration; (6) resource ownership; and (7) commercial relationship. The CEO will be involved in decisions at the portfolio level and will ensure processes and dedicated senior executives are in place to accomplish specific deals. That said, in a mega-deal the CEO will be actively involved in establishing the commercial relationship (Attribute 7), and, at Board level, its ongoing development.

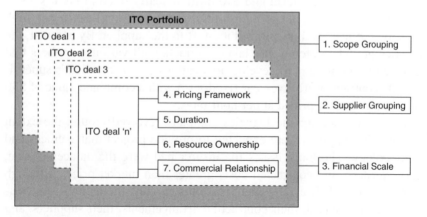

Figure 1.5 The seven attributes of configuration

Attribute 1: Scope grouping

Scope grouping describes what services are provided, to whom, and where, in terms of three facets: service, recipient, and geographic (see Table 1.1). *Service scope* describes the service bundles, or function segmentations

Table 1.1 Scope grouping

Facet	Options	Advantages	Disadvantage	Management issues
Service	1. Entire service scope	• Conducive to a sole or prime supplier	• Maintaining knowledge and control	• Retaining appropriate core competencies • Providing strategy and direction • Providing management focus and time
	2. Selected scope	• Conducive to best-of-bread and/or panels	• Integration of end-to-end processes and outcomes	• Total cost of ownership (TCO) management • Detailed performance metrics that aggregate to overall service metrics
Recipient	1. All business units	• Organizational consistency and standardization • Potential economies of scale	• Unique needs not met cost-effectively	• Getting buy-in from business unit management • Tailoring agreement to meet unique needs while keeping necessary items standard
	2. Business unit self select	• Accountability and ownership	• Integration between business units	• Extensive contract flexibility and rights (e.g., to merge or eliminate business units, move contract under a prime)
Geographic	1. All geographies	• Organizational consistency and standardization • Potential economies of scale	• Inconsistent market capabilities between regions	• Getting buy-in from regional management • Tailoring agreement to meet unique needs while keeping necessary items standard
	2. Geography self select	• Accountability and ownership	• Integration between regions	• Extensive contract flexibility and rights (e.g., to merge regions, and 'chop and change' scope, move contract under a prime)

that have been, or are to be outsourced, aligned with the traditional segmentation of a particular business function (e.g., IT, HR, Procurement). *Recipient scope* refers to the business groups (that is divisions, units, subsidiaries) that receive the outsourced services. *Geographic scope* refers to the physical locations that receive services. Any combination of service, recipient, and geographic scope may be configured.

Attribute 2: Supplier grouping

Supplier grouping refers to the approach taken to selecting suppliers (see Table 1.2). There are four options and any or all can be in place. The

Table 1.2 Supplier grouping options

Option	Advantage	Disadvantage	Management issues
Sole	• Single point of accountability • Potential to pass on economies • Streamlined contracting costs and processes • End-to-end key performance metrics	• Monopolistic behaviors by the sole supplier • Compromise quality where the sole supplier is not best of breed (in certain services, industries, or geographic locations)	• Extensive contract flexibility and rights due to the dependence on the one supplier • Need independent expertise to avoid solution channelling and ensure value for money (quotes reflect market values)
Prime	• Single point of accountability • Allows the potential for best-of-breed subcontracting • Streamlined, but a bit more complex, contracting costs and processes • End-to-end KPIs	• Prime supplier must be good at the subcontracting lifecycle (selection, management, disengagement) • Client may desire different subcontractors than those proposed by the prime supplier • Client often required to resolve issues between the prime and subcontractors when they cannot resolve them • Primes and subcontractors often encroach on each other's 'territory' without the permission of the client	• Contract design ensuring various rights over the subcontracting (access, selection, veto, etc) • Compliance auditing ensuring the prime supplier passes on obligations to the subcontractors • Oversight ensuring all parties are operating as an efficient united front

continued

Table 1.2 *continued*

Option	Advantage	Disadvantage	Management issues
Best of breed	• Greater control • Flexibility to chop and change • Promotes competition and prevents complacency	• Attracting the market for smaller 'slices' of work • Keeping suppliers interested, thereby giving management focus and allocating staff • Interdependent services and contracts • Integration complexity • Tracing accountability	• Designing inter-dependent contracts between independent suppliers • Multi-party interface and handover management • End-to-end process management is more difficult • Multiple lifecycle management
Panel (preferred suppliers)	• Buy services and assets when required • Promotes ongoing competition • Prevents complacency	• Attracting the market when panel membership is a pre-qualification and does not guarantee work • Adding new panel members due to market conditions changing • Potential limitation of client rights if suppliers not on the panel are desired	• Bidding process of panel members for contracts or work orders • Ongoing ranking of panel members based on performance • Managing and evaluating the total program

major options are sole supplier, prime supplier, best of breed, and panel. *Sole supplier* arrangements have one supplier providing the scope of the outsourced services. *A prime supplier* arrangement is when one head supplier is accountable, and contractually liable, for the outsourced services but uses any number of subcontractors to deliver part of the scope under contract to itself. A *best-of-breed* approach is where a client has any number of suppliers, each providing unique services. A *panel* is a list of preferred suppliers who compete for work over a defined period, and may not have any guaranteed work. There are issues and challenges with all these approaches, and getting decisions wrong here can have deleterious strategic consequences for the client organization.

Attribute 3: Financial scale

Financial scale indicates the degree of outsourcing performed in a financial sense measured in two ways: relative and absolute (see Table 1.3). *Relative financial scale* is the percentage of IT or business process/function spend

Table 1.3 Financial scale components

Component	Description	Examples	Management issues
Relative	The % of operating spend represented by the outsourcing portfolio	• >80% Majority outsourcing • >50% < 80% Major outsourcing • >20% <50% Moderate outsourcing • <20% Minor outsourcing	• Large scale is often high risk, and consumes significant management resources • Small scale often receives scant attention from both parties
Absolute	The per annum value of the outsourcing portfolio	• $1B Mega deal • $100M Major deal • $10M Moderate deal • $1M Minor deal	• Large deals attract market focus • Small may need to get the market's attention

represented by the outsourcing portfolio. It indicates financial criticality to the client. *Absolute* is the annual value of the outsourcing portfolio. It indicates importance to the outsourcing industry.

Attribute 4: Pricing framework

The pricing framework describes the payment method. There are three options: lump sum, unit, and cost-plus. *Lump-sum fixed-price* contracts are lump sum (e.g., $2 million annually for a call centre). *Unit-price* contracts charge per transaction unit (e.g., $13 per call). *Cost-plus* contracts have the supplier pass through actual costs plus a profit provision via a mark-up (e.g., operators at cost, with a 3 percent mark-up) or flat management fee (see Table 1.4).

Attribute 5: Duration

Duration reflects the contract length. There are three options: single-term, evergreen, or rollover. *Single-term* deals have a fixed duration that expires on a specified date (see Table 1.5). *Evergreen* deals have no expiry, rather it continues until either party terminates. *Rollover* contracts have a fixed initial term with options to extend. Extensions can be automatic (parties must agree not to extend) or optional (ends unless the extension is agreed). Any of these can be short or long term. For example, a single-term deal could be for one or ten years and an evergreen deal could end after one year or go on for a decade. A rollover could be any number of years, so a 3+2+2 deal could be three, five, or seven years depending upon the extensions taken up.

Table 1.4 Pricing options

Option	Advantage	Disadvantage	Management focus
Lump sum, fixed price	• Potential to lock in cost • Predictable costs within the specified volume bands • Explicit financial goal	• Misinterpretations over what is 'in' and 'out' of scope • Negotiating requirement changes • Lose track of individual cost drivers, when lumped into one sum • Difficult to reduce price when lesser volumes are required • Portion of the fixed price relates to the risk determined by the supplier in terms of the volatility of cost to supply	• Continuous forecasting again fixed price limitations such as volume constraints • Explicit scope definitions • Agreeing charges for 'out-of-scope' work • Unbundling lumped prices to assess cost drivers or benchmark
Unit pricing	• Ability to 'chop and change' services • Volume discounts • Can reduce costs by reducing demand • Can track unit costs, • Assists charge-back if usage is detailed	• Premium if supplier does not have a base guaranteed workload • Exceeding budget as supply is effectively 'unlimited', particularly if there has been pent up demand or latent demand created	• Demand tracking and management, as price is directed related to usage
Cost-based pricing	• Full knowledge of cost dynamics • Retain knowledge of operations • Can track unit costs, in particular when calculating total cost of operations (TCO)	• Costs are known, but in the control of the supplier • Costs incurred prior to scrutiny, can only correct future behavior, not recoup past losses' • Supplier often is reliant upon client directions • Supplier does not have inherent motivation to reduce cost	• Understanding of cost drivers and market prices • Directing supplier's efficiency • Auditing and benchmarking of supplier's costs and efficiency

Attribute 6: Resource ownership

Resource ownership describes which party controls or 'owns' the service resources. 'Ownership' is not literal; it identifies the party holding leases, licenses, or labor agreements. Figure 1.6 shows the various ownership alternatives that can exist in any given deal. It describes the various

Table 1.5 Contract duration options

Option	Advantage	Disadvantage	Management focus
Single term	• Can be aligned to life of assets or other contracts	• Often results in a retender, even if the supplier has performed well	• Preparing for end of contract
Roll-over	• Pre-set conditions for extending the contract past the initial term, • Motivates the supplier to do well	• Client tends to retain absolute rollover discretion, thus is not guaranteed • Rollovers occur with no competitive tension	• Assessing the rollover conditions as well as the current market conditions (to decide if a retender is warranted)
Ever-green	• Never 'out of contract'	• Complacency in either or both parties	• Continuous assessment of contract

	Party Owning the Resource (S = supplier, C = client)												
Resource	S	C	S	C	S	C	S	C	S	C	S	C	S
Assets (hardware and or software)	✓		✓			✓	✓			✓		✓	✓
Facilities (purpose built and/or office site)	✓			✓	✓			✓	✓			✓	✓
Labor (direct and/or management)		✓	✓		✓			✓		✓	✓		✓
	Infra-structure		Onsite		Service & Facility		Buy-in		Facility Host		Labor		Total
	Type of Outsourcing												

Figure 1.6 Resource ownership alternatives

options that resource ownership configuration may take and summarizes the advantages and disadvantages of the various options.

Attribute 7: Commercial relationship

Commercial relationship summarizes the overall nature of business transactions between the parties. Options are arms-length, value-add, co-sourced, and equity (Table 1.7). *Arms-length* is between independent parties for mutually exclusive accountabilities. *Value-add* is where the parties have arms-length services as well as shared business initiatives, such as the commercialization of a developed application. *Co-sourcing* is where both parties provide labor and assets, and have integrated accountability. *Equity* relationships are where related entities provide services or through a joint-owned entity such as a joint venture.

Table 1.6 Resource ownership options

Options	Advantage	Disadvantage	Management focus
Infra-structure	• Access to facilities and technology without capital investment • Pay for required capacity • Potential for volume discounts	• Potential switching costs • Often requires commodity or standard type asset use (vanilla solutions) • Contract length tends to reflect asset life, not business plan cycle	• Capacity planning • Ensuring security and disaster recovery at supplier • Ensuring asset refreshment is at market standards and prices
Onsite	• Co-location promotes interaction and understanding • Greater degree of confidentiality • Can observe supplier's staff • More seamless services	• No economies of scale from shared facilities with other clients • Supplier's staff adopt the culture of client rather than the supplier's	• Support, maintenance, and security of facilities • Maintaining a professional and effective relationship
Service and facility	• Assets are able to ported to alternative supplier or back inhouse at minimal cost • No novation of software licenses or asset leases required	• Ensuring assets are maintained in accordance with warranty • No economies of scale from shared assets with other clients	• Relationship management • Ongoing performance and compliance reviews • Ensuring security and disaster recovery at supplier
Buy-in	• Direct control of service delivery and outcomes • Pay for required assets • Can incorporate competition for each buy-in round via panel	• Supplier has little accountability other than to meet specifications	• Asset specification, implementation, integration and management
Facility host	• Direct control of service delivery and outcomes • No need to support and maintain purpose built facility	• Network link to host – another potential node fault • Limited physical access to site	• Network management • Ensuring good security and disaster recovery at supplier
Labour	• Access to skill base and expertise • Lower switching costs, if specialized organizational knowledge not required	• Service outcome accountability difficult to separate between parties • Site accommodation and access for supplier staff	• Providing clear directions to the supplier • Auditing of supplier timesheets

continued

Table 1.6 *continued*

Options	Advantage	Disadvantage	Management focus
Total	• Greater focus on 'core' business • Access to facilities and technology without capital investment • Centralized support • End-to-end performance metrics • Less integration issues	• Loss of control • Over-dependence on the supplier • High exit barriers and disengagement costs • Significant transition requirements • Extensive rights required in contract	• Relationship management • Ongoing performance and compliance reviews • Maintaining and obtaining knowledge without ongoing direct experience • Ensuring viable termination options and sourcing alternatives • Auditing internal controls at supplier

Table 1.7 Commercial relationship options

Options	Advantage	Disadvantage	Management focus
Arms-length	• Distinct accountabilities • Transparency	• Can result in a more adversarial approach	• Delivery of accountabilities
Value-add	• Ability to derive greater mutual value from the relationship	• The value-added component can get left behind in the need to deliver the 'core contract' • The risk/reward sharing of potential initiatives are often good concepts rarely worked out in advance and are difficult to implement	• Delivery of accountabilities plus planning and executing initiatives
Co-sourced	• Both parties contribute valuable expertise • Co-location facilitates shared commitment of field staff • Client tends to maintain directional control	• Shared accountability decreases 'answerability' • Often means client bears majority of risk • Disengagement turmoil	• Establishing and ensuring shared values when supplier wants profit and the client wants to control costs • Cost savings and overrun sharing

continued

Table 1.7 *continued*

Options	Advantage	Disadvantage	Management focus
Equity	• Shared governance and often board representation • Can facilitate the transition – asset, facility, and staff transfers • Both parties receive a return on investment if profitable	• Partners with different agendas – supplier to make profit and client to have low cost • Unwinding equity to cancel contract or vice versa • Makes use of alternative suppliers politically difficult and could be contractually prevented	• Managing the contract as well as the entity or equity investment • Ensuring a balance of political, economic, and legal power such that one party is not more dominant than the other

Configuration in action

How does this schema assemble itself in practice? And what are the consequences of getting it wrong?

Case example: Getting it wrong – and right

Take one of our researched cases – a state-owned enterprise – as an example. This organization has annual revenues of $1 billion. The initial outsourcing deal was for the entire IT function. Viewing the configuration at the portfolio-level described above, with references to the different configuration descriptors, the organization outsourced all its IT (1) to a prime supplier (2). This was worth $20 million yearly (3a), with 100 percent of the IT budget outsourced (3b). Viewed at the deal-level, this configuration involved a 5+5 year (4) fixed-price contract (5). Resource ownership (6) was such that the supplier owned the assets, bought from the client, and was responsible for labor. Facilities were split with the client owning the helpdesk facilities and the prime supplier subcontracting the datacenter. This was intended to be a partnering-style deal (7).

By the end, the client had no in-house expertise, costs had risen, service had dropped, and the promised strategic leadership never materialized. By most measures, the deal was not a success. Near the end of the deal, the organization hired a new CIO who reconfigured the arrangement. Viewed at the portfolio-level, services were re-scoped into three groups (1), which were contracted to three best-of-breed suppliers (2). These contracts (3a) amounted to a moderately large arrangement (3a), representing almost 100 percent of the IT budget (3b). At the deal level, each contract had different terms (4). One was 3+2, one 6+3+3 and one evergreen. Pricing was hybrid in all, with fixed and unit-priced elements (5). Resource ownership changed so that each supplier provided and managed the resource base (including facilities, assets, and labor) (6). Each contract was arms-length (7). At the end of the first year, savings for all three were significant; however, service quality was good for only two.

When it re-contracted, this government agency changed many configuration attributes. Particularly important changes were the move to arms-length relationships, the move to hybrid pricing, and the change of resource ownership where the suppliers now provide all resources.

In short, there is not a simple answer to achieving success with outsourcing. Nevertheless, the configuration attributes show the choices available to management for structuring deals that work for them. Each organization must design, and often re-design, the configuration levers that will work best. The CEO has a key role in making sure this happens.

Managing the process: The outsourcing lifecycle

Sourcing strategy means little without understanding and planning for the full journey a deal takes. We propose a systematic lifecycle process that optimizes results. This works because it links business strategy with sourcing strategy, and to the means by which they can be dynamically delivered across the lifetime of outsourcing contracts. A CIO of a major bank that had outsourced its IT in a 1997 ten-year deal commented in 2005: 'The major lesson? Getting sufficient granularity in plans, processes, and actions to give us transparency, then control.' Putting in place the process described in this section gives that granularity, transparency, and control. Outsourcing continues to raise expectations and pose challenges for all organizations. Repeatedly, we found even experienced organizations running into massive problems, suffering from slow organizational learning, and working in a reactive rather than an anticipatory mode. Unfortunately, for clients and service providers alike, outsourcing initiatives are usually conducted in a disjointed manner, with different individuals or teams independently carrying out, what are in fact, interrelated activities (as depicted in the 'common approach' shown in Figure 1.7).

For example, the CEO may determine the services to be outsourced, the legal team to prepare the contract, an operational team to prepare the Service level agreements (SLAs), a separate team to select the service provider, and a different team altogether formed to manage the service provider, and so on. In many cases, these teams have not fully understood the implications of the other team's outputs and more importantly, have not been privy to the debates and issue resolutions that took place to get there.

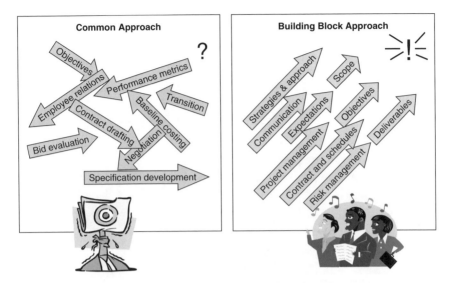

Figure 1.7 Streamlining the approach through the lifecycle

Because of this, they lack a thorough understanding of the basis for the final arrangement. Furthermore, the outputs of the various teams overlap, at a minimum, and in the worst case can contradict each other.

One of our profound frustrations has been to watch organizations repeat mistakes that others made over a decade ago. Another has been to watch organizations go through painstakingly long learning experiences that could easily be circumvented from the existing knowledge on outsourcing management. Our model intends to provide a missing piece to that knowledge. It answers the question: What process works best?

The need for such a model is apparent from our finding that 60 percent of organizations believed their own lack of experience was one of the most significant problems encountered during the contract term – more than any of the other 14 typical problems identified. It is this lack of experience that this research aims to counter – by accelerating the evolution of (our) hindsight into (your) foresight.

Using our structured approach helps to eliminate the mistakes others have made, and reap the benefits. Following it takes no more elapsed time than conducting error-prone approaches. Moreover, it guards against the 'cumulative damage' effect we observe regularly in our case studies. Failures and omissions early in the outsourcing cycle invariably have severe repercussions at a later stage. In outsourcing, a stitch in time really does save nine. Everything in this lifecycle has been tried, tested, and found to work effectively in over 100 actual outsourcing deals – large and small, complex and simple, in dozens of industries, in many countries, for 50 different business functions.[15] On the basis of the success and failings of the

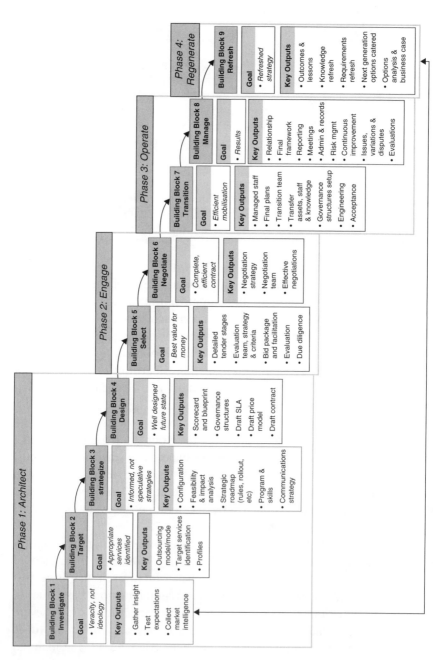

Figure 1.8 The outsourcing lifecycle – goals and key outputs

100 outsourcing cases and tested via in-depth interviews in 7 large organizations, and applied to many others, we present a 4-phase/9-building block lifecycle containing 54 key activities summarized in Figure 1.8.

The outsourcing lifecycle presented here is a structured way to make decisions, prepare for, and manage outsourcing from pre-contract to contract end. In the lifecycle, each phase, and the building blocks therein, prepares the way for the following phases and building blocks. Likewise, the success of each building block depends on the preceding ones, with the last one paving the way for the next-generation sourcing strategy and its lifecycle.

The concepts are presented as a comprehensive, high-level overview of the outsourcing lifecycle; showing *what* actions should take place, and *when* is the best time to conduct them. We found that organizations that followed the phases and building blocks in this sequence had more success and fewer problems than those that did not. However, the sequence of activities within each building block could be somewhat more fluid without deleterious results. We also found that organizations needed to 'walk through' the lifecycle before embarking on it, to decide what they would need to know and what events or actions would need to take place for the outsourcing to succeed as a multi-generational program. For this reason, in the Architect Phase, you essentially need to work backwards from the last building block to the first to understand the entire lifecycle. You then execute from the first building block onward.

One will ask where the supplier fits into the client's lifecycle. This is shown in Figure 1.9. Where potential suppliers begin to play a role in the lifecycle is up to you, as client. Nevertheless, suppliers are always involved in the Engage Phase. Many potential suppliers are often involved much earlier, of course, in helping clients architect the optimum deal or where a staged market testing approach is used before the final bidding process is undertaken.

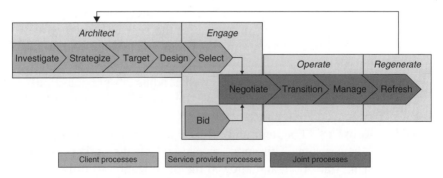

Figure 1.9 The outsourcing lifecycle – where the supplier fits in

The architect phase

As discussed earlier, *The Architect Phase*, where the foundation for outsourcing is laid, consists of the first four building blocks – investigate, target, strategize, design. At the end of this phase, the organization knows itself well enough to confidently publicize its needs.

The architecting process is critical because the ever-present risk of self-interest and conflict between client and supplier. Minimizing this risk requires significant forethought and planning. There are a huge number of details that must be handled; which is why planning, implementing, and operationalizing the details matters.

As all too many deals have shown, without this initial architecting work, high costs will show up later, typically as loss of control, inadequate service, extensive out-of-scope charges, excessive management time and effort, and constant renegotiation. The Architect Phase puts a premium on developing an evidence-based sourcing strategy that pinpoints the services required and the outsourcing configuration that is most likely to deliver on expectations. Without this up-front work, significant issues will accumulate, and cost a lot more to resolve later in the lifecycle. Suppliers, too, recognize the eventual pain that ill-thought-out plans can cause. As one executive told us: 'There is generally an expectation that here is this knight in shining armour…. I'll get three times better service at half the price. So you have this large gap in expectations from the start'.

Case example: A state agency gains acumen, changes plans

A state government agency beginning a BPO initiative had formed some preliminary ideas and expectations, but believed it was prudent to investigate further. It investigated two state government agencies like itself, as well as a federal agency, and two private sector companies, studying in particular the service structure and strategy in each case, the sourcing decisions and lessons, and implications for itself.

This investigation helped form, as well as adjust, its previous thinking. Management learned, for example, that market offerings did not have IT systems up to their expectations. Therefore, they required the bidders to use its IT system and propose a development process to move to a new system. This approach caused little disruption to operations during transition, and allowed the organization to fully retain all its information during the term of the contract.

Management also found the market to be immature and disparate. So it opted for a staged open tender (public) rather than a direct closed tender (invitation only), which had been the original plan. The winning bid ended up being from a firm it would not have originally invited.

In its investigation, management also observed the importance of having both a dedicated transition team and a dedicated contract management team. When these were missing, they saw significant problems. So these team members were identified right away and formed the core project team for the entirety of the lifecycle. They also gave all other employees significant professional and personal assistance in making the transition. As a result, this agency did not suffer the typical staff morale plunge and loss of key personnel that have plagued others.

Most importantly, the investigation taught management the value of the Service Level Agreement (SLAs) schedule and the need to develop Key Performance Indicators (KPIs), which it had not known about. Management invested two months in getting the SLAs and KPIs right. Both parties credit that work with making the deal work smoothly over the entire term of the contract.

Building block 1: Investigate – discard the myths

Many misconceptions exist about what outsourcing can and cannot do for an organization. In practice each firm, and its circumstances, is different. In this building block, the primary goal is to replace ideological beliefs with goals appropriate to the organization's circumstances, its industry, and the markets where it procures services. Because outsourcing can be highly imitative behavior, where organizations attempt to duplicate the imperfectly observed success of others, there is a real need to discard myths and simplistic beliefs. An organization will never know what really made another deal successful: it may not be in the same position (e.g., the other client may have been a loss leader for the winning supplier); it may not be in the same market; it may not have the same structure; and it may not even be outsourcing the same mix of activities. The need, then, is to develop acumen about claimed benefits so that you can focus outsourcing on your own goals and organization's characteristics. Some sample CEO myths to discard before they bite back at you now follow. Remember: all myths have a grain of truth in them. Do not discount the promises, but analyze them very carefully, indeed, and take real steps to secure the outcomes you really need, which may be different from the ones on offer.[16]

1. 'Outsourcing IT and complex business processes is much like outsourcing anything else (e.g., catering, rubbish disposal, premises security).'
2. 'Vendors have inherent advantages in superior management practices and economies of scale. Therefore they will achieve lower costs while improving service.'
3. 'Longer term single supplier deals secure partnering relationships, lower transaction costs, and greater business advantage.'
4. 'Outsourcing is about spending as little as possible and monitoring outcomes, not managing. That can be left to the supplier.'
5. 'Drive the hardest commercial bargain possible. The supplier will look after its own profit margins. The contract is everything.'
6. 'Outsource your problems. The market is now mature enough to provide superior capability handle them.'
7. 'Client and supplier buying shares in each other secures superior partnering, technical innovation, risk sharing, and greater business leverage.'
8. 'Anything is going to be better than your existing department (IT HR, Procurement ... .)'.

Building block 2: Target – identify the right activities to outsource

There are no hard and fast rules about what should and should not be outsourced. Certainly, some types of services have been more popular targets, particularly those with mature markets, predictable demand, predictability of service costs, and well-known performance standards. The goal of this building block is for organizations to identify and then profile those areas where they can actually achieve sought-after benefits. (see above how to accomplish this. The matrices in Figures 1.3 and 1.4 also assist in this analysis).

Building block 3: Strategize – get prepared

The purpose of this building block is to conduct the planning that enables objective and knowledgeable decisions to be made throughout the remainder of the lifecycle. It is important to get this right. Wrong strategies create pathway inflexibilities that are difficult and expensive to change later. The strategies developed in this building block include:

• Rollout strategy: How the outsourcing initiative will be rolled out as a program.

- Organizational 'rules of the game' strategy: The underlying rules to be followed in outsourcing, such as allowing or not allowing in-house bids, conditions for transferring staff, the use of penalties and rewards in the contract, to name but a few.
- Lifecycle strategy: The detailed program for the outsourcing lifecycle, focusing particularly on building blocks 4–7.
- Staffing strategy: The expertise and people needed to manage and execute the program.
- Communication strategy: The how, what, when, where, and who to communicate.
- Decision-making strategy: The business case rules for key decisions, as well as the base case for the outsourcing 'go/no go' decision.
- Analysis strategy: The feasibility, risk, and impact assessment over the outsourcing initiative.

Building block 4: Design – detail the future

This building block wraps up the Architect Phase. Together with the other three building blocks, this phase leads to defining the planned *configuration* of the deal. These configuration choices define the 'rules for the upcoming game', so they need to be detailed (see the discussion on configuration above).

Accordingly, building block 4 results in detailed documents that articulate the future arrangement using commercial language, that is, in language potential providers understand and can bid on. The intent is to balance the often-competing interests of client and suppliers, while, at the same time, motivating the suppliers to provide the services and quality its client desires. The three main documents are the desired contract terms, the detailed SLAs, and the pricing model for the services. If these key governing documents are prepared in as close to final form as possible, and used as the baseline for the bidding process (in building block 5), the client increases the probability of obtaining exactly the services it requires, under the conditions it requires. Moreover, by leaving little to chance or opportunism, it gains considerable negotiating leverage and efficiency.

By the end of building block 4, you should also have designed the retained organization (the portion of your organization that will remain part of the service delivery chain – see Chapter 4), the contract management function that will monitor the relationship (see Chapter 7), and the desired inter-party relationship (see Chapters 2 and 3).

The time to decide what needs to be done, and by whom, is before opening bidding, not after the deal has been signed and everyone knows where they will be working. While it is tempting to wait and 'make a go of it', delaying organizational decisions is rarely successful. More likely, the organization suffers out-of-control costs, high staff turnover, inadequate supplier monitoring, and poor coordination among the parties.

Case example: An international airline's handshake agreement costs it plenty

The CEO of an international airline made an agreement with the top executive of a service provider because they had worked together before and trusted each other. The deal was simple enough. The service provider would take over call centre operations, its core business, so that the airline could focus on *its* core business. This was to be a *strategic partnership*, so both parties believed they only needed a brief, high-level memorandum of understanding (MOU). The contract and other specifications would be developed over time.

Years later, after both executives had left their companies, an internal audit revealed that (a) there was never a signed contract or a specification, and (b) the service provider had been over-billing for years. Each business unit was being charged a price per call, and simultaneously, the centralized accounts payable section was being charged for full cost recovery (even for such items as toilet paper at the service provider's facility). The over-billing resulted from there being no detailed descriptions of the services included in *price per call* nor the items to be charged as *reimbursable costs*.

The lesson this airline learned, and knowledgeable firms know, is that they should never give service providers complete discretion over what to charge or how to charge. We found successful organizations preparing their service level agreement, price framework, and contract *before* selecting their service provider so that the deal they want is put to market. In that way, negotiation is constrained to just a few elements, rather than the entire deal.

In all the cases we have studied where substantial portions of the deal were negotiated after selecting the service provider, or after the service provider had begun work, significant problems arose.[17]

The engage phase

The *Engage Phase*, where one or more suppliers are selected and the deal is negotiated, consists of the fifth and sixth building blocks – select and negotiate. Unfortunately, many organizations start their lifecycle here at the Engage Phase. However, skipping the Architect Phase is equivalent to starting to build a house before it is designed, hoping everything will turn out right in the end. Organizations need to spend and invest prior to the Engage Phase if they are really to save money. We return to this theme of getting on the optimal cost-effective path in Chapter 4. Meanwhile consider the following illustrative case.

Case example: A bank approaches the market without understanding its full needs

A bank issued a voluminous expression of interest (EOI) in an open tender process before determining its evaluation criteria. After receiving 14 widely varying bids, the evaluation team realized it needed a structured evaluation methodology to select a supplier.

The 11-member team therefore convened a methodology workshop to develop the evaluation criteria. By its close, the team realized the voluminous EOI had elicited only 30 percent of the information it needed to select a supplier.

To maintain the bank's credibility in the market, rather than shortlist to fewer suppliers, the team issued its request for tender (RFT) to all 14 suppliers.

Evaluating all RFTs added two months to evaluation and cost an extra $200,000 (not to mention the cost to the 14 suppliers). It took only one day to develop the criteria and the evaluation methodology, which would have prevented this excessive cost.

Building block 5: Select – choose the best supplier(s)

Building block 5 begins the Engage Phase. Its activities involve the competitive bidding process, facilitating and evaluating the bids, and conducting discovery and due diligence. This building block is where all organizations should increase their bargaining power by leveraging the competitive tension that naturally occurs in this phase. As discussed earlier, once the contract has been awarded, the organization's bargaining power plummets.

Competitive bidding is the most common selection technique, with most organizations using a tender (a request for proposal) to see how the marketplace will respond to its needs. This approach not only pressures suppliers to deliver their best value for money against their peers, but it also gives the client information to evolve and mature its selection decision. Determining which supplier(s) to depend upon for many years is akin to acting as the matchmaker for an arranged marriage. Vigilant selection delivers the best match – if the organization truly knows itself.

Our casework shows that appropriate selection depends on:

- The client's knowledge of the market and its players, including standard capabilities and processes, niche competences, geographic reach and differentiation, price ranges, and approaches. To gain all this information, the organization may need to issue a request for information (RFI) in BB1.
- The stability of the market's offerings. If the work to be outsourced is characterized by a short lifecycle, the client may need to scan offerings more than once. Again, an RFI is one way to assess market changes.
- The degree of influx of new entrants into the market. New entrants can change price/performance dynamics, competitiveness of the market, and current once-off opportunities. If this is the situation, the organization may need to issue a registration of interest (ROI) in BB1 to identify interested parties and their capabilities.
- The number of potential service providers. If sizeable, the organization may need to create a culling process to, say, evaluate only 5 bids rather than 20. An ROI in BB1 helps determine market size, and an EOI in BB3 helps create a shortlist for the BB5 tender.
- The degree to which the organization knows what it wants. If requirements are not certain and have not been commercially articulated (via the contract, service level agreement, and pro forma price schedule), then it may need to explore options and alternatives – typically done through an EOI.
- The completeness and competitiveness of preceding bids. If the organization does not receive enough information to make the right decision on solutions, pricing and providers, it can conduct a post-RFT. RFTs commonly involve (1) asking for a best and final offer (BAFO), (2) conducting parallel negotiations with two bidders to down-select to one, or (3) extending the clarification period after the bids have been received until all concerns have been ameliorated.

We discuss selecting and leveraging suppliers in much more detail in Chapter 3.

Building block 6: Negotiate – seal the deal

So much emphasis has been placed on negotiation in outsourcing contracts that an inexperienced person could believe it is the pinnacle of the outsourcing lifecycle – involving the greatest amount of work and the greatest risk of signing a bad contract. If it does become the pinnacle, then something has gone seriously wrong earlier.

At this stage organizations place themselves at risk in at least four ways.

- The organization has not drafted its desired contract and SLA requirements prior to opening the competitive process.
- Its business case is based on invalid baselines.
- It has not developed a feasible best alternative to a negotiated agreement (BATNA), so it has no well-thought-out alternative if a supplier radically changes its offer once at the negotiation table. This does happen.
- It has made itself vulnerable, perhaps by being on a firm, short deadline, thereby giving the supplier the leverage to act opportunistically.

When the Lifecycle Model is followed, negotiation simply involves refining the exact wording of various documents. It should not involve give-and-take negotiations over the intent of the deal because that is when parties win or lose depending upon the particular individuals involved. As one experienced respondent put it to us:

'Don't negotiate, calculate'

The contract and SLA should have already been developed (in BB4), the supplier's preferred alternatives declared, the discovery/due diligence by both parties concluded (in BB5), and the preparations for transition completed (novated or assigned licenses, asset inventories and audits, and so on, in BB4). But when prior lifecycle activities have not been conducted thoroughly, inevitably there will be issues that require negotiation.

The key is planning the negotiation in detail, by prioritizing the issues, determining the organization's position on each issue, knowing the individuals involved from both parties, and having BATNAs in hand and reviewed and approved by management beforehand.

The operate phase

The *Operate Phase* – where the deal is put in place, operationalized, and managed through its term – covers the seventh and eighth building blocks: transition and manage. In this phase the benefits and consequences of the previous work done (or not done) come home to roost. The Operate Phase either proceeds smoothly as a result of the strategies, processes, documents, and relationship management designed in the earlier building blocks, or the phase suffers, due to misinterpretations, ambiguities, disagreements, and disputes. At this stage, such problems can only be corrected through huge, and tedious, remedial efforts. Consider the following case, drawn from our database.

Case example: A finance organization learns how not to manage a provider

A financial organization assumed that compliance with the contract was a foregone conclusion, so no oversight of a HR/BPO contract was required. Thus, it handed oversight over to a low-level contract administrator and did not perform any compliance reviews until four years into the five-year contract. At that point, it hired an independent audit firm to evaluate the situation.

After an extensive process, the auditors determined that the supplier was only 40 percent compliant with the contract. Work totaling $US200,000 a year had not been performed, many KPIs were not being reported, many reports were not being generated, and the list went on. The auditors further noted that the client had been negligent in its contract management responsibilities. The supplier failed to carry out the required work because the contract required the client to request the work, which it had not done. Furthermore, the client did not follow up on KPIs or request missing reports, did not ask for performance review or planning forums, and so on. Another key finding of the audit report was that the client did not install any governance over the contract, so the supplier was allowed almost complete discretion in what it did.

Because of this audit, and to better manage its next-generation deal, the government organization put in place a seven-person contract management team, led by a senior contract manager. This contract-management function cost $US360,000 a year, but it was required to ensure savings of $US830,000 a year through specific contract-management activities, experienced personnel, and proactive management.

Building block 7: Transition – the starting gate

The Operate Phase starts with transition, which officially begins at contract commencement and ends on a specified date or when both parties sign a transition acceptance form confirming that all aspects of the arrangement are fully operational. Irrespective of the official start- and end-dates, the transition actually begins much earlier, and actually ends much later. In fact, if not managed properly, transition may never end. Therefore, all parties need to begin planning the transition as soon as it is reasonable to believe the deal may go ahead.

Just as 'Select' (building block 5) is not the beginning of the outsourcing lifecycle, 'Transition' is not the first building block for planning its operation. This transition building block should merely execute the plans made earlier. Inevitably, of course, there will be contingencies and adjustments needed when, as one CIO put it: 'the rubber hits the road'.

Building block 8: Manage – get the results

In essence, all previous seven building blocks prepare for this building block: manage. The game is actually played out in this part of the Operate Phase. This is where the benefits (and problems) of outsourcing appear. A decade of in-depth studies demonstrates that outsourcing cannot be contracted for, and then left largely unmanaged. Unfortunately a regular finding is that organizations greatly underestimate the amount, and different type, of management required when outsourcing on any sort of substantial scale.

The goal of the activities in this building block is to manage for results. Depending on the extent of the outsourcing, it can require the client to make profound changes in its strategic and operational mechanisms. Basically, clients must learn to manage outputs, rather than inputs, use negotiation and relationship management in place of direct control, and rely on periodic planning and reviews to take the place of day-to-day oversight of service delivery operations. These changes in management work are so significant, that we devote the whole of chapter 4 to them, though we also touch on more issues below, including details of the costs of outsourcing management.

The regenerate phase

The *Regenerate Phase*, where next-generation options are assessed, consists of one building block: refresh. Following this phase, the lifecycle begins anew, returning to the Architect Phase, where the organization prepares for its next-generation deal(s). An illustrative case shows how one organization managed this effectively.

Case example: A power utility re-invents the next generation deal

A utility was nearing the end of a third generation BPO contract for plant, equipment, and systems maintenance. It believed this was particularly necessary, as it had amalgamated three geographic regions, which had five quite different contracts, into two regions, each under a standard contract. The client was planning to conduct a re-tender for only one region. The other region was to be backsourced to a wholly owned subsidiary, to regain the operational competence it had lost from nearly 15 years of outsourcing. The contract management function was very concerned about having a related entity as a supplier, because that ran a high risk of substandard services and high cost.

The utility, then, conducted a detailed SWOT of the incumbent contracts to ensure that the third generation agreements built in the strengths of the previous, took advantage of the opportunities, addressed the weaknesses, and had contingencies for the threats. Based on the SWOT, the key areas of strength identified were a comprehensive and 'reader-friendly' contract, diligent contract management, monthly detailed performance review, retaining of in-house operation of core operational systems, and benchmarking between the suppliers. Weaknesses were a fixed price contract when the client needed to be able to chop and change services (changed to a fixed-price base-load, with interchangeable service units, and volume discounts for work above that). The key opportunity, to grow the subsidiary, was also the key threat. The threat was addressed by first, maintaining alternative competitive supply, secondly having substantially the same agreement with the subsidiary as it did with the independent supplier and thirdly, putting in the same governance.

After some initial politicking, the subsidiary 'fell into line as an arms-length provider' and was soon delivering the market equivalent standard of service. In fact, the utility was delighted by the speed in which it reached market performance. Furthermore, the subsidiary used the third-generation contract as the template for winning work outside the utility, which gave it a substantial advantage in competing for work as other competitors were blatantly less evolved.

Building block 9: Refresh – toward the next generation

All contracts end, either through early termination, or by reaching the natural end of the term. During a contract's life, firms and markets change, perhaps in ways that render past decisions inappropriate in a current context. For example, market growth may have created more competition, supplier capabilities have likely changed, and information disparities between the parties may have decreased. Thus, each client should re-assess its initial sourcing decisions before coming to the end of the current contract. Then the lifecycle begins anew.

Depending on the decisions made – the work to be re-tendered, backsourced (brought back in-house), or renegotiated with the incumbent supplier – the lifecycle is repeated, individually, for each option chosen. If the outsourcing configuration will differ significantly, the entire lifecycle may need to be repeated. However, if only re-tendering the same scope of work with little change to the deal, the organization may be able to begin at the Engage Phase. If backsourcing, the transition within the Operate Phase may be the appropriate starting point. In addition, if renegotiating the same scope but an improved deal, the organization might begin at building block 4 (design) then skip to building block 6 (negotiate).

It is important not to underestimate the investment needed in this phase. As a guideline, one very large organization, The UK Inland Revenue began its BB9 work 2.5 years before the end of a 10 year contract. Because of this work, it successfully switched suppliers and signed a further ten-year deal with the new suppliers in 2004. Interestingly, the CIO, John Yard paid out US$12 million to serious bidders to attract them, also signaling that the re-bid would be truly competitive, with the incumbent having no 'inside track' advantage.

The Refresh Phase receives more detailed treatment in Chapter 9. A comprehensive overview of the activities, and client and supplier responsibilities described in this section appears in Figure 1.10.

Challenges

This chapter has presented the CEO and senior team with two major outsourcing challenges: How do you arrive at a viable sourcing strategy that underpins business mission and direction? What process can you put in place to ensure that the strategy is implemented and pays off?

The CEO can deal with the strategy challenge by strategizing, configuring, and monitoring sourcing arrangements. The CEO can handle the process challenge by resourcing implementing, and being selectively involved in the outsourcing lifecycle. Our research evidence shows that outsourcing will be most successful if it is viewed as a strategy with a lifecycle rather than as a one-off transaction. The CEO and his/her organization will have more successful outcomes, and ITO/BPO deals that operate in

	Building Block	Key Activity	
		Client	
Architect	BB1: Investigate	1. Gather insight via experts and experienced organizations 2. Determine and test goals/expectations 3. Collect intelligence on market conditions and potential suppliers 4. Investigate similar decisions and peer organizations	
Architect	BB2: Target	5. Match goals to appropriate outsourcing model 6. Identify, with objective criteria, suitable services to outsource 7. Prepare the 7 baseline and future state profiles: service, cost, asset, staff, stakeholder, current contracts, and governance	
Architect	BB3: Strategize	8. Decide the rollout approach (big bang, phased, piecemeal) 9. Determine key 'rules' (e.g., governing docs, # suppliers, asset ownership, risk/reward) 10. Design the detailed end-to-end lifecycle program/projects 11. Identify and source the lifecycle skills 12. Prepare the lifecycle communications strategy 13. Prepare the business case rules and the base case 14. Assess feasibility, risk and impact to the organization	
Architect	BB4: Design	15. Prepare the commercial and operating blueprint 16. Develop the 4 balanced score metrics – service, financial, relationship and strategic 17. Draft the service level agreement – scope, metrics/incentives, reporting, & governance 18. Draft the price framework (fixed, variable and cost plus items) 19. Draft the contract considering the standard 100 issues (Attachment x) 20. Design the inter-party relationship (structure, roles, authorities, etc) 21. Design the retained organization (kept functions) 22. Design the contract management function (governance)	
			Service Provider
Engage	BB5: Select	23. Plan and detail the tender stages 24. Identify the right evaluation team/s – breadth and depth 25. Determine the right evaluation criteria and strategy for each tender stage 26. Request the right, clear and comprehensive bid data for each tender stage 27. Facilitate the best responses (briefings, Q&A, data room, tours, etc) 28. Use interactive evaluation techniques (interviews, site visits, etc) 29. Select supplier based on value for money 30. Conduct due diligence on supplier (company, price, solution, contract, and customer references)	23. Plan the approach to the tender stages 24. Identify the right bid team/s – breadth and depth 25. Determine the bid/no bid, or go/no go, criteria for each stage 26. Request the right, clear and comprehensive client data for each tender stage 27. Prepare the best response/s 28. Prepare for the interactive evaluation techniques 29. Conduct due diligence on client and data
		Both Parties (separate and joint as applicable)	
Engage	BB6: Negotiate	31. Prepare negotiation strategy and prioritise negotiation items 32. Conduct effective negotiations	

Figure 1.10 Key activities and responsibilities in the lifecycle: A comprehensive view

Building Block	Key Activity
	Client
BB7: Transition	33. Finalize and mobilize all plans (e.g., communications, risk, set-up, acceptance)
	34. Resource the transition project
	35. Manage the impact on staff (retained, transferring and departing)
	36. Manage the transfers (staff, asset, 3rd party contracts, work-in-progress, etc)
	37. Manage knowledge retention and transfer
	38. Implement retained organization and contract management
	39. Engineer workflows, communication channels, authorities, etc
	40. Conduct acceptance, closeout and post-implementation review
BB8: Manage	41. Invest in the relationship (plan, assess and improve)
	42. Meaningful reporting and analyses
	43. Regular communication and meetings
	44. Diligent documentation and administration
	45. Manage risks and plan contingencies
	46. Manage issues, variations and disputes
	47. Effect continuous improvement and streamlining
	48. Evaluate and audit supplier (controls, performance, compliance)
	49. Evaluate organization both as a customer and contract manager
BB9: Refresh	50. Assess next generation options (backsource, retain, handover)
	51. Assess contract outcomes and lessons
	52. Knowledge refreshment (e.g., market, technology, price, metrics)
	53. Reassess requirements – re-scope, re-bundle and re-design
	54. Determine the strategy and business case for each option

(Operate / Regenerate row labels on left)

Figure 1.10 *continued*

a cost-effective manner when they pro-actively ensure management of the entire outsourcing lifecycle.

As discussed, there is a recommended path and a flawed path. The difference is management. But this initially costs money. Although organizations outsource for a range of reasons, they all generally also aim to reduce costs. CEOs, CFOs, COOS, and CIOs are going to need to get their heads around the notion that the organization needs to invest in the outsourcing management process and requisite human resource capabilities in order to save real money.

Addressing the costs of management

Spending to save is the third big challenge in outsourcing for senior management. In this respect it is worth looking at outsourcing management costs. In re-analyzing our multiple research bases – by 2010 representing over 1200 deals,[18] we made three findings:

1. **Costs of getting to contract** fell between **0.4 percent and 2.5 percent** of contract value. As one example, in 1997 DuPont spent $US100 million when signing their seven year, $4 billion deals with CSC and Andersen Consulting.
2. These costs rise as a percentage as the size of the deal increases.
3. These costs rise as the percentage of IT/business processes outsourced increases.

We found **on-going outsourcing management costs** ranging from **3 percent to 10 percent** of total contract value.[19] Our 2001 survey found the average contract management cost to be 4.2 percent of total contract value. By 2009, for ITO this was averaging 5 percent, for BPO 7 percent. Managing offshoring costs more, from 10 percent to 12 percent in 2000, from 10 percent to 15 percent in 2003–04, and ranging from 12 percent to16 percent from 2005–09.[19]

As outsourcing becomes a core competency, wise organizations invest more in its management, even though spending more runs counter to most Boards' goal of spending less. Their real goal should be to continually spend less on contract management *per dollar outsourced*. We have found, though, that managing costs is less important than managing portfolio configuration, complexity, and risk.

Low spenders do not perform contract management; they perform what we call *contract administration*. We will develop the distinction in Chapter 5, where we discuss the evolution of client and market capabilities. Administering contracts may work where no significant contracts exist and where the outsourced activities are relatively simple to define, discrete, and easy to monitor. But for all other situations, simply administering a contract slowly, but ultimately, leads to an expensive erosion of control over the client organization's IT and business process destinies. Ironically, this can then result in a rapid growth in management costs as problems arise, and the client tries to claw back the ground lost.

Three further CEO challenges

These management cost considerations raise three further challenges for the CEO, because essentially these costs relate to relationship and people. The challenges are:

1. How do we create and sustain value-adding win–win relationships with our supplier(s)?

2. What people capabilities do we look for in the supplier, and
3. What capabilities do we retain in-house in order to keep on the optimal, cost-effective outsourcing path?

These challenges are critical because getting them right incurs costs, but also result in superior pay-offs from outsourcing. As a result we now devote a chapter to each of them, before moving to Chapter 5 and what then becomes possible, once these challenges have been addressed effectively.

Conclusion: Lessons on moving to the strategic agenda

In this chapter, we have provided an overview of why the CEO should care. Moreover we have detailed what the CEO should care about, make decisions on, and ensure is in place if the outsourcing enterprise is to show a strategic return on investment. The strategic lessons are:

1. Organizations fail because they outsource problems, messes, and things they do not understand. The lower risk option is to outsource activities you understand and can write detailed contracts for, and can monitor. Partnering arrangements are for mature clients to undertake. Buying-in resources to operate under your management is also a viable lower risk way to use the external services market.
2. Outsourcing disappoints where the CEO and senior management see it as about spending a little as possible on an activity or function, and about stepping aside from management. In fact, outsourcing is still about managing but in a different way, with different skill sets, if the organization is to retain control of its own destiny.
3. Signing long-term outsourcing contracts for short-term reasons has been, and will continue to be a regular source of serious disappointment.
4. Vendors still tend to be better at selling their services than clients are at buying them. This book is dedicated to developing better customers, as well as suppliers.
5. Client organizations, and their CEOs, still expect too much from ITO/ BPO vendors, and not enough from themselves. So what should they be able to do?

    a. Formulate and monitor sourcing strategy that fits with dynamically changing strategic and operational business needs for the next five years.
    b. Configure outsourcing arrangements that are optimal, making judicious, complementary choices across the seven attributes of configuration.

   c. Understand in detail the external services market, vendor strategies and capabilities, where vendors are coming from, and what a good deal with *this* vendor looks like.

   d. Put in place a process for managing across the lifecycle of all the organization's outsourcing arrangements.

   e. Arrive at a contract that delivers what you expect and need without sustaining high hidden or switching costs over the next three to five years.

   f. Put in place and sustain a post-contract in-house management capability that keeps control of the organization's IT/business function destiny, and leverages supplier capabilities and performance to mutual advantage.

Notes

1. Recent publications that distill this research are Willcocks, L. and Lacity, M. (2009) *The Practice of Outsourcing: From Information Systems to BPO and Offshoring.* Palgrave, London; Lacity, M. and Willcocks, L. (2009) *Information Systems and Outsourcing: Studies in Theory and Practice.* Palgrave, London; Willcocks, L. and Lacity, M. (2006) *Global Sourcing of Business and IT Services.* Palgrave, London; Oshri, I., Kotlarsky, J. and Willcocks, L. (2009) *Handbook of Global Outsourcing and Offshoring.* Palgrave, London; and Lacity, M., Willcocks, L. and Zheng, Y. (eds) (2010) *China's Emerging Outsourcing Capabilities.* Palgrave, London. See also Willcocks, L. and Craig, A (2009) *Outsourcing Enterprise5: Step-Change – Collaborate to Innovate.* Logica, London; and Willcocks, L., Grifiths, C. and Kotlarsky, J. (2009) *Beyond BRIC: Offshoring in non-BRIC Countries – Egypt A New Growth Market.* ITIDA, London. Further details and downloads are on www.outsourcingunit.org

2. See Willcocks, L. and Lacity, M. (2009) *The Practice of Outsourcing: From Information Systems to BPO and Offshoring.* Palgrave, London.

3. For evidence see Cullen, S. and Willcocks, L. (2003) *Intelligent IT Outsourcing.* Butterworth Heinemann, Oxford; Kern, T. and Willcocks, L. (2001) *The Relationship Advantage: Information Technology, Outsourcing and Management.* Oxford University Press, Oxford; Kern, T., Willcocks, L. and Van Heck, E. (2002) 'The winner's curse in IT outsourcing: how to avoid relational trauma', *California Management Review,* 44, 2, pp. 47–69; Lacity, M. and Willcocks, L. (2003) 'Information technology sourcing reflections', *Wirtschaftsinformatik,* Special Issue on Outsourcing, 45, 2, pp. 115–25.

4. Reported in Rohde, L. (2004) 'Sainsbury, Accenture to redo outsourcing pact', *Computer Weekly,* October 25.

5. Reported in Earle, A. (2004) 'End of the affair: bringing outsourced operations back in-house', *Computerworld,* May 31.

6. Wighton, D. (2004) 'JP Morgan scraps IT deal with IBM', *Financial Times,* September 16.

7. Reported by Miller, A. (2004) 'Outsourcing options and performance management in the private and public sectors', Presentation at *the Outsourcing Summit*, London, November 22.

8. Collins, T. (2004) 'MPs given little comfort on state of child support agency systems', *Computer Weekly*, October 28. As an example of parliamentary reports, see House of Commons Public Accounts Committee (2009) Central Government's Management of Service Contracts. Stationery Office, London.

9. Smith, H. (2010) 'The sky's the limit: liability for IT and outsourcing projects', *Herbert Smith Bulletin*, February.

10. Lacity, M. and Willcocks, L. (2009) *Information Systems Outsourcing: Studies in Theory and Practice*. Palgrave, London. Also Lacity, M. and Willcocks, L. (2001) *Global IT Outsourcing: In Search Of Business Advantage*. Wiley, Chichester.

11. Kern, T. and Willcocks, L. (2001) *The Relationship Advantage*. OUP, Oxford.

12. See also Willcocks, L. and Craig, A. (2009) *Outsourcing Enterprise5: Step-Change- Collaborate To Innovate*. Logica, London.

13. See Lacity, M. and Willcocks, L. (2001) op. cit. and Kern and Willcocks (2001) op. cit.

14. Talking in 2004, Kevin Rollins, the CEO who replaced Michael Dell, felt that outsourcing could cause a company to lose key knowledge in critical areas such as IT or raise costs as in manufacturing: *'philosophically, I'm opposed to outsourcing ... I don't like it for Dell clearly because I think it makes us higher cost, not lower cost.'*. Under Rollins, Dell kept all its manufacturing in-house, and in 2004 was planning to build a manufacturing plant in North Carolina to be close to Canadian and US customers. Other plants were being planned in Europe and Asia to be close to their customers there. These plans assumed sustained growth that did not always materialize in all markets. See Spooner, J. (2004) 'Dell's dirty words: outsourcing, proprietary', *CNET News* November 5.

15. Cullen, S. Willcocks, L. and Seddon, P. (2001) *Information Technology Outsourcing Practices in Australia*. Deloitte Touche Tohmatsu/University of Melbourne. The detailed research and academic underpinning appear in Cullen, S., Seddon, P. and Willcocks, l. (2005) 'Managing outsourcing: the lifecycle imperative', *MISQE* 4, 21, pp. 229–46. A much more detailed description for practitioners appears in Cullen, S. and Willcocks, L. (2003) *Intelligent IT Outsourcing*. Butterworth, Oxford.

16. A debunking of these myths appears in Cullen, S. and Willcocks, L. (2003) *Intelligent IT Outsourcing*. Butterworth, Oxford.

17. Cullen and Willcocks (2003) op. cit. is rife with examples. See also Willoccks and Lacity (2006) op. cit.

18. The first research base is the 106-case base used as the basis of the outsourcing lifecycle. The second is a 750 plus longitudinal case study database held at London School of Economics. An early publication drawing on this research base this was Lacity, M. and Willcocks, L. (1998) 'An empirical investigation of information technology sourcing practices: lessons from experience,' *MIS*

Quarterly, 22, 3, pp. 363–408. The third research study is a 2000 survey of over 280 deals described in Cullen, S., Willcocks, L. and Seddon, P. (2001) *IT Outsourcing Practices In Australia*. Joint Deloitte Touche Tohmatsu/ University of Melbourne, Melbourne. We also draw upon recent studies of offshoring covering some 85 case studies to date, for example Willcocks, L., Griffiths, C. and Kotlarsky, J. (2009) *Beyond BRIC: Offshoring in Non-BRIC Countries – Egypt as a Growth Market*. LSE, London; Lacity, M., Willcocks, L. and Zheng, Y. (2010) *China's Emerging Outsourcing Capabilities*. Palgrave, London.

19. In one of our studies, the deals that outsourced over 65 percent of the IT budget averaged a 10 percent management cost, while those under 25 percent of the IT budget averaged 3 percent. Management costs fell between 1 percent and 10 percent of contract value. Detailed case study research allows us to make some judgments about effective spend. If one excludes from these figures the organizations having poor experiences, those doing contract administration rather than effective management, and those playing catch-up due to early lack of investment, the figures of 3 percent to 10 percent are reliable for domestic outsourcing, checked across all our separate studies.

CHAPTER 2

Building the relationship advantage

Outsourcing contracts are agreed in concept but delivered in detail, and that's how the relationship can break down; the devil is in the detail.

          – CEO of a major supplier

We had to clean up our act ... we weren't as professional as they were.

          – Senior executive, US government agency

We want them to be successful. No-one wants a failing supplier.

          – COO, European Oil Company

Introduction

In trying to identify what makes for success in outsourcing, practitioners invariably highlight 'relationships' – but the study of how such successful relationships could be developed is quite recent, and relatively neglected.[1] Successful relationships don't just happen. In this chapter we show that overall strategic business intention must determine the nature of the relationship and the contract. A detailed design is essential to build effective relationships throughout the life of the deal. This determines the key underlying drivers of behavior, and whether power-based or trust-based relations emerge. Positive intervention by top management is vital to make the 'chemistry' work. We also point to the criticality of establishing targets. Thus a relationship values charter sets a benchmark for behavior, while regular health checks and contract card monitoring to assess the success of the relationship are crucial throughout. In practice, including relationships into a key metrics scorecard, covering also strategy, finance, and service is a significant move, signaling that an organization is willing not just to speak about how relationships are important, but monitor whether the parties enact the right behaviors to leverage those relationships.

Paying attention to outsourcing relationships

Outsourcing in itself is neither good nor bad. Its outcomes are determined by how it is managed before and after the contract has been signed. For example, our own study of organizations seeking IT cost savings found that good management made a 40 percent difference in cost savings achieved. Another study found client–supplier partnering arrangements were a major factor in explaining perceptions of outsourcing success. Our study of 235 client organizations identified good relationships as one of the most important factors contributing to effective delivery and successful contract management. Significantly, none of the organizations cited a good contract as the key factor. Good relationship management techniques, such as flexible working arrangements, willingness to change, and frequent and effective communication, were, however, regularly highlighted.[2]

Strategic intent

Outsourcing is more successful if it is viewed as a strategy, not as a transaction. Relationships form part of that strategy and are not an inadvertent by-product of executing a contract. By working proactively, the client organization can ensure relationships are effective and outcomes successful. Relationships, especially in large-scale deals, matter to the extent that they must be planned strategically at CEO and Board level. Only CEOs can determine the strategic intention of the relationship. CEOs can establish the major contractual parameters and determine ultimately whether the relationship is power- or trust-based. And only CEOs can ensure that the mechanisms, people, and incentives are in place to build the desired relationship.

In formulating an outsourcing relationship strategy, executives must first look at the business intention behind the deal. One useful model analyses outsourcing relationships as choices on strategy and capability (see Figure 2.1). According to this model, clients choose between degrees of operational efficiency or business value, and also between degrees of resource accessibility or leadership from the supplier.[3] Organizations that do not make choices in this deliberate and coherent way end up with confused and uncertain, often conflicting expectations that are very difficult to fulfill.

Case example

One major organization we studied treated outsourcing as a strategy to achieve organizational change, and planned their strategy with care. It did not assume cultural innovation as a guaranteed benefit naturally occurring

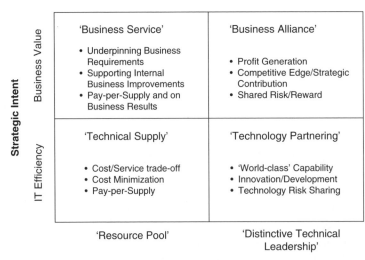

Figure 2.1 Outsourcing as the choice between strategic intent and business capability

from outsourcing. Management was preparing a whole-of-IT outsourcing contract but wanted more that just an operations contract. It believed the supplier would be well placed to introduce innovation and re-engineering sorely needed in a business that had not had the return on investment from IT. Accordingly, it knew it needed more than the 'standard agreement' for this to occur – akin to an operational alliance. It evaluated different re-engineering approaches to determine the one best suited. It designed detailed evaluation criteria and 'real life' scenarios to which the bidders were to respond. It tested various models with the industry (different payment and risk/reward schemes) until it had a model that it believed would work. The model chosen recognized that the supplier should be paid to generate ideas and business cases first. After the business cases were accepted or rejected, the supplier was remunerated for implementing them (but also putting some 'skin in the game' itself). Within the first year, it had received more innovation ideas than it had ever generated internally. The actual number of innovations implemented remained less than had been hoped, however, as the client had very entrenched ways of operating and was change-resistant. Nonetheless, management believed the introduction of the ideas and supporting business cases, alone, provided substantial benefits in unfreezing current mindsets on how and why technology was under-employed to move the organization from a change-resistant mentality to a change-embracing one. Thus the desired relationship, that of the supplier delivering operational services as well as being a vital change agent, was successful.

The nature of relationships

The contract is an obvious – but ultimately superficial – driver of day-to-day behavior. Less successful outsourcing deals over-emphasize the forces that drive behavior as shown in the upper region of the 'iceberg' in Figure 2.2. But these will only get you so far. The deeper and more powerful drivers are rooted in the values and attitudes of the people responsible for carrying out the agreement. These need to be expressed and secured in the processes and in the people involved across the outsourcing relationship.

These deep drivers in turn determine whether the relationship will be more power- or trust-based. Trust and power represent alternative ways to minimize risk and secure cooperation. Power-based relationships are based on the negative threat of sanctions that might be applied to gain compliance. In power-based relationships communication tends to be secretive, while conflict resolution becomes paramount as manipulation and blame spread. Short-term gains, 'more for less' and self-interest are the abiding motifs. However, power is a poor substitute for trust, given the high costs involved in monitoring and imposing sanctions, the negative orientations and behaviors adopted, and the limited goals that can be pursued by the parties.

How do you know when you are in a power-based relationship? Some typical quotes from our power-based case histories include:

- 'They always wait for us (the client) to react to something ... they play dead until we kick them.'

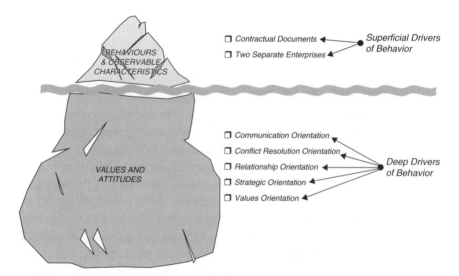

Figure 2.2 Outsourcing: The underlying drivers of behavior

- 'We know where they have problems but damned if I am going to tell them.'
- 'The supplier is only in it to make money.'
- 'It's tougher dealing with the supplier people than our helpful in-house staff.'

Contrast these statements with some typical ones we found in more trust-based outsourcing arrangements:

- 'We really handed them over a mess, so we're going to give them time to clean it up ... we couldn't do it ...'
- 'We had to clean up our act ... we weren't as professional as they were'.
- 'Our contract wouldn't let them hire any of our people for two years, but we had to cut them some slack on that one.'
- 'We want them to be successful. No-one wants a failing supplier.'

Our finding is that relations that generate trust offer an important competitive advantage over those that do not. And this means moving to more open and collaborative communications, resolving conflicts constructively, and seeing the arrangement as a co-dependent long-term investment designed to benefit both parties.

This is not to say that power, and especially the balance of power, is not important. Outsourcing relationships where power is more equally distributed are much more successful for both sides than those in which one side dominates. At the same time, trust is not won automatically but is built on regular delivery of what is expected and what has been promised. Without delivery, trust will not build – or will slowly erode – and both sides resort to power-based relationships and tight contract terms in order to try to get what they want.[4]

In most cases the client will want a balance between the two alternatives of power and trust. Extremes of either are generally unacceptable to clients or suppliers and rarely sustainable over longer periods. A more typical pragmatic pattern is for relationships to start more contract- and power-based, then move to more trust-based as trust is earned over time by performance. Chapter 5 develops this theme further in the context of moving to collaborative innovation.

The power of people

The outsourcing relationship is amorphous and ambiguous, but it is crucial to the success of the whole outsourcing initiative. There continues to be a blindly naive belief that outsourcing is a relatively straightforward transaction involving the simple transfer of services to a supplier, and that benefits will automatically follow. But outsourcing is not a straight-forward transaction: it is a complex strategy for managing the delivery of what is often a range of services. Like all management strategies, the key to success lies in how that strategy is planned, implemented, and managed. This depends, first, on the people involved, and, secondly, on how productive relationships are built and sustained throughout the lifecycle of the arrangement.

Have no doubt, individual people can get in the way of outsourcing success. In a major oil company the CIO commented: 'When X was in place as a demand manager nothing got done; when Y took his place it all began to happen.' In the major UK Inland Revenue deal we researched, both client and supplier contract managers fought adversarially over the contract for the first 18 months. Eventually both were replaced by people more competent to build and sustain the ten-year relationship. Very frequently we found senior managers admitting an initial over-focus on contract management and large under-estimations of change in mind-set and skills needed to staff up outsourcing arrangements.

Some manager types are definitely unhelpful.[5] For example, on the client side we have seen people far too passive or over-dependent on the supplier. One variant here is the client who forces the supplier to make all the decisions. Others manage what is most familiar, and may well get involved in its technical detail, rather than accepting the broader management remit needed. Some define themselves as administrators, seeing their role as passive – processing, dissemination, and filing. Others see the supplier as untrustworthy and one to blame for most things that go wrong in the deal. This can breed adversarial behavior among all parties, over time and can become a self-fulfilling prophecy.

On the supplier side, we have seen other dysfunctional role types. Some focus entirely on profit, no matter what was agreed, or over-focus on selling new work, rather than delivering what is actually in the contract. Some are the polar opposite and are willing to deliver whatever the client insists on, and may well be at odds with their own management as a result. Others we have seen include those who block changes and want to reduce everything to routine; and those who are waiting to be caught out and see quick apology as their main weapon (in outsourcing it's not a sustainable one). Our classification of unhelpful client and supplier types are shown in Table 2.1.

In Table 2.2 we collect together the much more positive role models emerging from our research studies. For the listing of negative and positive roles we can populate each role with scores of people whose performances we have researched and monitored. In looking down the client roles note

Table 2.1 Contract manager stereotypes – 'Baddies'

Client	Supplier

• **The Administrator**
  – Passive processing, dissemination, and filing
	• **The Apologizer**
	  – Waits to be caught out, then quick to say sorry

• **The Adversary**
  – Supplier is evil and to blame for all things
	• **The Caged Animal**
	  – Can't deliver, but being forced to try anyway

• **The Comfort Seeker**
  – Manages what is most familiar
	• **The Freezer**
	  – Tries to block changes, wants routine

• **The Defensive Posturer**
  – Forces the supplier to make all decisions
	• **The Obliger**
	  – Willing to do whatever the Client wants, often at odds with own management

• **The Mouse**
  – Disempowered and doesn't want to upset the supplier
	• **The Shark**
	  – Focused on selling new work, not deliver 'old' work

• **The Virgin**
  – Naive and completely trusting
	• **The Chainsaw**
	  – Must make a profit no matter what was agreed

that each is concerned with making sure that the interests and views of all parties are considered, and with trying to move the deal on to mutual advantage.

Some additional roles need to be inherent across all parties to a relationship. Any one of these present in an outsourcing arrangement will make a noticeable difference. In the best arrangements all will be present across the organizations and their contract management teams (see Figure 2.3). What makes the chemistry work? Our observations suggest there are six underlying, deep attributes that combine in these positive roles across both parties to the deal. The first is monitoring and protecting, that is ensuring the organization is protected, risks are addressed, and compliance is comprehensive. The second is facilitation and problem solving – making things happen, breaking down barriers. A third is organizing by planning processes, maintaining records, audit trails and controls. Relationship development is the fourth, by which we mean facilitating trust, respect, and interpersonal relationships. Entrepreneurship is also needed in order to seek innovation, better ways of doing things and leverage the long-term potential inherent in the relationship. Finally, both parties will have scanners who are well networked and connected, are natural explorers, know the details of other agreements and relationships, and are natural benchmarkers on issues such as practices, costs, risks, and contract clauses.

Table 2.2 Contract management – positive role models

Client	Supplier
• **The Empathizer** – Takes into account the supplier's needs and motivations	• **The Saviour** – Turns the shop around and continues to produce answers
• **The Collaborator** – Involves the supplier and seeks their perspective	• **The Pleaser** – Continuously trying to satisfy the client and introduce improvements
• **The Wise Owl** – Knows the industry well, has managed a multitude of deals before, and knows how to manage both sides	• **The Straight Shooter** – Tells it like it is, forthright
• **The Progresser** – Focused on continuous improvement in both parties, an entrepreneur of sorts	• **The Trusted Colleague** – Can be relied upon, is a good sound board and even provides mentoring
• **The Facilitator** – Problem solver, makes things happen	• **The Value Maximizer** – Seeks to add value and long-term potential to the deal
	• **The Relationship Developer** – People person: facilitates trust and respect at all levels

- **Monitor/protector**
  - ensures the organization is protected, risks are addressed, and compliance is comprehensive
- **Facilitator/problem solver**
  - makes things happen, gets over 'hiccups', breaks barriers
- **Organizer**
  - maintains records, audit trails, and controls; plans processes
- **Relationship developer**
  - facilitates trust, respect, and interpersonal relationships
- **Entrepreneur**
  - seeks innovation, better ways of doing things, and long-term potential out of the relationship
- **Scanner**
  - well networked/connected, natural explorer, knows details of other agreements and relationships, natural benchmarker (practices, costs, risk, contract clauses)

Figure 2.3 Contract management: Team chemistry

Round and round we go: The relationship cycle

But it is not just people. It is also the process and structures they work in. The first chapter introduced a comprehensive lifecycle comprising four phases and

Table 2.3 Building relationships across the lifecycle

Building block	Relationship technique highlighted
1 – Investigate	investigate relationships that have worked (or not) and why
2 – Target	craft the type of relationship best suited to the envisioned deal
3 – Strategize	profile the services, in particular the stakeholder profile
4 – Design	articulate desired behaviors through a relationship charter/code of conduct
5 – Select	choose a supplier that has demonstrated the desired relationship
6 – Negotiate	signal desired relationships and win–win. Involve delivery people in the process
7 – Transition	define clear and comprehensive transition roles
8 – Manage	put in place continuous improvement through relationship health checks
9 – Reconsider	incorporate lessons via a relationship SWOT near the contract end

nine key building blocks (see Figures 1.1 and 1.8). The lifecycle represents only the activities of one party – the client. The need for a client model is evident from our survey analysis, which found 60 percent of clients attributing their own lack of experience as one of the most significant problems encountered – more than the other 14 typical problems identified.[6] It is this lack of experience that the lifecycle aims to counter. Here we use the lifecycle to highlight techniques for clients to design the relationship they desire. A particular focus is given to the design of sustainable relationships and the issues and practices regarding such design. These are highlighted in Table 2.3.

Building block 1: Investigate relationships that work and ask why

The purpose of building block 1 is to replace ideological concepts with realistic expectations appropriate to the client's circumstances and the outsourcing markets in which it may procure services. An organization considering outsourcing may not have a safe general set of assumptions – including about relationships – from which to make outsourcing decisions. It is therefore important to go out and test those assumptions with experts, other organizations, and the market before embarking on the outsourcing journey.

Case example

One regional government did this assumption testing to good effect. As part of formulating their outsourcing strategy, they investigated peer organizations in the commercial and public sectors regarding the commercial relationships they had in practice, identifying what worked and did not. In doing so, the government achieved a significant learning breakthrough.

The management team had previously not attributed any importance to the transition and, in particular, the client's role in the transition. But it found several instances of transition mishaps and underestimating the role the client played, that it recognized it needed a dedicated transition team and needed to include the transition plan as part of the tender. This was not only critical to a smooth transition, but also critical to relationship formation because it set precedence regarding the ongoing operational relationship to follow. As one organization that was investigated stated: 'begin how you intend to continue'.

Building block 2: Target the most appropriate kind of relationship

A detailed understanding of the current state of the target services is essential if one is to approach the market knowledgeably. Building block 2 provides invaluable information for one's own piece of mind, but also when dealing with the supplier's pitch on service delivery. Being fact-based is vital; this enables the client to sit down and analyze with the supplier, rather than have to negotiate in an ill-informed way. The recommended profiles are made up of the components detailed in Table 2.4.

Table 2.4 Profiles

Type of Profile	Components
1. Service	• Service Environment • Current and future service requirements • Volume, trend and load data (i.e. # users, transactions, desktops, calls, etc) • Performance criteria, service levels, measurement methods • Customer satisfaction indices
2. Baseline Costs	• Costs at current service levels and loads • Estimated costs at required or future service levels • Future capital expenditure program
3. Balance Sheet	• Assets (including intellectual property) – type, age, quantity, location • Liabilities
4. Staffing	• Organization chart(s) • Job descriptions • Staff numbers and full time equivalents • Remuneration • Accrued and contingent liabilities

5. Commercial Relationships	• For each current contract, licence, lease, agreement, etc
	  – Scope
	  – Value
	  – Inception and end dates
	  – Assignment, novation and termination options

continued

Table 2.4 *continued*

Type of Profile	Components
6. Stakeholder	• Internal (i.e. users, management, departments) • External (i.e. end customers, other suppliers, affiliated organizations, media)
7. Governance	• Management • Administration • Control • Reporting • Systems • Risks and mitigation

Of particular importance to the design of an effective relationship is the internal and external stakeholder profile. This profile identifies who cares about the service and what they care about – the people with whom the supplier is likely to require some form of relationship.

Case example

A government agency responsible for the management of owned and leased property wanted to conduct a BPO initiative. It knew that any supplier would have difficulty in managing the various stakeholders that made up the organization and understanding the various disparate needs. Senior management wanted assurance of best practice and quality service, value for money, and assurance that the government's best interests were represented. The finance department wanted accurate and timely financial data delivered in formats compatible with the various financial systems used. The IT department wanted data compatibility, accurate and timely updates, and a secure environment. Tenants wanted timely response and resolution. The special projects group wanted expert recommendations. The policy group wanted assurance that policy has been complied with, knowledge of areas in which the supplier was having difficulties, and recommendations for policy changes. The third-party subcontractors wanted timely payments for services rendered, fair assessment and feedback, and information to facilitate service performance. The agency prepared individual stakeholder profiles and facilitated the bidders in meeting the stakeholders to better understand their requirements. Each bid came up with innovative solutions in stakeholder management and the final agreement with the winning supplier had Key Performance Indicators (KPIs) reflecting all the stakeholder needs, not just the standard industry metrics.

Building block 3: Establish a strategy for the relationship

Building block 3 is crucial to the effective navigation of the entire outsourcing lifecycle. It defines the vision regarding the use of outsourcing within the client as well as setting up outsourcing as a program identifying the right skills at the right time, and developing the communications framework. Strategy sets the parameters for what subsequently will happen. It is important to get this right. Wrong strategies create pathway inflexibilities that are difficult and expensive to shift.

Building block 4: Design a framework for the relationship

Building block 4 builds on the previous blocks to convert the desired arrangement into a commercially sound framework. It covers the detailed design of the arrangement with the desired relationship as part of that design. Determining who the client is going to live with and depend upon for many years is akin to an arranged marriage, albeit one in which the client, initially, has the major discretion.

Building block 5: Choose a supplier that meets your relationship needs

A competitive process is the most common selection technique and most clients employ a tender to select their ITO suppliers. Such an approach provides pressure on suppliers to deliver best value for money against their industry peers, exposes the organization to a variety of capabilities and potential solutions, and allows an informed selection decision to evolve and mature.

Where the bid price is the sole criterion, the evaluation process is relatively straightforward. However, where 'value for money' is the key criterion, the tender evaluation becomes more complex. Service delivery is often the foremost criteria, as well it should be. We found it the number one factor for successful outsourcing. However, the more successful deals had the supplier exhibiting a far greater range of skills, as we will discuss in Chapter 3.

Case example

A telecommunications client that selected a newly formed consortium to deliver a wide range of services. The qualitative criteria revolved around technical proficiency only. No single party had all the core technical competencies, thus a consortium of three best-of-breed suppliers was the winning bid. Within the first few months of operations, the client realized that the contract would be unworkable. These parties had never worked together before and every meeting required a representative of each consortium member to be there. In addition, no decision could be reached without achieving time-consuming tri-supplier consensus. The client had only assessed technical proficiency of the bidders; it never assessed the business skills of the consortium as a business entity and their customer governance and account management strategies. It lived with this situation through the initial three-year term and then went to market for a sole supplier.

Building block 6: Negotiate the kind of relationship you want

A great deal of the good work in signaling and building the type of relationship required can be thrown away during block 6 phase of negotiation. The classic way of cutting across suitable relationship building is to have, on each side, one team for developing the outsourcing proposal, another for carrying out the negotiations, and quite another responsible for delivery. Not involving the delivery managers in the negotiation process can create strong barriers to subsequent relationship development. So can negotiating deals with stiff penalties, slim supplier margins, and little subsequent additional work to bid for. Not allowing the vendor a reasonable profit ultimately translates into a 'Winner's Curse' deal. This is harmful to performance, relationships, and satisfaction for all parties. Looking at 85 outsourcing contracts, we found nearly 20 percent of them to be ones where the supplier stood to make no profit. In 75 percent of such cases what looked to be a win/lose for the client turned into a lose/lose. The relationships we observed in those deals were all adversarial; the relationships were tentative to non-existent.[7] In Chapter 3 we elaborate further on the Winner's Curse and how to avoid such a scenario.

Building block 7: Work at the transition relationship

The transition process in building block 7 officially begins at contract commencement and ends on a specified date or by the signing of a transition acceptance form. Irrespective of the official start and end dates, the transition actually begins much earlier and ends much later; or, if not managed properly, may not end at all. Accordingly, it is critical that both parties begin planning for the transition as soon as it believes outsourcing may go ahead.

A good jump out of the starting gate will pave the way for a smooth process thereafter. One key to the jump is to have clearly defined roles regarding the transition. The client organization will typically have the following transition roles (Table 2.5), for which a counterpart (or counterparts) exist with the supplier.

The relationship prior to transition will now further change, and hopefully develop, as emerging problems have to be engaged with. Those

Table 2.5 Client transition roles

Transition Roles	Description
Steering Committee or Joint Reference Panel	1. guide the project and provide strategic input to the implementation process 2. facilitate timely decision-making and resolve issues escalated from the transition team 3. monitor the quality of key deliverables 4. provide a forum for communicating progress and achievement of project milestones
Transition Program Leader	5. manage all the transition activities across all the divisions to ensure consistency 6. report to the steering committee
Transition Project Team Leaders	7. manage the transition for a specific service, geography or customer group
Human Resource (HR) Representative(s)	8. provide HR specific advice 9. coordinate the HR initiatives and services to staff 10. assist in setting up the retained organisation
Business Representative(s)	11. provide business unit specific advice 12. coordinate business unit transition activities 13. liaise with business unit line management 14. test and accept the business unit's data migration and functioning
Technical Representative(s)	15. provide technical advice 16. coordinate technical transition activities 17. liaise with supplier's technicians and system integrators 18. test and accept technical migration, configuration and operational functioning
Business Process Representative(s), if applicable	19. provide business process advice 20. coordinate business process transition activities 21. liaise with the supplier's business process re-engineering team and service set-up team 22. test and accept business process migration, configuration and functioning
Communications Representative(s)	23. provide communication and change leadership advice 24. develop communications messages and media 25. liaise with supplier's communications representative 26. manage the feedback loop
Administration Resource	27. coordinate logistical support 28. create and manage control files

recognizing that this is a resource-intensive period for both parties and that plan a bi-party program are in a much better position to have a successful outsourcing arrangement.

Case example

A global mining company that ensured the parties worked efficiently and effectively from the start. It had multiple transition teams, a detailed transition program, numerous transition planning workshops, and test runs with the supplier. The parties were able to perform a 48-hour weekend transition moving assets to the supplier's facility, connecting the network, and getting all applications up and running. On Monday morning, it was business as usual.

Building block 8: Manage your relationship

Building block 8 involves implementing and managing a new way of operating. New workflows, communications, paper flows, and signoffs are required. New relationships will need to be quickly formed, and people accustomed to a certain way of operating will need to operate in a completely different manner. Whether the relationship exhibits more power-based characteristics or more trust-based characteristics as explained earlier, long-term success will be dependent upon how the relationship is managed. The best governing documents (e.g., contract, service level agreement, governance charter – see Chapter 6) become merely weapons in a poorly functioning relationship – to be used against the other party rather than to guide successful outcomes. A successful relationship requires the investment of time and effort at all levels of both parties, where many times the journey is more important than the destination. It is an investment well worth making to establish fundamental understandings and insights into the other party, establish key interpersonal relationships in order to overcome inevitable hurdles, and establish shared as well as discrete values.

Building block 9: Review your relationship

In building block 9 typical options, for any or all of the scope of work, includes renewal, renegotiation, retender, return to in-house and/or discontinue service. In large-scale deals, some services are backsourced, some eliminated, some the incumbent supplier provides, and some a new supplier provides. To what extent this occurs varies widely (see Chapter 9 for a fuller discussion). There is one new assessment of particular relevance to the potential future relationship under any option – the prior generation outsourcing Strengths, Weaknesses, Opportunities, and Threats (SWOT) assessment, which includes paying attention to the relationship aspects.

Case example

A utility company conducted a detailed SWOT of the incumbent contract relationships. It believed this was particularly necessary, as it had amalgamated three geographic regions comprising five contracts into two regions. It was planning on conducting a tender for one region and backsourcing the other region, to a wholly owned subsidiary, to regain the operational competence it had lost from nearly 15 years of outsourcing (this was the third generation). The contract management function was concerned that having a related entity as a supplier would throw out the very successful governance and relationship management processes that had evolved. Based on the SWOT, the key areas of strength were a comprehensive and 'reader-friendly' contract, diligent contract management, monthly detailed performance review, retaining of in-house operation of core operational systems and benchmarking between the parties. Weaknesses were a fixed price contract when the client needed to be able to chop and change services (changed to a fixed-price base-load, with interchangeable service units, and volume discounts for work above that). The company signed substantially the same agreement with the subsidiary as it did with the independent supplier and put in the same governance. After some initial politicking, the subsidiary 'fell into line as an arms-length provider' and was soon delivering the market equivalent standard of service.

How healthy is your outsourcing relationship?

Relationships are not just about subjective feelings – 'feel-good' or 'feel-bad' factors. Establishing outsourcing relationships, keeping them on track, and getting the most out of them means measurement. All parties will benefit from negotiating and clarifying a relationship values charter at the beginning of the deal, from regular health checks during its course, and from monitoring – using a contract scorecard – the alignment of strategy, service, relationships, and financial outcomes. But getting the right culture between the parties has proven to be one of the most difficult aspects of an outsourcing agreement.

The relationship values charter

For this reason, experienced outsourcing clients have adopted a form of agreement, called a 'Relationship Values Charter' or a 'Code of Conduct' that describes and agrees the behavior to be demonstrated during the course of the relationship. Modeling the desired behaviors at this stage is invaluable as it significantly contributes to selecting a supplier that best 'lives' these values. Getting the right value and culture between the parties has proven to be one of the most difficult aspects of an outsourcing agreement.

A relationship values charter agreed between a communications manufacturer and its Tier 1 IT infrastructure supplier is shown in Figure 2.4. This charter was designed during building block 4 and was used in the remainder of the lifecycle – in building block 5 to draft the relationship-related questions in the request for tender and to guide customer reference checking, and in building block 7 to evaluate the relationship on a bi-annual basis. As a result, the client selected a supplier who had demonstrated

---

- **Service** – We do not desire to apply penalties. The Services will be of a consistent high standard, comparable to market standards, and customers will be delighted.
- **Financial** – We will achieve our financial goals:
  - o Client – reduce cost over time and have competitive pricing at all times
  - o Contractor – reasonable profits
- **Communication** – We will communicate frequently, openly and honestly with each other.
- **Meet Needs** – We will be both proactive and reactive to each other's needs.
- **Creative Solutions** – We will constantly search for better ways of doing things.
- **Conflict** – We recognised conflict as natural and will focus on solving the problem, not apportioning blame.We will resolve conflict at the lowest level.
- **Fairness** – We will be fair to all parties.
- **Time** – We will provide each other time and management focus.
- **External Relations** – We will project a united front and will not discuss sensitive issues outside of the relationship.
- **Industry Model** – Our relationship will be seen as an industry model.
- **Enjoyment** – We enjoy working together and respect one another.
- **Added Value** – We will both derive more value from our relationship than just the exchange of money for services.
- **Works Seamlessly** – The services value chain will appear seamless.
- **Technology Leadership** – We both wish to have recognised technology leadership

---

Figure 2.4 A specimen relationship values charter

the behavior with other clients and the parties had a mechanism for gauging the degree to which the behavior was exhibited in their deal.

Clients who do not specify the behaviors they seek must work with the behaviors they get, as well as the behaviors the client itself exhibits.

Case example

In this case, the spiraling adversarial behavior was initiated by the client. A property company and a supplier agreed to an 'outsourcing alliance' – a partnering style of relationship. All worked very well together during negotiation and planning the transition. Then, on the first day of the contract, the supplier walked into the client's office asking where the relationship manager would be accommodated (expecting an office next to the director in the spirit of 'partnering'). The director was quite surprised – he had expected the supplier's staff to be offsite and certainly was not going to provide free office accommodation. Reluctantly, the director gave the supplier an office in the basement. The supplier was wounded by what it thought was an overt gesture normally found in a 'master–slave' relationship. Rather than discuss expectations of partnering behaviors, the supplier went on the defensive stating that 'if that's how they're going to treat us, fine'. The supplier instructed staff to perform only the letter of the contract and rely on the client's instructions as opposed to introducing the potential innovation ideas that were enthusiastically thrown about during negotiation. The client to be then interpreted this behavior exhibited by the supplier 'typical: say anything to get the deal, then run it the way they like' and the adversarial relationship began.

Client–supplier relationships diagnostic

Given the importance of the relationship, a 'health check' diagnostic is vital for determining whether an outsourcing relationship is exhibiting vital signs of health. Table 2.6 provides an abbreviated diagnostic as used in one successful arrangement we studied.

Case example

An electric utility evaluated the relationship every quarter, and had an improvement agenda to focus on the key gaps. In fact, the relationship was deemed so unusually superior that an independent consultant was brought in when a new general manager took over at the client. This was to verify that it was, in fact, arms-length (no collusion, etc.) and good governance was in place. Nothing

Table 2.6 A specimen relationship health check diagnostic

Category	Diagnostic Questions
Behaviours Exhibited	1. Do both parties display ethical behaviour?
	2. Is there an 'us' vs. 'them' mentality?
	3. Are both parties proactive?
	4. Does either party blame the other when problems arise?
	5. Does either party misrepresent the relationship to others?
	6. Do the parties give each other recognition when it is due?
	7. Are there key individuals who dislike each other?
Perceptions of the parties regarding one another	8. Do both parties respect one another?
	9. Do both parties think the other party is a good listener?
	10. Do both parties believe the relationship is a role model for the industry?
	11. Do both parties use the relationship as an example of good practice within their respective organizations?
	12. Are both parties reliable?
	13. Are there unfulfilled promises by either party?
	14. Does either party think the other party is not pulling their weight or living up to their accountabilities?
	15. Do the parties think of the other party as trustworthy?
	16. Does either party display the NIH (not invented here) syndrome (i.e. 'it's not our problem, it's their problem')?
	17. Do both parties understand each other's business, underlying drivers and motivations, politics?
Investment in the relationship	18. Are both parties investing management time and effort?
	19. Are there solid relationships at all appropriate levels?
	20. Does each party get the management attention it needs from the other?
	21. Is the client organization an enthusiastic customer reference site for the supplier?
Communication	22. Is there regular communication?
	23. Is there regular feedback?
	24. Do the parties provide early warning to each other?
	25. Do the parties suggest improvements to one another?
Relationship processes	26. Are there clear protocols between the parties?
	27. Does each party assess the satisfaction of the other party?
	28. Do the parties plan together?
	29. If the contract has financial rewards for superior performance, have such awards been applied?
	30. If the contract has financial consequences for poor performance, has such recourse needed to be continually applied?
	31. Do the parties continuously seek better ways of doing things?

unseemly was found. Only minor 'tweaking' of process transparency (forms and signoffs) was recommended, stating 'the commercial relationship and behaviors exhibited were what parties everywhere aspire to'.

The contract scorecard

Outsourcing is not a goal in itself, but a management technique for achieving any number of business goals – and whether outsourcing has achieved these goals cannot be assumed, it needs to be monitored and kept on track. As one CEO told us, 'Outsourcing contracts are agreed in concept but delivered in detail, and that's how the relationship can break down; the devil is in the detail.' How then to keep account of the detail? Organizations that are veterans at the outsourcing game know that the success of a deal has more than a single dimension. For example, they know it is not just the cost, but also the quality of the service that matters. They also know it is more than just getting what you pay for, but whether the relationship is productive or dysfunctional. Further, they know that outsourcing is not just an operational exercise; there are strategic goals to achieve, or at least not to disable, as well. In other words, when an organization looks to outsource, it is important to understand the potential total value that lies on the table. It is also very unwise to assume that goals are achieved inherently upon signing an agreement. Since outsourcing is rarely a reversible option and can consume a large part of the budget, management's ability to drive and demonstrate success has become a basic expectation.

To assess the myriad criteria that an outsourcing deal may need to demonstrate to be deemed 'successful' – we regularly find organizations pursuing five or six major objectives, and some, inadvisably, up to 17 – the industry is now recognizing the value of applying a balanced scorecard approach. The balanced scorecard hit the corporate scene in the early 1990s through the work of Kaplan and Norton.[8] Originally designed for companies to measure non-financial attributes of firm performance, it has since proliferated into many forms. Our application of the balanced scorecard to outsourcing is adapted from Kaplan and Norton's theoretical base – that is, it treats success as having more attributes than purely financial. The technique has been developed further in our advisory work, and from our research findings, and is presented in this book in adapted form to induce organizations to think more strategically about their outsourcing deals.

With regard to outsourcing arrangements, our contract scorecard is a method used to evaluate the success of the arrangement in a more holistic manner than just meeting KPIs (e.g., availability) and reducing cost. The contract scorecard helps the parties to establish how the quality of the service will be evaluated, but also how the financial outcomes will be judged, how the relationship is conducted and if the outsourcing deal is achieving its strategic aims. In sum, it provides a valuable senior executive dashboard for representing the overall success of the deal from a holistic perspective.

The four quadrants for assessing an outsourcing deal are service quality, finance, relationship, and strategy (Figure 2.5).

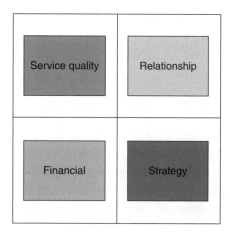

Figure 2.5 The contract scorecard quadrants

One part of the approach is a focus on monitoring relationships. It has to be said that this is in practice rarely done in a concerted manner. It is precisely the use of a scorecard approach that disciplines both clients and suppliers to pay attention to this key area. Given the theme of this chapter we will look here mainly at the relationship quadrant, but bearing in mind that the scorecard approach assumes an inter-dependence and balance between the quadrants and metrics (see Chapter 8).

Relationship

Relationship embodies the perception metrics assessing behaviors exhibited by one party in the eyes of the other. Examples include:

- communication – frequent, honest
- meeting needs – proactive and reactive
- creative solutions – continuously search for better ways of doing things
- conflict resolution – focus on problem solving, not apportioning blame
- fairness – act even-handed to each other
- management time – provide time and focus to each other
- external relations cohesion – project a united front
- industry model – the relationship seen as an industry model
- positive interaction – enjoy working together, mutual respect
- integration – the supply chain appears seamless

The case that follows gives a practical example of how an organization tailored its outsourcing measurement through the lens of the four quadrants.

Case example of a contract scorecard

The logistics division of an Armed Forces was looking to outsource most of the logistics functions it performed such as maintenance, security, warehousing, inventory, and asset management. For 6 months, 15 people were working on a penalty scheme that would nail the supplier for poor performance. This was prior to any KPIs having been developed.

Upon a consultant's advice, the team dropped the penalty system and began to work on the metrics themselves. To facilitate its thinking, it adopted the scorecard approach. Service quality metrics were focused on accuracy, availability, and timeliness. The financial metrics focused on planned vs. actual cost. The relationship metric focused on the satisfaction of the Army units and the integrity of the supplier's conduct, and the strategic metrics focused on continuous improvement. These were further broken down, and detailed, into each of the 22 functions the supplier was to perform.

Rather than continue with the extensive penalty regime they had begun with, which was likely to be constantly the cause of disputes, they implemented a simple points system whereby under/over achievement resulted in (+/−) a number of points. Each of the 22 areas had a floor, which then gave the organization the right to temporarily step-in at the supplier's cost until the supplier demonstrated it was able to perform at the expected standard, or remove that area from the scope. The achievement of a significant points surplus resulted in the granting of specified extensions, provided that the organization could substantiate that the prices in the market have not fallen significantly.

Whether you choose to use a balanced scorecard approach to evaluate the overall success of an outsourcing deal will depend upon: (1) how actively you intend to ensure the myriad of desired outcomes are achieved and (2) what the key stakeholders to the deal want to know on a regular basis. When an organization uses the contract scorecard, it will tend to publish the results on a very high-level dashboard. This is then supported by a comprehensive performance report describing, at a minimum, the detailed metrics, root cause, and actions to be taken. The scorecard technique is sufficiently important to merit Chapter 8 being devoted to how effective scorecards can be constructed.

Conclusion – lessons on the relationship advantage

This chapter deliberately appears very early in this book, precisely because it is a neglected practice area. Senior executives must constantly pay attention to relationship development and link the type of relationship to their strategic outsourcing intent. Relationships need to be managed across the outsourcing lifecycle and are heavily dependent on the right processes and people being in place. Monitoring relationships is a key management task. This chapter points to the following lessons:

1. Outsourcing relationships accounting for 20 percent of the IT or business process budget are themselves strategic assets and demand ongoing senior executive investment and attention.
2. Outsourcing arrangements with well-managed relationships are more likely to be successful. Reviewing our case work, relationship management can create a 20 percent to 40 percent difference on service, quality, cost, and other performance indicators. Globally, organizations investing most in developing successful relationships consistently perform better than competitors or agencies in the same sector.
3. There is no such thing as an instant relationship: trust is earned and relationships built through performance, day by day.
4. Management needs to be proactive and sow the seeds for a successful relationship before the start of the deal and cultivate it thereafter at three levels – executive, managerial, and operational.
5. For all but short-term arrangements, power-based relationships are poor substitutes for co-operation and trust building processes given the high transaction costs of monitoring and of imposing sanctions, the negative orientations and behaviors adopted, and the limited goals that can be pursued by the parties. This theme is developed further in Chapter 5.
6. The contract is a necessary but not sufficient governance tool for outsourcing. That said, badly constructed contracts, based on faulty cost-service analyses, and containing ambiguities, loopholes and incomplete terms, can seriously damage outsourcing health. Poor contracts spiral down, taking relationships with them.
7. In outsourcing relationships, you mainly hit what you aim at. Using measures like relationship values charters, regular relationship health checks and contract scorecards sets and aligns targets and encourages superior performance.

Notes

1. See Willcocks, L. and Lacity, M. (2009) *The Practice of Outsourcing: From Information Systems to BPO and Offshoring.* Palgrave, London; especially chapters 3, 4, and 13. Also Goles, T. (2001) *The Impact of the Client–Vendor Relationship on Information Systems Outsourcing Success.* Unpublished Ph.D. Thesis, University of Houston. Also Kern T. and Willcocks, L. (2001) *The Relationship Advantage: Information Technologies, Sourcing and Management.* Oxford University Press, Oxford.
2. See Willcocks, L. and Fitzgerald, G. (1994) *A Business Guide to IT Outsourcing.* Business Intelligence, London; Grover, V., Cheon, M. J. and Teng, J. (1996) 'The effect of service quality and partnership on the outsourcing of information systems functions', *Journal of Management Information Systems*, 12, 4, pp. 89–116; Cullen, S., Seddon P., and Willcocks L. (2001) *IT Outsourcing Practices in Australia.* Deloitte Touche Tohmatsu, Sydney. Also Lacity, M. and Willcocks, L. (2009) *Information Systems and Outsourcing: Studies in Theory and Practice.* Palgrave, London; chapter 12. These findings also emerge from our most recent research detailed in Chapter 5.
3. From Kern T. and Willcocks, L. (2001) *The Relationship Advantage: Information Technologies, Sourcing and Management.* Oxford University Press, Oxford.
4. These are conclusions drawn from 100 plus case studies in Lacity, M. and Willcocks, L. (2001) *Global IT Outsourcing: Search For Business Advantage.* Wiley, Chichester; they are reinforced by later findings in Willcocks, L. and Lacity, M. (2006) *Global Sourcing of Business and IT Services.* Palgrave, London.
5. This is based on unpublished PhD research into 107 case studies by Cullen, S. (2005) 'Towards Reframing Outsourcing: A Study of Choices in Process, Structures and Success', Melbourne University, Melbourne.
6. Cullen, S., Seddon P. and Willcocks L. (2001) *IT Outsourcing Practices in Australia.* Deloitte Touche Tohmatsu, Sydney. See also Lacity, M. and Willcocks, L. (2009) *Information Systems and Outsourcing: Studies in Theory and Practice.* Palgrave, London; especially chapter 12. See also Willcocks, L. and Lacity, M. (2006), op. cit; especially chapter 2.
7. Reported in Kern, T., Willcocks, L. and Heck, E. (2002) 'The winner's curse in IT Outsourcing: Strategies to Avoid Relational Trauma', *California Management Review*, 44, 2, pp. 47–69. See also Willcocks and Lacity (2006) op. cit.
8. For a more detailed perspective see Chapter 9 of the present book. There is also Cullen, S. (2009) *The Contract Scorecard.* Gower, London, which provides a comprehensive description of how to devise, tailor, and implement outsourcing contract scorecards.

CHAPTER 3

Selecting and leveraging suppliers

I see myself in competition with all its other clients for the supplier's prime attention and resources.

– John Yard, CIO UK Inland Revenue

It's unwise to pay too much, but it's unwise to pay too little. When you pay too much you lose a little money, that is all. When you pay too little, you sometimes lose everything, because the thing you bought was incapable of doing the thing you bought it to do ...

– John Ruskin

Introduction

The evidence we have accumulated shows clearly: organizations that have the CEO and a multidisciplinary team involved in sourcing strategy and configuration make more effective decisions. The CEO ensures the identification of clear business needs and objectives, and the availability of in-house IT sourcing capabilities and resources. As we demonstrated in Chapter 1, the CEO brings brain and influence, but also responsibility to key risk areas, because getting sourcing strategy and selection of supplier(s) wrong can hit share price, disable business strategy, as well as being very costly operationally. Our first chapter focused on the CEO role and strategic advantage, the second on the power of relationships. In this chapter we focus on the supplier selection process, and acquiring the right supplier people and competencies.

The CEO and senior management team must be involved in selecting and managing the supplier because, while some organizations see outsourcing as an opportunity to pass on risk, in practice such risk displacement is largely illusory. In reality, an organization is left very exposed when it chooses the wrong supplier. Moreover, as we shall see in the Chapter 4, the organization itself can inhibit or facilitate supplier performance enormously. The CEO is responsible for making sure superior supplier performance is possible. One key part of the answer lies in helping to shape the supplier selection process.

As shown in our first two chapters, outsourcing is most successful when managed as a life-cycle not a one-off transaction. It will be recalled that the outsourcing lifecycle consists of nine building blocks in four phases. The client's bargaining power fluctuates throughout this lifecycle, as will be recalled from Figure 1.2. Here we focus on the *Engage Phase* – the select and negotiate phase, when the client's power is at its height. Clients can emerge from this phase with unrealistic expectations of what their responsibilities are, what the service provider will actually do for the price and how the deal will work out in practice. So the more a client uses its power well during this phase, the greater will be the eventual chances of success. This is why the CEO, in particular, must bring his/her considerable influence to bear in this process.

Capabilities and competencies

When evaluating suppliers, clients tend to focus on suppliers' resources because these are highly visible on site tours, balance sheets, and resumes. But they should be more interested in suppliers' ability to turn these resources – its physical and human assets such as physical facilities, technologies, tools, and workforce – into capabilities that, in turn, can be combined to create high-level customer-facing competencies. Figure 3.1 illustrates the relationship between these three types of asset.

Our research has identified 12 key supplier capabilities:[1]

1. *Leadership* – the capability to identify and deliver success overall. Look out for leaders only focused on meeting contractual service levels and margins. Check that the leader has strong relationships with the client-side

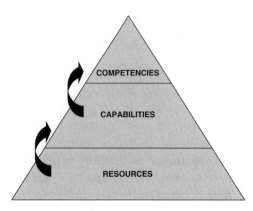

Figure 3.1 The relationship between supplier resources, capabilities, and competencies

leader, but also with the top management of the supplier's own organization.

2. *Business management* – the ability to deliver in line with service agreements and its and the client's business plans. For what happens when this is lacking see 'The Winner's Curse' and the case study later in this chapter.

3. *Domain expertise* – the capability to retain and apply professional knowledge. Look not just for technical know-how but for the much harder-to-acquire ability to understand the business, and experience in your specific kind of sectoral back-office environment, for example procurement, IT, or human resources in a manufacturing environment.

4. *Behavior management* – the ability to motivate and inspire people to deliver high-level service. Suppliers who have patchy human resource records and also manage transferees indifferently will not deliver the qualitative service improvements you expect.

5. *Sourcing* – the ability to access resources as needed. Check out economies of scale claims, the availability of specialized professional skills you might need, and the dynamic areas of quality and costs of staff in offshore locations. Also claims of superior infrastructure, and superior procurement practices.

6. *Process improvement* – the capability to incorporate changes to the service process to meet dramatic improvement targets. Check the supplier track record on re-engineering for clients, and also its skills and change capability.

7. *Technology exploitation* – the capacity to swiftly and effectively deploy new technology. A major reason we found for BPO is harnessing supplier IT capability here, and getting them to make the IT investment you are reluctant to make. Is the capability available and are you contracting for its deployment, or just riding on a promise?

8. *Program management* – the capability to deliver a series of inter-related projects. This goes beyond project-level capabilities. Remember, you might want to expand use of the supplier, and the supplier will also have many other clients.

9. *Customer development* – the ability to help customers make informed decisions. This is the difficult area of relating to users to enable to them to become customers able to make informed choices about service level, functionality, and costs. How customer-focused is the supplier?

10. *Planning and contracting* – the capability to deliver 'win/win' results for customer and supplier. Does the supplier share with you its vision of the potential prize for both parties, and a coherent process for achieving it? Do they contract in ways that facilitate or contradict this process and prize?

11. *Organizational design* – the ability to design and implement successful organizational arrangements. In practice suppliers vary greatly on their

flexibility here. Some emphasize a 'thin' front end client team, interfacing with consolidated service units. This could constrain the ability to customize service and deliver to a specific client business plan. As a client, what degree of flexibility do you need? Others allocate most of their resources to 'enterprise partnerships' created for each major deal. Our research found quite major deals sometimes taking two years to optimize client–supplier organization fit. On offshore, we found clients frequently experimenting. Thus Figure 3.2 shows a large US organization using a funnel design. This clarified and controlled demand but could also lead to delays in interpreting and delivering performance. Offshore suppliers sometimes adopt a Mirror design reflecting exactly in their design the client's own organization, thus lowering risk, but possibly increasing immediate cost.

12. *Governance* – the capability to track and measure performance. The overriding responsibility for governance arrangements lies with the client, but every supplier will have some type of joint service review committee that defines, tracks and evaluates performance over time. Figure 3.3 shows the larger arrangements in an enterprise partnership deal where a third entity run by a joint Board of Directors was created to deliver service to, in this case, the London Insurance Market by service supplier Xchanging. One latent tension here is of managerial schizophrenia among the third entity Board members: whom do they ultimately represent?

These 12 capabilities, in turn, can be leveraged into three important competencies (Figure 3.4):

- *Delivery competency* based on the supplier's ability and willingness to respond to a customer's day-to-day operational needs.

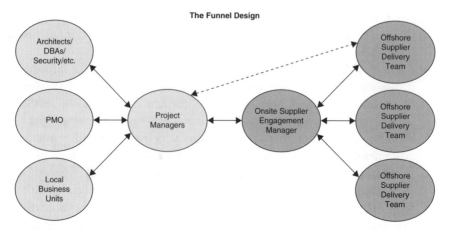

Figure 3.2 Going offshore: Funnel design

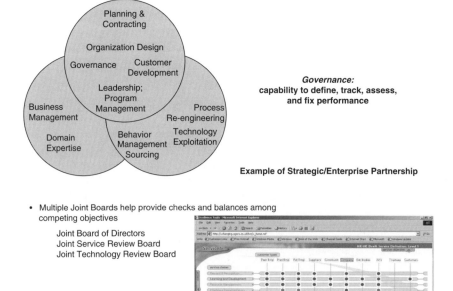

Figure 3.3 Governance in the London Insurance Market 2001–07

- *Transformation competency* based on the supplier's ability to deliver radically improved services in terms of cost and quality.
- *Relationship competency* based on the supplier's capacity and will to align itself with the customer's values, goals, and needs. By far, this is the hardest competency to find in a supplier.

The *delivery competency* primarily involves the supplier's leadership, business management, domain expertise, behavior management, sourcing, program management, and governance capabilities. The *transformation competency* mainly involves the supplier's leadership, behavior management, sourcing, process improvement, technology exploitation, program management, and customer development capabilities.

The *relationship competency* primarily relies on the supplier's leadership, customer development, planning and contracting, organizational design, governance, and program management capabilities. Among these, the planning and contracting capability presents the greatest challenges because it is very difficult to align customer and supplier incentives. Most outsourcing relationships are still based on fee-for-service contracts, in which a customer pays

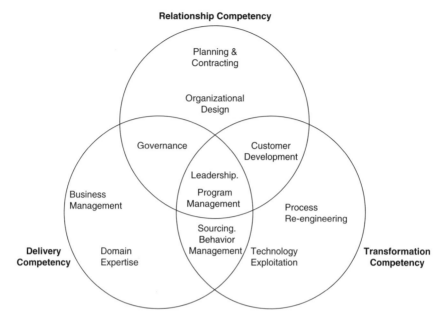

Figure 3.4 Twelve supplier capabilities

the supplier a fee for delivery of a service. With a fee-for-service contract, the customer is motivated to squeeze the supplier for more resources and services without wanting to pay more. The supplier is motivated to squeeze as much profit margin as possible through contract add-ons and delivering only to service levels agreed. The customer has to ensure that the plans and contracts motivate the supplier to meet sourcing expectations.

Customers should focus on the supplier's delivery competency when they primarily want the supplier to maintain or slightly improve existing services, such as maintaining legacy systems, operating data centers, or servicing a fleet of desktop devices. They should focus on the supplier's transformation competency when they are seeking radical improvements in costs and services and on the relationship competency when they are seeking a substantial and long-term commitment from the supplier. Our strong finding is that suppliers cannot properly focus and utilize such competencies unless pro-actively enabled by the client (for how to achieve this see Chapters 4 and 5).

Get the supplier configuration right

As we sketched in Chapter 1, there are a number of ways to choose suppliers. The first involves deciding which configuration of suppliers best fits the client's purposes. The reader will recall from Chapter 1 four options: *Sole Supplier, Prime Contractor, Best-of-Breed,* and *Panel.* Let us give more detail on these.

- *Sole Supplier* is where a single supplier provides the entire portfolio or deal. The benefits include sole accountability and seamless service, but this model can compromise service quality, as no one supplier is outstanding in all areas.
- A *Prime Contractor* arrangement consists of a network, with several suppliers under the control of the head contractor. It is a well-recognized form of supply chain contracting. The head supplier is accountable, and contractually liable, for the entirety of the contract but uses any number of subcontractors to deliver all or part of it. Typically, the subcontractors have expertise or operate in regions, that the head contractor does not, or they are deployed by the client to support its local customers. Alliance networks where two or more suppliers to offer services as a package have identified as a long-term trend in outsourcing. However, they require contract provisions that limit what can be sub-contracted, and to which firms, and how the sub-contractors will be monitored and controlled.
- In a *Best-of-Breed* network (also known as multi-vendor, multi-sourcing, or selective sourcing) the organization has a number of suppliers and thus is in effect the head contractor itself. It represents a low risk outsourcing option that has been adopted by 75 percent of UK and 82 percent of US organizations.[2] The benefits and problems associated with this option relate to competition: although competitive tension leads to continuous improvement and cost-effective benchmarking, it is often difficult to constructively manage suppliers working in keen competition with one another.
- In a *Panel* arrangement there is a list of preferred suppliers working in continuous competition. Interactions are many and brief, and work is not guaranteed: each supplier competes on a regular basis for various contracts or work orders over a defined period. This approach is often used in applications development, hardware purchasing, and consulting, as the work tends to be periodic and the requirements vary with each initiative.

Table 3.1 provides a summary of the benefits, risks, and issues associated with each configuration.

Another way to choose suppliers relates the supplier market in which the client wants to operate. It involves three main choices:

Domestic versus offshore

Offshoring has been predominately a 'best-of-breed' approach, although some organizations have set up a prime contractor to manage offshore

Table 3.1 Supplier configuration options

Option	Benefits	Risks	Management issues
Sole supplier	• Sole accountability • Potential to pass on economies • Streamlined contracting costs and processes • End-to-end key performance metrics	• Monopolistic supplier behaviors • Compromise quality where the supplier is not best of breed (in services, industries, or geographic locations)	• Extensive contract flexibility rights due to the dependence on supplier • Independent expertise to avoid solution channeling and ensure value for money (quotes are market values)
Prime contractor	• Single point of accountability • Allows best-of-breed subcontracting • Streamlined, but a bit more complex, contracting costs and processes • End-to-end KPIs	• Prime must be expert at subcontracting (selection, management, disengagement) • Client may desire different subcontractors • Client often required to resolve issues between the prime and subcontractor/s • Primes and subcontractors often encroach 'territories'	• Contract ensuring various rights over the subcontracting (access, selection, veto, etc) • Compliance auditing ensuring the prime passes obligations to the subcontractors • Oversight ensuring all parties are operating as an efficient and united front
Best of breed	• Greater control • Flexibility to chop and change • Promotes competition and prevents complacency	• Attracting the market for small 'slices' of work • Keeping suppliers interested, giving management focus, and allocating staff • Interdependent services and contracts • Integration complexity • Tracing accountability	• Designing interdependent contracts between independent suppliers • Multi-party interface and handover management • End-to-end process management is more difficult • Multiple lifecycle management
Panel	• Buy services and assets when required • Promotes ongoing competition • Prevents complacency	• Attracting the market when panel is a pre-qualification and does not guarantee work • Adding new panel members or wanting to use suppliers not on the panel	• Panel bidding process for work • Ongoing ranking of panel members based on performance • Managing and evaluating the total program

suppliers. Typical services for which the overseas labor market has demonstrated superior cost advantages include applications coding, call centre operations, data entry, and transaction processing. As a result, the offshore market has tended to be very niche-orientated. This is changing as the bigger offshoring suppliers become more global in intent and build their capabilities for wider markets including most forms of business process services. In this they are of course competing with extant global suppliers. Partly due to offshore price pressure, all of these have also stretched, in reverse direction, to securing offshore facilities. The interesting development here is 'bestshoring' that is a mix of offshore, near shore, and onshore in the same deal. For example in its 2005 deal signed with ABNAmro bank, TCS has resources in Mumbai, Budapest, Netherlands, Luxembourg, and Sao Paulo in an attempt to locate capabilities where they are best employed at the best price to the customer. A further development has been the many emerging offshoring locations dotted around the globe and outside the BRIC (Brazil, Russia, India, China) countries[3] (see also Chapter 10).

Local versus global

Global providers are a common choice if an organization opts for the sole supplier configuration, due to their international reach and broad service offerings. Such large suppliers have access to more resources and are better able to assemble and deploy SWAT teams as needed.

Niche versus broad

The respective advantages of these two types of supplier are described in Table 3.2. In their limited service offerings niche suppliers represent a best-of-breed option and are either contracted directly with the client, or indirectly through a prime contractor.

Supplier modeling: A case study

Case study: Domestic versus offshore

This case study shows how customers can compare current domestic suppliers with an offshore supplier by assessing their relative capabilities and competencies. The customer was a large US retailer with an eight-year relationship with a domestic supplier for legacy system maintenance and enhancement. The existing contract was quite large, with the supplier

Table 3.2 Niche versus broad

Supplier capability	Niche supplier	Broad supplier
Leadership	Supplier leaders will be well known and there will be easy access to CEO and straightforward deployment of resources	Harder to contact top management
Planning and contracting	Suppliers have more vested interest in the relationship because they cannot absorb or afford failures	The client should push hard for creative contracts, as suppliers have greater ability to absorb risk than niche players
Organization design	Less formal design is required and the deal is more based on personal relationships	Formal organizational design is more important.
Process improvement	Niche suppliers may rely less on processes (like Six Sigma, CMM) but make up for this with domain expertise	Broad suppliers may rigidly use CMM
Domain expertise	There will be better domain knowledge because of specialization, but specific elements of business knowledge will still need to be transferred to the supplier	Clients need to pay special attention to knowledge transfer. Large suppliers can gain domain knowledge through the transfer of relevant employees

assigning nearly 500 IT workers to the account. The question was whether to award a large re-platforming project (from Visual Basic to Java) to the existing supplier or an Indian supplier. The existing supplier was seen as capable but costly. It charged $US100 per hour for programming, while the Indian supplier charged $US30 per hour. The Indian supplier had already performed well on some pilot projects, but the retailer had underestimated the extra burden of managing remote teams and the volume of re-work required because the supplier did not understand the business. These issues eroded much of the cost savings. Rather than letting the hourly rates dominate the decision, we show how the 12-point capabilities model can help bring about an informed decision.

In this scenario, the retailer was primarily interested in the following supplier capabilities (see Table 3.3):

- leadership (who will be responsible?)
- business management (can the supplier earn a margin on this bid?)
- program management (can the supplier organize, manage, test, and transfer the large number of program rewrites?)
- sourcing (will we get the supplier's best programmers and project managers?)

- behavior management (will supplier employees be motivated, productive, and easy to work with?)
- organizational design (where will supplier employees be located and how will we interface with the supplier organization?)
- technology exploitation (does the supplier have automated tools to develop and test the new platform?)
- planning and contracting (what is the fixed price?)
- governance (how will the supplier track, report, and fix performance?)

Because the re-platforming project was primarily technical and involved clear requirements, the supplier would not have to interact with end-users, so customer development and domain expertise capabilities were not pertinent. Furthermore, the retailer was not seeking new processes, so the process design capability was also irrelevant.

Looking at the analysis in Table 3.3, it is quite clear that the domestic supplier had superior capabilities to deliver the project compared to the offshore supplier. But the Indian supplier clearly won on contract price. The retailer decided to use the offshore supplier bid to pressure the domestic

Table 3.3 The relative capabilities of the two suppliers

Supplier capability	Domestic supplier	Offshore supplier
1. Leadership	*Strong*	*Good*
	The supplier had named a well-respected manager with a good support team	The supplier had named a well-respected manager but is less clear on who will serve in the supporting team
2. Business management	*Strong*	*Strong*
	Given the high cost bid, the supplier should have been able to deliver the project and still earn a profit	Although the bid was low, the supplier cost base was low and should have been able to deliver and still earn a profit
3. Domain expertise	N/A	N/A
4. Behavior management	*Strong*	*Weak*
	Supplier employees would ask the customer if they needed clarification. Many of supplier staff will have worked with the client before	Supplier employees were eager to please but did not share bad news promptly. The supplier staff were mostly new to the client
5. Sourcing	*Weak*	*Weak*
	It was likely that the supplier would assign low-level programmers	It was likely that the supplier would primarily use new hires from Indian universities
6. Process improvement	N/A	N/A

continued

Table 3.3 *continued*

Supplier capability	Domestic supplier	Offshore supplier
7. Technology exploitation	*Strong* The supplier had performed this work in the past and had automated tools.	*Strong* The supplier had performed this work in the past and had automated tools.
8. Program management	*Strong* The supplier had demonstrated this capability in the past	*Weak* The supplier relied heavily on an on-site engagement manager who was expected to fulfil too many roles.
9. Customer development	N/A	N/A
10. Planning and contracting	*Weak* The supplier was very expensive	*Strong* The supplier's bid was 60% lower than the domestic supplier
11. Organizational design	*Strong* Supplier staff were primarily on-site	*Weak* The supplier staff would be offshore, with an on-site engagement manager as the contact
12. Governance	*Strong* The supplier already had reporting processes in place and reported twice a week	*Weak* Although the supplier was CMM5, internal supplier reports were not shared, and in the past the client had had to request daily reporting

supplier to reduce its price by 10–50 percent.

> 'We were paying about $100 for commodity type coding (with domestic suppliers),' commented the Director of Contract Management. 'The domestic suppliers saw the writing on the wall. We put out a bid to the approved list of domestic contractors and the current director of the PMO made it very clear that we were not going to pay those kinds of prices anymore. Our domestic prices dropped from about $100 per hour to $80 and some of the rates even dropped into the $50 range for some services.'

However, by forcing the domestic supplier to reduce their costs the retailer weakened the domestic supplier's business management capability (its ability to earn a profit while delivering the service). Significantly, our research has found that domestic suppliers are increasingly using offshore captive centers to compete with Indian suppliers on costs, while leveraging their domestic presence to keep customer service levels high.

Case study 2: Small versus large

The senior managers of a large US company decided that the Applications Development Director should outsource at least a third of new development work offshore. Such senior management decisions are common in the large US organizations that we have studied and are based solely on the lower hourly wages of offshore workers. However, typically they neglect or underestimate the high transaction costs involved in coordinating and managing offshore suppliers.

The context was a new software development for a large intranet that would connect the customer's sales force with a centralized customer ordering, inventory, and logistics centre. This required new technologies (wireless) and a good understanding of the customer's business. The Applications Development Director was considering two Indian suppliers of very different sizes. The larger Indian supplier had over 40,000 employees. The smaller one had only 250 employees, of which 220 resided in Hyderabad and 30 in the US.

Respective analyses of the suppliers' salient capabilities (governance was similar) are summarized in Table 3.4. They indicated that the larger Indian supplier had superior business management, domain expertise, sourcing, and

Table 3.4 Small versus large supplier

Supplier capability	Smaller supplier	Larger supplier
1. Leadership	*Strong*	*Weak*
	The CEO was personally committed to the customer. He had handpicked the supplier's leaders, and the CEO would personally oversee and help them deploy resources to ensure contract success	The customer knew it would be difficult to get through to the supplier's top team
2. Business management	*Weak*	*Strong*
	The supplier was just starting to build the business and incurring substantial start-up costs. The customer was worried that it would be responsible for the supplier's survival	The supplier had annual revenues of $1 billion and had earned substantial net revenues

continued

Table 3.4 *continued*

Supplier capability	Smaller supplier	Larger supplier
3. Domain expertise	*Questionable* The supplier's CEO had a good understanding of the business context because he had worked closely with the Application Development Director before. But it was doubtful whether the rest of the supplier's employees had the same understanding	*Strong* The supplier organization had previously created similar applications for other clients
4. Behavior management	*Strong* The supplier had a unique strategy to attract and retain top talent. He had built a compound in Hyderabad that integrated the families of the employees physically and socially. He had only a 7% turnover. His team was highly geared toward customer service and willingly deferred holidays and worked through weekends to deliver	*Weak* The supplier relied heavily on new hires and people with less than five years' experience. Turnover was nearly 25%. The employees worked rigidly within the confines of the supplier's CMM processes
5. Sourcing	*Weak* The small supplier did not have much breadth or depth of resources.	*Strong* The large supplier had access to more resources and was better able to assemble and deploy specialist teams as needed.
6. Process improvement	*Weak* The supplier would not help re-design business processes but expected the client to articulate requirements clearly	*Weak* The supplier would not help re-design business processes but expected the client to articulate requirements clearly
7. Technology exploitation	*Weak* The customer had expertise with intranets but not in wireless technologies	*Strong* The supplier had proven wireless and intranet expertise
8. Program management	*Weak* The supplier was still finding its way, tailoring work processes to each new customer. While this resulted in higher customer service, it could equally have resulted in cost escalation, scope creep, or lower quality.	*Slightly weak* The supplier relied heavily on CMM processes. In the past the customer had complained that the rigidity of these processes had increased costs. One possibility might have been negotiating 'flexible CMM' in which the customer specifies which documents they will or will not pay for

continued

Table 3.4 *continued*

Supplier capability	Smaller supplier	Larger supplier
9. Customer development	*Strong* Many of the supplier's project managers had lived and worked in the US on similar accounts. They understood US culture and feel comfortable interacting directly with users	*Weak* The supplier did not generally interact directly with end-users but relied on the customer's project managers to document user requirements
10. Planning & contracting	*Strong* The supplier would have more vested interest in the relationship because it could not absorb or afford failure	*Strong* The customer might have been able to push harder for creative contracts as the supplier had greater ability to accept risk than a smaller supplier
11. Organizational design	*Strong* The supplier's US-based project managers nearly all lived within 30 miles of the customer's headquarters. For the customer this was a big plus	*Weak* The supplier was willing to release 30% of the staff to the customer's site but the customer would be charged on-shore rates plus expenses (hotels, transportation, visas, etc)

technology exploitation capabilities. However, the smaller supplier had superior leadership, behavior management, customer development, and organizational design capabilities. The Application Development Director finally chose the smaller supplier, mainly because its CEO was hungry for the business and personally committed to the success of the project. Furthermore, the supplier's project managers were local, and the supplier's employees seemed highly motivated. He rejected the large supplier because he was afraid that his company would be only a 'small fish in the big supplier's pond.'

Apply appropriate selection criteria

Not every business context requires suppliers to excel in all 12 capabilities and all three competencies. Every supplier does not have to be a 'partner' possessing a strong relationship competency. Some suppliers may be better at delivering commodity services, such as desktop services, for which the typical vendor management practices apply. Customers who want suppliers to maintain legacy systems will focus on the capabilities that enable the delivery competency. Customers should seek a supplier with a strong relationship competency if they are looking for a long-term partner to serve as the primary source of IT services. Customers who want the supplier to transform their IT functions should focus on capabilities that enable the transformation competency.

Clients need to assess a supplier's capabilities and competencies in each new business context. A supplier's ability and willingness to deliver the 12 capabilities is not fixed across the supplier organization, nor is it fixed in time. Because supplier organizations can be very large (some suppliers employ more than 100,000 people worldwide) and complex, a single supplier can present many different faces.

Suppliers' willingness to deliver the 12 capabilities also largely depends on their perception of the desirability of the customer. Customers falsely assume that all suppliers are vying to have their business. A supplier's willingness to 'go the extra mile' for a particular customer depends on:

- the prestige of the customer
- the size of the contract
- the potential for additional supplier revenues and good profit margins with this client and with other clients because of this deal
- the opportunity to enter into new markets
- the opportunity for knowledge transfer to supplier
- the perceived risks
- the supplier headquarters' sales targets or other financial considerations like meeting quarterly sales quotas.

The job of the client is to do the analysis and work out ways in which the supplier can be influenced to go that 'extra mile'. As John Yard, former CIO of the UK Inland Revenue observed wisely: 'I see myself in competition with all its other clients for the supplier's prime attention and resources'.

There are three main types of criteria that are used to evaluate suppliers:

1. Mandatory – the first gate in which the bidders must pass
2. Qualitative – the 'value' part of the value for money equation
3. Price – the 'money' part of the value for money equation

Mandatory criteria are 'drop dead' criteria – the first cut that eliminates non-compliant responses and disqualifies providers who cannot meet even the most basic expectations. Typically, mandatory criteria are of such importance that if these criteria are not met it does not matter what else is in the bid or how low the offered price.

Qualitative criteria are the criteria applied to the non-financial attributes and solutions the provider is offering. These criteria (and their importance relative to one another), determines what kind of information clients request from bidders, and it makes most sense to develop the information requirements after deciding what criteria will drive the selection process.

Table 3.5 Qualitative criteria list

Criteria	Description
General capabilities	These relate to the overall character of the provider and include: • its twelve core capabilities • its service and product offerings • its market share, strategies, and focus • the geographic areas where it has current operations • stratification of its client base • its financial viability
Track record	These relate to the provider's experience and proven skills and competencies in relevant areas including: • the client's industry • the geographical areas of operation required by the client • specific services and assets required in the deal • the nature of the proposed arrangement • prime contracting and managing subcontractors • customer reference checks
Proposed approach	These reflect the detailed solutions proposed by the provider such as: • service delivery • staffing and staff management • transition in and out of the deal • risk management • account and client relationship management • compliance with the contract and Service Level Agreement (SLA) • continuous improvement • industry development (if applicable) • price approach and viability

The task of evaluation is simplified, and providers do not waste time on low-priority items.

On *price criteria*, all too many come unstuck and it is worth looking how to avoid this.

Bid effectively – avoid the 'winner's curse'

> It's unwise to pay too much, but it's unwise to pay too little. When you pay too much you lose a little money, that is all. When you pay too little, you sometimes lose everything, because the thing you bought was incapable of doing the thing you bought it to do ...
>
> – John Ruskin

Successful outsourcing is not about getting the lowest price at all costs. It is about getting the lowest price for a sustainable solution under a fair contract from a superior service provider. Outsourcing is not an isolated economic transaction that automatically implements itself after the parties sign an agreement but an ongoing commercial relationship with long-term economic and strategic consequences that depend on the choices the parties make and how they subsequently conduct themselves. If a client chooses unwisely, these consequences can be very bad.

There can be severe repercussions when the provider is saddled with a contract from which it stands to make no money – the so-called 'winner's curse' (see Figure 3.5).

The consequences can be devastating, not only for the service provider but also the client. A 2002 study of 85 contracts found the winner's curse came into play in nearly 20 percent of the cases and that in over 75 percent of those cases it was also visited on the client.[4] We have found similar winner's curse deals signed, with similar outcomes in the 2000–03 and 2007–10 economic downturns (see Chapter 10).

Clients should be on their guard. A provider may deliberately offer a very low price to get the organization's brand into its portfolio. Alternatively, it may be so desperate for business that it undercuts other bids in the hope that, once the contract is secured, it can recoup profits by selling additional services to the client – in other words, the provider is prepared to take a hit in one area in order to make it up in others. Under worst-case scenarios providers may even bank on securing a profit through restricted interpretations of the contract and exploiting contract loopholes and ambiguities.

Clients, therefore, should not automatically select the least expensive option. Nor should they leap to the opposite extreme and opt for the service

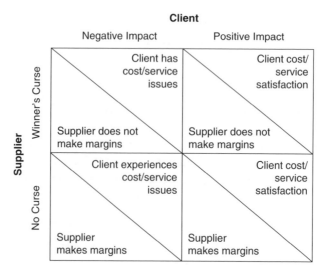

Figure 3.5 Winners curse – and other options

provider that is qualitatively ranked highest. Instead, they should weigh price against quality to get the best value for money. Indeed, choosing service providers on a 'best value for money' basis has become the norm in outsourcing. Organizations have learnt that the lowest bid price does not mean the lowest cost overall. In fact, the opposite is often the case. The costs involved in additional oversight, out-of-scope charges, constant renegotiation, dispute resolution, re-working and backsourcing, can make the price originally agreed no more than a distant memory.

These considerations also apply to modern offshoring deals – from 2000 often pointed to as the 'magic bullet' on price. There is reality to the dramatic lower cost of labor, though this has also been changing, as Indian suppliers in particular experience high labor turnover issues and necessary wage hikes. Moreover, new locations are emerging continually, bringing into play new economic equations.[5] But a client needs to look at the price-cost equation carefully in every instance, and how it is likely to change over time.

Transaction/coordination costs can be higher than you think in offshoring deals; infrastructure and communication costs need to be fastidiously calculated, but may be dynamic and decreasing over the five-year period you sign for. Also look at the long-term strategy of the supplier. Is it pricing low just to get new clients and meet aggressive revenue expansion plans. Does it assume that making an initial loss on your business can be made up by securing much more of your business, even though you have only vague plans on this yourself? Take care to avoid the winner's curse in offshoring as in any other form.

Most organizations use tendering to select service providers. Such an approach has the advantage of putting pressure on service providers to deliver best value for money against their industry peers and of disclosing a variety of capabilities and potential solutions, thus allowing a well-informed selection decision to take place. The alternative is direct negotiation with appropriately placed organizations. However, this strategy is only likely to be successful if:

- One service provider is so outstanding that there is no benefit in evaluating alternative service providers.
- The client is an informed buyer and knows the market prices and industry norms regarding service definitions, technology, and key performance indicators.
- The organization knows exactly what it wants and can quickly draw up an effective contract, service level agreement, and price schedule.
- Speed is more important than cost or exploring alternative solutions comparing service providers. But organizations must be careful not to throw away advantages in speed by poor preparation.

- The client is an experienced outsourcing manager and can expertly manage the provider and the arrangement.
- The client has significantly more bargaining power than the service provider.

In contrast, non-competitive processes such as direct negotiation may seem easier to carry out and faster to put in place. But they may not get the best results. For most organizations tendering is the most appropriate strategy. In addition many organizations, particularly in the public sector, require competitive tendering.

Turning to the detail of the bidding process, paper transactions – issuing documentation and expecting an informed and comprehensive response – is unrealistic. Bidders require interaction to be effective. The more an organization can help potential providers understand its organization, strategies, and ways of operating, the better the responses will be. There are also a number of interactive techniques by which clients can increase their knowledge of potential suppliers, the most common being presentations by bidders, interviews with key supplier personnel, site visits to the supplier and its other customers, and joint workshops to pilot working together (Table 3.6).

Table 3.6 Bid facilitation techniques

Facilitation technique	Description
Bidder discovery/ due diligence	The aim of this is to allow bidders to verify the representations made by the client in its market package and other communications. Due diligence by the provider helps clarify the assumptions on which their proposals are based. This has the benefit of limiting potential caveats, disclaimers, and risk contingencies in bids. It can include:
	• reviewing existing service agreements, contracts, subcontracts, service provider agreements, lease agreements, supply and equipment sources, maintenance practices and related items for which the service provider will take responsibility
	• verifying the inventory of all assets to be purchased, or provided by the organization, verifying the ownership, determining the condition and market value
	• validating service definitions, KPIs, baseline costs, capacities, loads, backlogs
	• confirming configuration, systems software, documentation, security, change control
	• reviewing applicable organizational standards, policies and procedures that they will need to comply with
	• confirming the employment conditions of staff that may be transferred under conditions no less favourable to those they currently enjoy
	• interviewing management, users and other key stakeholders
	• running integration tests and diagnostics.

continued

Table 3.6 *continued*

Facilitation technique	Description
Briefings	Most providers welcome opportunities to meet and obtain information from the client. At a market briefing providers are usually presented with: • background information on the organization, its history, and its future strategies • reasons for outsourcing, discussion of key requirements, and the organization's expectations of the service provider • introductions to key stakeholders and their views • a overview of the market package; evaluation criteria, key dates, and further stages in the selection process • objectives, issues, and other items that are difficult to communicate or emphasize in a voluminous market package.
Data rooms	When it is not practical to include information or data in the market package, a data room can play a useful role. This is a secure room containing data, bulk information and, if appropriate, a secure terminal to assist prospective providers in formulating bids. All registered prospective bidders are allowed an opportunity to visit the room and view the data but usually are not allowed to copy documents without authorization.
Questions and answers	Service providers generally have questions throughout the response period. The best way to handle these is to have a written request/response procedure. Only information clarifying the Market Package is sent out and never any proprietary information relating to other bidders
Site visits	When documentation cannot adequately convey the full range of information, bidders can be offered the opportunity to visit sites.
Workshops	Workshops can help providers explore options with the organization so that they can tailor responses more sensitively and effectively. These can take a number of forms – brainstorming, problem solving sessions or discussions to increase understanding of how the organization works.

Conversely, there are a number of interactive techniques by which clients can increase their knowledge of potential suppliers, as shown in Table 3.7:

The winner's curse: An experience to avoid

Case study 1: A global manufacturer

A well-known global equipment manufacturer had a successful outsourcing business in Europe and wanted to enter the Asia-Pacific market. It cut a deal with an industrial manufacturer that wanted to outsource its IT function. The service provider created a new wholly owned subsidiary for the region. The deal was the first of what were planned to be many.

Table 3.7 Interactive bid evaluation techniques

Evaluation technique	Description
Presentations	It is worthwhile having bidders present their proposals, so that the client can see how they interpret the bid, what they see as important and what their strengths are
Interviews with key supplier personnel	Interviews with the key individuals in the supplier's account and service delivery teams can help the client better understand what bidders are proposing and how well they understand its needs. They also allow the client to assess the personal capabilities of the individuals concerned and their ability to work with the client
Site visits	Inspecting the provider's operations is invaluable in gaining understanding of how they conduct their business and manage relationships in practice
Workshops	Workshops or field experiments provide an opportunity to see how well the parties can work together. Such opportunities to exchange views and problem-solve, whether focused on real or hypothetical issues, are almost always worthwhile. However, government probity rules, which dictate that all bidders must receive exactly the same information, may not permit them in the public sector, given the fluidity of conversations in such workshops.

In order to get the first critical deal with the client, the supplier's sales team bid a price that was below cost. It did not realize that, however, since it was dealing with its first client and had no idea what the actual cost would be. It basically bid the price it thought necessary to win he contract without having a firm grasp of what price was needed to make a reasonable profit. The client knew the service provider could not be making money on the deal but took comfort in the strength of its well-known global brand.

After 18 months the service provider still had not won any further clients. A review of the subsidiary by its parent organization showed that it was making unacceptable losses and there was little possibility of a rapid turnaround. So it had to start making money from its one client. The service provider assigned a new account manager – a lawyer. His mission was to re-interpret the contract and reclaim any possible money he could. This was possible because the contract had no date limitations regarding when work could be billed and reimbursements claimed.

Nine months of intense dispute followed. Invoices were raised for work deemed out of scope, a number of additional charges and reimbursements were claimed which went right back to the start of the contract. Work that the client had been obtaining was stopped if the account manager interpreted the work as out-of-scope. Eventually the two parties reached a settlement through a third-party intermediary. The wholly owned subsidiary was wound-up, and the client had to find a new service provider.

However, further difficulties followed with the new service provider. The client had developed a deep distrust of service providers, and the new service provider had to invest a lot of time and effort in relationship management – and repair – to regain enough trust to be able to function effectively.

Case study 2: A major retailer

The IT department of a retailing company had recently been transferred to its Corporate Services division. The general manager believed that commodity functions should be outsourced so the division could focus on adding value to the operational business units. She saw IT services as a commodity and put data centre operations out to tender. As a commodity market, she believed the providers were undifferentiated in their services and approaches, and the contract was awarded solely on the basis of price. The successful bid was 30 percent lower than the nearest other bid.

Things soon began to go wrong. Scope and price variations became common. Eventually a post had to be dedicated to variation management. Service levels were rarely achieved, because they had been set up as targets not minimum standards. This was because the client accepted the service provider's 'standard' service level agreement rather than developing one that represented its needs. The service provider capped the amount of resources they would provide for the price and would only provide more if more money was paid. In time, the general manager had to hire specialists to work in the data centre in order to restore service to previous levels and meet peak demands.

Within a year the total cost of contract outstripped the bid and the in-house baseline. Moreover – and most telling – the efforts of the division's remaining IT people had become focused on fighting the contract, not on adding value to the business.

Conclusion – lessons on selecting and leveraging suppliers

An organization can be left very exposed if it chooses the wrong supplier. The displacement of risk on to a supplier is invariably illusory. This is why the CEO and senior executive team must be involved in ensuring that the supplier selection process, and that the supplier's capabilities are requisite. This chapter suggests the following lessons:

1. The selection and negotiation phase is when the client enjoys most bargaining power and, if this power is not used wisely at this point, there

can be very negative repercussions. The CEO's authority and influence is a key resource in this process.

2. Customers need to assess suppliers' capabilities and competencies rather than their resources. We have identified 12 key capabilities that in turn can be converted into three competencies of overriding importance to clients – delivery, transformation, and relationship competencies.

3. Choosing the right supplier model or configuration of suppliers is the essential first step. This is part of sourcing strategy and the CEO should be involved (see also Chapter 1).

4. Customers should assess a supplier's capabilities and competencies for each new business context: not every business context requires suppliers to excel in all 12 capabilities and all three competencies. In assessing suppliers there are three different sets of criteria – mandatory, qualitative, and price.

5. It is vital to avoid the 'winner's curse' – bids which excessively favor the client at the expense of the supplier, as these do not work to the client's advantage in the long run. The key is getting the best *value* in return for a fair price.

6. Tendering is generally the most common and effective strategy to select suppliers. Direct negotiation without tendering and competition is only for highly experienced clients.

7. The more interaction and transparency between client and potential supplier at bid and negotiation stage the better. A range of techniques have been developed to facilitate this on both sides.

Notes

1. More detail can be found in Willcocks, L. and Lacity, M. (2006) *Global Sourcing of Business and IT Services*. Palgrave, London. The original article is Feeny, D., Lacity, M. and Willcocks, L. (2005) 'Taking a measure of outsourcing providers', *Sloan Management Review*, 46, 3, pp. 41–48. See also Oshri, I., Kotlarsky, J. and Willcocks, L. (2009) *The Handbook of Global Outsourcing and Offshoring*. Palgrave, London, chapter 4.

2. This finding comes from Willcocks, L. and Lacity, M. (2009) *The Practice of Outsourcing: From Information Systems to BPO and Offshoring*. Palgrave, London.

3. See Willcocks, L. Griffiths, C. and Kotlarsky, J. (2009). *Beyond BRIC – Offshoring in Non-BRIC Countries: Egypt a New Growth Market*. LSE, London

4. See Kern, T. and Willcocks, I. and Van Heck, E. (2002) ,The winners curse in IT outsourcing: strategies for avoiding relational trauma', *California Management Review*, 44, 2, pp. 47–69. Also Willcocks and Lacity (2009)

op. cit. and Chapter 10 which reports on research during the 2007–10 economic downturn

5. See Willcocks, L. Griffiths, C. and Kotlarsky, J. (2009). op. cit. – By 2009 we found Indian supplier companies themselves moving, at least in part, to cheaper locations, for example Sri Lanka.

CHAPTER 4

Keeping control through core retained capabilities

What keeps me up at night? I think our challenge now is probably more internal than external. And that is how to get all of our internal stakeholders lined up behind whatever we execute. Get them to understand this is the way we need to manage.

– Senior executive, multinational resource company

You've got to be able to upskill your organization and to have a human resource policy which provides such training to people in your organization.

– Senior executive, major oil company

We never resolve the issues. It's unresolvable because the bank still doesn't lead on or own the outcome. So while they continue to blame the outsourcer for not delivering something which they can neither describe nor write down or articulate or agree on, it's just not going to work.

– Senior bank executive, four years into a large-scale
IT outsourcing contact

Introduction

As Chapter 3 showed, outsourcing offers opportunities to acquire new capabilities from outside the organization. These capabilities can be used to reduce the cost and improve service levels, provide access to new skills, improve capital management and, indeed, offer a range of other often strategic, benefits. In this respect, one fundamental client question has guided this book: how to leverage the growing, increasingly globalizing, ITO/BPO services markets to achieve business advantage? This chapter deals with the most critical, all too often neglected, leveraging and risk mitigating practice, namely retaining key internal capabilities that underpin the business's future capacity to exploit business and IT services. There is an uncomfortable reality here – our research indicates that few organizations, even those that have outsourced for several years, have in place such capabilities. As consequent problems mount, organizations then have to play 'catch-up', often on a large scale. As one practitioner (IT executive, international bank) put it: 'The problem is putting the genie back into the bottle. It's really, really hard work.' Five years into another large-scale deal, a business manager reflected on the source of the mixed outcomes they were getting: 'It was all owned by and driven through the outsourcer – almost a black magic relationship. They were seen as the experts and holders of the knowledge. And the interesting thing is they were seen as the only people that had the knowledge as well.'

This book is designed to show how an organization can dramatically climb the learning curve from limited contract administration and management to outsourcing leadership and collaborative innovation (see Chapter 5, Figure 5.1, for a diagram of this evolution). Expanding leadership capacity enables wider goals to be achieved, moving from tactical back office cost reductions and service streamlining through quality, and value-added objectives, to innovation and strategic contributions to business positioning and competitiveness.

In this chapter we bring together the necessary learning through the lens of the core retained capabilities needed to keep control of back-office functions. We show how these capabilities provide governance, control, risk mitigation, and flexibility in outsourcing arrangements, and form the basis for maturing an organization's ability to lead and innovate through outsourcing.

Core retained capabilities for IT and back-office functions

Across 20 years research a key challenge we found organizations wrestling with has been: where, at this moment in time, should we draw the line between what can be outsourced and what needs to be retained? Looking at just IT, strong, informed decisions are frequently made about activities and assets, for example:

> We have our infrastructure, mainframe, midrange, servers, all that sort of stuff is outsourced, likewise our bulk printing and mailing. We don't outsource strategy, we don't outsource architecture, we don't outsource service management or security, any of that. All of that is retained in-house, with full-time resource; the other commoditized-type IT services are outsourced. (BH Billiton, Resources and Manufacturing Company, 2007)

Service management, strategy, architecture, finance, security, they were all what we saw as our key capabilities within IT. (Axa Insurance Company, 2007)

But the really difficult area is deciding on what needs to be retained and developed in terms of leadership, management, and staffing. And, as will emerge, getting this wrong can have highly damaging consequences for any outsourcing arrangement. Where then should the line be drawn? Our own work finds that high performing back-offices are managed by a residual team of highly capable, demand-led and strategy-focused people. In this section we provide a framework for describing and discussing the substance of such a team, and what happens when it is, and if it is not, in place.

Defining capabilities

The framework in Figure 4.1 identifies nine core retained capabilities required for high-performing back-office functions, along with associated skills and inter-relationships. We define a capability as a distinctive set of human-based skills, orientations, attitudes, motivations, and behaviors that, when applied, can transform resources into specific business activities. Collections of capabilities, in turn, create high-level strategic competencies

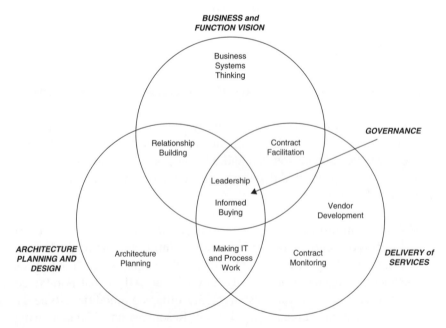

Figure 4.1 Nine core capabilities for high-performing IT and back-office functions

that positively influence business performance.[1] We found the skills supporting a capability to be in each case a distinctive mix of interpersonal, technical, and business skills. In this chapter we focus specifically on the IT function. Here, distinctive 'core IS capabilities' are needed to manage the demand side of, and exploit information and communications technologies. These capabilities are measurable in terms of IT activities supported, and resulting business performance. Throughout we use the word 'role' to refer to a person formally enacting a capability. For example in the role of CIO a person enacts the leadership capability. In the role of, say, procurement manager the role holder will enact informed buying.

Four tasks

Our research demonstrates that the modern high-performing IT function has four fundamental tasks:

- *Governance, including leadership and coordination.* This involves aligning dynamically the IT function's activities internally, and with those of the organization as a whole.
- *Eliciting and delivering on business requirements.* A demand-driven task concerned with defining the systems, information, and processes to be provided, and how they can be leveraged for business purpose.
- *Ensuring technical capability.* A supply-focused task about defining the blueprint or architecture of the technical platform used over time to support the target systems and processes, and dealing with risks inherent in non-routine technical issues.
- *Managing external supply.* This concerns arriving at and managing sourcing strategy. It requires understanding of the external services market, and the ability to select, engage, and manage internal and external IT resources and services over time.

Note that each task has both strategic and operational dimensions.

Nine capabilities

These four tasks are delivered through nine capabilities (see Figure 4.1). These populate seven spaces. Three spaces are essentially business, technology, or service facing. A fourth is a lynchpin governance position covered by two capabilities (leadership and informed buying). Finally, there are three spaces that represent various interfaces. The capabilities that populate these interfaces are crucial for facilitating the integration of effort

Table 4.1 Nine core capabilities

Capability	Primary agenda
Leadership	Integrate the IT effort with business purpose and activity
Business systems thinking	Ensure that IT capabilities are envisioned in every business process
Relationship building	Get the business constructively engaged in operational IT issues, and the potential IT offers
Architecture planning and design	Create the coherent blueprint for a technical platform that responds to present and future business needs
Making technology and process work	Rapidly trouble-shoot problems being disowned by others across the technical supply chain
Informed buying	Manage the IT sourcing strategy to meet the interests of the business
Contract facilitation	Ensure the success of existing contracts for external IT services
Contract monitoring	Protect the business's contractual position present and future
Vendor development	Identify the potential added value from IT service suppliers

across the four fundamental tasks. An overview is shown in Table 4.1. Let us look at these capabilities in more detail.

Capability 1: Leadership – The central task here is to devise and engage in organizational arrangements – governance, structures, processes, and staffing – that successfully manage internal and business interdependencies, in ways that ensure the IT function delivers business value for money. Leaders also influence the overall business perception of IT's role and contribution, and establish strong relationships at senior business executive level in order to achieve a shared vision of IT. Leaders also determine the values and culture of the IT function, and instill the belief that IT staff's primary duty is to contribute to the business. Bob Sellwood, senior IT executive at BH Billiton gives some insight seven years into a $900 million outsourcing arrangement with CSC:

> What keeps me up at night? I think our challenge now is probably more internal than external. And that is how to get all of our internal stakeholders lined up behind whatever we execute. Get them to understand this is the way we need to manage. What does governance success look like? How do you measure governance success? What is the right way of measuring the goodness of any of these deals? And what is the right kind of framework to pull this together?

Capability 2: Business systems thinking – In leading practice organizations we study, business systems thinkers from the IT function are important contributors to teams charged with business problem solving, process re-engineering, strategic development, and delivering e-business. Such organizations recognize that business processes should be redesigned in the light of technology potential. The business systems thinker applies an holistic perspective, focusing on optimal integration of strategy, process, technology, systems, and people.

Without such staffing and vision, a major insurance company we studied contracted a supplier to deliver a strategic IT system aimed at transforming administrative and customer service systems. However, the business transformation was conceived as an IT project, and the supplier was given primary responsibility and aggressive deadlines. In the event the supplier failed to deliver detailed business requirements on time and the project was cancelled nine months into the two-year implementation.[2]

Capability 3: Relationship building – Here role holders facilitate the wider dialogue, establishing understanding, trust, and cooperation among business users and IT specialists. Relationship builders develop users' understanding of IT and its potential for their lines of business. They help users and specialists to work together, help to identify business requirements, ensure user ownership and support user satisfaction with IT services. To achieve these things they need a distinctive blend of high technical and relationship skills.

When it works, even one individual can make a difference. As one retailer business unit head commented: 'things are quite different now; we feel our contact point with IT is really one of us'. In contrast, at DuPont four years into a major outsourcing deal with Accenture and CSC, we found several regional business units losing touch with under-staffed local IT functions, where IT leaders had to undertake multiple leadership, relationship building, and contract facilitation roles. In time mounting problems led to better staffing and a stronger focus on career development.

Capability 4: Architectural planning and design – The principal challenge to the architect is, through insight into technology, suppliers, and business directions, to anticipate technology trends so that the organization is consistently able to operate from an effective and efficient IT platform – without major investments into major migration efforts. Planners shape the IT architecture and infrastructure through developing the vision of an appropriate technical platform, and through formulating associated policies that ensure necessary integration and flexibility in IT services.

Any outsourcing arrangement provides a strong test of the value of retaining this capability. We saw a bank and a manufacturer give away their architects, assuming that the task of architecture planning was technical and therefore one for the suppliers. Three years into outsourcing found each of them rebuilding this capability, because they could not understand, let alone talk with and influence the suppliers about how to address existing and fresh demand through a new technology platform with better economics. Looking at organizing new contracts in 2007, Jo Hein of Australian Customs and Excise said: 'We need internal knowledge to make decisions about where we are going rather than having to rely on the provider to say – this new technology has come up, how are we going to deal with it?' In support, a CIO of a major UK public sector agency told us: 'They are going to take your architecture where their business is going, not where you need to go … It's dangerous to let all your architects go, and I am skilling up my group to build an expertise that can keep up'.

Capability 5: Making technology and process work – Operating in the overlap between the challenges of IT architecture design and delivery of IT services is the core capability of making technology and process work. Technology 'fixers' are needed to troubleshoot problems and identify how to address business needs which cannot be properly satisfied by standard technical approaches. They understand the idiosyncrasies of the inherited infrastructure and business applications, enabling them to make rapid technical progress – by one means or another. In outsourced environments they also assess and challenge third party suppliers' claims about technical problems and proposed solutions. The capability requires a broad and strong understanding of technology fundamentals, and the insight of an architecture planner, together with a pragmatic and short-term orientation to problem resolution.

The need to retain high-quality technical 'doing' capability was widely recognized among the organizations we studied. For example the lead IT executive in a public sector agency in charge of a five-year deal: 'We can't retain too much skill because we will be paying twice for it. But we are retaining a modicum in the systems analysis and requirements definition area, and, for example, for rapid application development, prototyping and hybrid skills.'

Chris Rawson at Lloyds of London commented: 'I have a network team, I would get no value by outsourcing them, they have an intimate knowledge of our network at Lloyds. They installed IP technology, a relatively new technology then, and I do not want to put that at risk.' Commonwealth Bank Australia (CBA) was more typical in under-estimating the need. Faced with a major business transformation eight years into a $3.4 billion ten-year single-source outsourcing arrangement with EDS, it began rebuilding its IS development capability. Fortunately, one recently acquired business unit had retained resource, leading the bank to be able to deliver successfully a cross-organizational CRM implementation between 2003 and 2005.[3]

Capability 6: Informed buying – In an organization that has decided to outsource most of its IT services, this role is the most prominent after the CIO. Informed buyers analyze and benchmark regularly the external market for IT services; select the 5–10-year sourcing strategy to meet business needs and technology issues; and lead the tendering, contracting, and service management processes. Informed buying also requires an intimate knowledge of suppliers – their strategies, financial strength, and their capabilities and incapabilities in different sectors, services, and regions. One informed buyer also described the pragmatic aspect to the role: 'If you are a senior manager ... and you want something done, you come to me and I will ... go outside, select and draw up the contract with the outsourcer, and if anything goes wrong, it's my butt that gets kicked by you'. (IT manager, energy company)

The ABNAmro bank $US1.2 billion global deal signed in late 2005 with five suppliers, three of them India-based, helped to point the way to the likely future challenges faced by informed buying. To be frank, we rarely come across an organization that invests nearly enough in this capability. But the signs are that as organizations outsource increasingly more of their IT budget, and on a multi-sourcing basis, they are going to need to invest much more in this capability – the need, indeed, for what we have called 'informed buying on steroids'.[4]

Capability 7: Contract facilitation – Here the contract facilitator lubricates the relationship between supplier(s) and the business users, not least by ensuring that problems and conflicts are seen to be resolved fairly and promptly within what are usually long-term relationships. It is an action-orientated capability. If service agreements, suppliers, and user behavior were perfect, contract facilitation would not be a core IS capability. The reality is that IT service delivery is invariably complex and messy. As one CIO stated: 'The users have been bitten a few times when they have dealt directly with suppliers, and it's a service we can provide, so we do.' Interestingly, the need for this role is rarely spotted straight away when outsourcing. The capability tends to grow in response to ongoing issues for which it emerges as an adequate response, such as:

- users may demand too much and incur excessive charges,
- the business user asks for 'one-stop' shopping,
- the supplier demands it,
- multiple supplier services need coordinating, and
- easier monitoring of usage and services is required.

However, the role is not just problem resolution. Contract facilitation is fundamentally a coordinating role, and includes managing the expectations of the different parties to supply agreements, both internal and external.

Capability 8: Contract monitoring – Located in the exclusive space of the supply face, contract monitoring involves making inputs into the development and maintenance of a robust contract as the basis for a sound governance framework. The role then involves holding suppliers to account against both existing service contracts and the developing performance standards of the services market. Not all potential issues and expectations can be identified at the onset of a relationship, and the contract will be subject to differing interpretations as issues arise. Moreover there is no standard contract, only standard headings, as each outsourcing arrangement has its own set of issues and dynamics. All this makes contract monitoring a highly skilled core capability focused on preserving the integrity of the organization's contractual position across the lifetime of the outsourcing arrangement.

While all organizations we have studied recognized the importance of contract monitoring and staffed it at the beginning of their outsourcing deals, they all too frequently put the wrong people in place, especially in the large deals, underestimating the dynamic nature and extent of the task.

Capability 9: Vendor development – Anchored in the supply face of our model, the vendor developer is concerned with leveraging the long-term potential for suppliers to add value, creating 'win–win' situations in which the supplier increases its revenues by providing services that increase business benefits. Given the prohibitive size of switching costs, it is in the client company's interest to maximize the contribution from existing suppliers and guard against what we call 'mid-contract sag' where the supplier delivers to the contract, but only to the letter: 'Yes the supplier can achieve all the things that were proposed – but where is the famous 'value-added service'? We are not getting anything over and above what any old outsourcer could provide.' IT service director, aerospace company. Compare this with a retail multinational that meets suppliers formally at senior levels to find new ways forward. According to the CIO: 'there are certain things we force on our suppliers like understanding our business and growing the business together'.

In their 2001 five year, annually renewable back-office outsourcing arrangement, the London insurance market and Xchanging developed an innovative approach by forming a jointly owned third entity, XIS, to deliver services. Joint ownership and management, together with shared risk and reward, has placed considerable emphasis on win–win innovations beyond the original contract.[5]

So you want to under-resource the retained IT function ….

It is easy to see why building such capabilities may not be the most obvious senior executive priority. If IT is mainly a commodity why do you want to invest rather than divest? And is not handing over responsibility for management and delivery at the heart of why you outsource in the first place? Moreover, as we saw in Chapter 1, the process of getting to contract is costly (between 0.4 percent and 2.4 percent of contract value), time-consuming and effortful, even before you then get into the big challenges of transition. The urgent drives out the seemingly less important... until problems keep coming back, and new problems arise for which you cannot find the resource, or knowledge, to handle.

But low spenders on core capabilities do not perform contract management; as we pointed out earlier, they perform what we call contract *administration*. (We develop this theme in more detail in Chapter 5). This may work where no significant contracts exist, and the outsourced activities are simple to define, discrete, and easy to monitor. But for all other outsourcing situations contract administration leads slowly and ultimately to an expensive erosion of control over the client organization's IT destiny. One symptom of this we regularly observe is the spreading of a person over several different roles. Thus in some business units at DuPont we found 'leaders' in fact doing contract facilitation, contract monitoring, and relationship building work as well. At a major bank the contract manager was at the same time informed buyer, leader, contract facilitator, relationship builder, and occasional technical fixer and architect – basically a one-man in-house IT function. Both situations were subsequently corrected.

But all too often we find organizations building core capabilities after experiencing serious problems, rather than pre-empting these, by evolving core IS capabilities at a speed able to absorb increasing degrees and different types of outsourcing. The need in outsourcing is to get on to the optimal, most cost-effective path (see Figure 4.2). This is done by managing the nine stage, 54 activity lifecycle process and activities as described in earlier chapters. In particular we have highlighted the shaping role of strategy and executive involvement, the power of building and managing relationships, and the criticality of selecting and leveraging requisite supplier capabilities. In this chapter we focus on the most neglected factor, but in many ways the most critical, not least because core IS capabilities are the final, and best insurance, policy you take out against having a poor outsourcing experience.

However, building and retaining core retained capabilities costs money. How much exactly has been detailed in Chapter 1. But on core IS capabilities you really do have to spend in order to save. Figure 4.2 shows the optimal path, but also the flawed path down which all too many organizations take their outsourcing arrangements. Without architecting and capability building work up-front, significant issue will accumulate, typically as loss of control, inadequate service, extensive out-of-scope charges, excessive management time and effort, constant renegotiation,

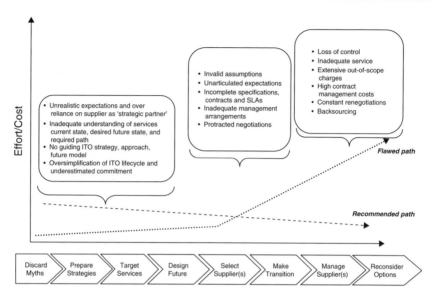

Figure 4.2 Getting on the optimal cost-effective path

Source: Intelligent IT Outsourcing – Cullen and Willcocks, 2003

and a growing belief during the Regeneration phase that the organization either needs to backsource the activities, or switch to another provider. Even without legal disputes, all these issues cost a lot more to resolve later in the cycle. Suppliers, too, recognize the eventual pain poor architecting work and inadequate internal capability can cause. Asked to comment on the impact of indifferent client retained capability one supplier account executive told us: 'In one deal we spent much more time filling in for client weaknesses than we seemed to spend on the actual work we were contracted to do! We had to second guess and propose all the time – to be frank it was very hard work for everybody to hold the thing together – not a good experience'.

The problem is that, traditionally in outsourcing, clients prioritize short-term cost reduction gains over any 'invest to save' philosophy. For example, in their 1997–2007 deal with EDS, CBA greatly under-invested in their core capabilities. To get off what was manifestly becoming a flawed path, they had to strengthen their internal capabilities dramatically. From 2001 to 2005, with CEO approved funding, staff numbers were increased from 32 to 126. This turned an adversarial, cost-focused relationship with the supplier into a much better controlled one – indeed the contract was renewed after ten years. It also underpinned two successful IT-enabled bank transformation efforts between 2001 and 2007.[6]

Core retained capabilities are a mature, realistic, tried-and-tested way of getting on the optimal cost-effective outsourcing path. The message?

Under-invest in core retained capabilities at your peril. Get on the optimal cost-effective path before it is too late.

Core capabilities: The key challenges

Throughout this book we have stressed that outsourcing is best seen not as the handing over of management, but as a radical change in the way management is done. As the finance director of oil major BP told us: 'To overcome the problems we have seen developing in other outsourcing contracts, we need to create a culture supported by process; the key thread is our internal behavior.' Commenting on HR outsourcing at British Aerospace, Steve Hodgson put it this way: 'The fact is you have given up managerial control, you don't control resources any more, you manage the service.'

In practice outsourcing creates five major adaptive challenges for the client organization. Let us look at these.

1. Human resource challenges

The nine roles all demand high performers who can develop into a high-performance team. In contrast to the more traditional skills found in IT functions, there needs to be a much greater emphasis on business skills and business orientation in nearly all roles, the exceptions being the 'technical fixer', and to some extent the 'technical architect' roles. There is a significantly increased requirement for 'soft' skills across all roles, the exception being the 'contract monitor' role. The major shift we have been observing in organizations such as Esso, ICI, DuPont, Commonwealth Bank, Lloyds of London, BP, and GE is toward fewer personnel, but of very high quality.

Each role requires a specific set of skills, attributes, and drivers. Through possessing one set, a person will be potentially disabled from high performance in the other roles. Our experience to date is that one person could deliver high performance in no more than two or three roles at any single point in their career path. This has considerable implications for staffing, personal, and career development. The set of skills and orientations are shown in Table 4.2. Our experience is that, typically, retained functions and staff tend to have some of the technical skills required for their jobs, lack business skills, but are most weak in interpersonal skills.

In practice, recruitment and retention of a small high-quality group is a major human resource challenge. The people being targeted here would look more familiar as senior professionals within a major management consulting firm. Two solutions that need to be faced up to are upskilling and

Table 4.2 Retained capabilities: Skills, orientations, and time horizons

Core IT capability	Skills			Time horizons	Motivating values
	Business	**Technical**	**Interpersonal**		
IS/IT leadership	High	Medium	High	Future/ Present	• Strategy • Structure • Individuals
Business systems thinking	High	Medium	Medium	Future	• Strategy
Relationship building	Medium	High	High	Present	• Structure • Individuals
Architecture planning	Low-Medium	High	Medium	Future	• Technology
Making technology work	Low	High	Low-Medium	Present	• Technology
Informed buying	High	Medium	High	Future/ Present	• Strategy • Structure
Contract facilitation	Medium	Medium	High	Present	• Structure • Individuals
Contract Monitoring	Medium	Medium	Low-Medium	Future	• Structure
Vendor Development	High	Medium	Medium-High	Future	• Strategy • Individuals

hiring. As one multinational oil company executive commented: 'You've got to be able to upskill your organization and to have a human resource policy which provides such training to people in your organization.'

The logistics manager at a major retailer said: 'To be honest, we had to recruit a few people.' Moreover you will need to:

• pay them at a level within striking distance of that provided by alternative employers;
• provide them consistently with the level of challenge they look for in the job;
• provide them with a career path despite the very small numbers.

A further human resource challenge rests with what one respondent termed 'the legacy people' problem. In other words, what about existing IT staff that the high-performance model specifically excludes? Some approaches we have observed in various combinations are: early retirement, redundancy packages, making people redundant as the in-house legacy systems become redundant, and relocation and retraining. In outsourcing situations one common response has been to transfer such staff to suppliers. One difficulty is that suppliers, understandably, prefer to take only the better motivated and skilled staff; sometimes the result has been that the staff that remain are not sufficiently motivated, or capable, of delivering on the in-house high-performance requirement.

2. The supplier challenge

What is the role of suppliers in supporting the high-performance concept? In the ongoing Xchanging-London insurance market back office deal, one supplier executive offered the following insight: 'The essence was maintaining active involvement from senior management on both sides, coupled with the availability within the supplying company of the necessary range of skills, often deficient in previous supplier models.'

In specific projects or services, suppliers need to have complementary rather than competing or duplicating capabilities and skills. Furthermore, it is important to develop mutual cooperation and understanding between the in-house and supplier groups. In some cases, however, different terms and conditions have been a source of friction and resentment; suppliers may turn lack of in-house skills to their own opportunistic advantage; and in-house employees may stand back and let supplier staff take all responsibility. Some of the ways toward a more constructive relationship are indicated by the following:

> They (the supplier staff) are part of my team, they sit with my team, so for all intents and purposes they could be working for me. We have brought them into the organization almost, because they are running a very important production system for us ... they also deal directly with the business users of the system ... it's worked well because they actually get a sense of responsibility for the service like the internal people. (IT Manager, UK retailing company)

With multi-supplier outsourcing being the dominant trend, the supplier's ability to work with other suppliers also supports the high-performance concept. In practice we find this capacity varies considerably from supplier to supplier, and can make a tremendous difference on how much time the internal team puts into intervention and management. Chapter 3 provides more detailed discussion of the 12 capabilities needed by a supplier.

3. The perennial challenge – relationships

In Chapter 2 we detailed the power of relationships in securing effective outsourcing outcomes. Part of this is not allowing a large power imbalance to develop in favor of the supplier. A senior IT executive outlines his chastening experience of this: 'The bank outsourced the whole thing, and the supplier was seen as the holders of knowledge. Now four years in, if you want anything done, you have to have one of those "Come to Jesus" meetings with the outsourcer.'

This is very different from other experiences we have noted, for example Chris Rawson IT director at Lloyds of London: 'We play very strongly the partnership ticket with our suppliers and ensure they are seen as part of the IT group at Lloyds in their dealings with internal customers.' Relationships with suppliers can turn into strategic assets – if leveraged properly. In particular many organizations are still finding their way in doing this when moving to multi-supplier arrangements. The evidence here supports having strong retained capabilities, rather than getting suppliers to manage each other.[7] Thus, in moving from a single supplier arrangement one public sector IT executive said: 'We want the focus now to come back on our people being responsible for the service, regardless of whether we now sign up three or four contractors.'

Taking a step back from this issue, we concluded in Chapter 2 that relationships become strategic assets only under certain conditions. First, senior management, including the CEO, need to sew the seeds for a successful relationship before the start of the deal, and cultivate it thereafter at three levels – executive, managerial, and operational. The contract cannot guarantee effective relationships but a poorly drafted one can seriously damage outsourcing health. There needs to be put in place the right structures and processes to facilitate the development of relationships within and across client and suppliers. The core retained capabilities detailed above have immense relationship building and leveraging power built into them. As we described in Chapter 2, on our evidence such relationship management – through senior management attention, contract, structure, process, and retained capabilities – can create a 20–40 percent difference on service, quality, cost, and other performance indicators. In addition, we saw that using measures like relationship value charters, regular relationship health checks, and contract and relationship scorecards sets and aligns targets, and encourages superior performance.

4. The project management challenge

An additional challenge relates to project management capability, which does not appear in Figure 4.1. Why is this? In dynamic business environments, the emphasis has shifted from hierarchical, functionally based organizations toward task and project-based ways of operating. The logic here is that project management skills will be spread throughout such organizations. Project management must be an *organizational* core capability, and not the preserve of one function or department. Whatever the IT component in a project, in practice its project manager can come from anywhere in the business, the main primary criteria being his/her credibility, which in turn relates to proven successful project experience.

In the core capabilities framework of Figure 4.1, candidates for the project manager role are most likely to be found in the relationship builder and technical fixer roles. Without this internal capability, in a pharmaceuticals company we saw a project manager, appointed from the business to implement an ERP system, fail through lack of technical credibility. Conversely, in a bank and insurance company several projects managed by IT personnel failed to deliver effective business systems through a narrow, technical view of the requirement.

Organizations experienced in outsourcing frequently tell us what we learned at BH Billiton in 2007:

> We outsourced too much project management capability in our first deal, and even if you have somebody doing projects for you, you can never give up project sponsorship, ownership and accountability. We don't believe you can let your hands off the wheel, and to do that you have to have a core capability and a core discipline.

That said, after one or two generations of outsourcing, many organizations begin to rebuild some of their specific IT project management capability and IT applications teams. For example, CBA in the 2002–06 period found this an effective way to manage large-scale IT-enabled business transformation projects. DuPont also began to develop an internal application strategy and team once it had started on a major global ERP implementation with its suppliers. In such organizations, the organizational project management capability was patchy at best; IT needed strengthening in its ability to have informed technical dialogue with suppliers and influence and contribute to IT supply; and the IT requirement was large and had to be shaped carefully to changing business needs. An emerging challenge, then, is to gauge how far your organization needs to create a core IT project management capability.

5. Rising challenges – move to the core?

In the last five years fresh challenges around the outsourcing decision have presented themselves. In principle one can outsource critical commodities but not differentiators or core capabilities (see Chapter 1). IT Security has leapt up the organizational agenda in this period, not least because of increased offshoring, and heightened awareness of hacking, and potential terrorism. The senior IT executive of a multinational resource company suggests how to deal with the challenge:

> 'We have internal capability around security. Probably not enough I think in our original outsource, we overlooked the detailed requirement. Clearly we don't want to do security administration. Happy for that to be outsourced. But all the monitoring and compliance, all that sort of thing, we believe we need to keep a pretty tight control over.'

We found many organizations concluding that they also should retain capability around the processing of an issue *through incident, change, and problem management.* Relatedly, one respondent stressed the need to manage external communications: 'There is also incident management. If we were to get a serious technical problem or security incident there is a whole load of issues associated with that which we don't necessarily want to expose, or have exposed, to external organizations.' The retained core capabilities management team will need to take responsibility for these emerging issues. And this leads to looking at the leadership role this team has in sourcing strategy and implementation.

Achieving leadership through the high-performance team

This book is built on a central research observation. Over two decades and more outsourcing practice has slowly, often painfully, moved up the learning curve, and matured in many organizations into relatively effective outcomes for stable, discrete, back-office activities. However, this represents improvements in the *management* of outsourcing. Most organizations still have to make the further step of *leading and innovating* through outsourcing. The essential pillars supporting such a development appear in the first four chapters of this book. But if leadership runs though all these chapters and the practices described therein, leadership is also a slippery concept that needs to be pinned down.

Ronald Heifetz in his excellent book *Leadership Without Easy Answers*[8] makes an important distinction between technical and adaptive work. Technical problems are rarely trivial but what makes them technical is that the solution, in the form of specialist know-how, techniques, and routine processes, already exists within the organization's (or a supplier's) repertoire. Managers can delegate such work to specialists and monitor the outcomes.

By contrast, leadership deals with adaptive challenges. In fact, Heifetz defines leadership as shaping and mobilizing adaptive work, that is, engaging people to make progress on the adaptive problems they face. For him, the hardest and most valuable task of leadership is advancing goals and designing strategy that promote adaptive work. An adaptive challenge is a particular problem, often difficult to specify precisely, where the gap between values and aspirations on the one hand, and circumstances on the other, cannot be closed by the application of current technical know-how and routine behavior. Adaptive challenges require experiments, discoveries, and adjustments from many parts of an organization.

'Technical' versus 'adaptive' challenges in outsourcing

Many will see outsourcing as essentially technical work. This is substantially correct for mature, stable, discrete activities. Typical examples include applications support and maintenance, data centre processing, networks, and communications. Risks are low when you understand such activities, can write detailed contracts, can monitor the outcomes, and where the supplier has requisite technical specialist capability. But even here the shaping work of leadership, outlined above, is critical. Moreover, there is adaptive work inherent in all forms of outsourcing – it is *never* just plug-and-play.

Internal leadership is required because the service, technologies, and business requirement will start to outdate before the ink on the contract is dry. Transitioning – 'when the rubber hits the road' – provides a specific set of adaptive issues that supplier leadership can also help with. Transferring staff internally or to a supplier, redundancies, or training people for new IT roles can be minefields. Moreover, there are all too many unknowns. A major one is precisely how the relationship between business unit users, the in-house IT function and suppliers service delivery will play out. Much of outsourcing is emergent – as managers, customers, and suppliers learn and re-learn to work with each other in the face of dynamic demands, staffing, technologies, and settings.

When one adds into the mix typical modern developments – large-scale, multiple suppliers, offshoring, the outsourcing of IT-enabled back offices like HR, procurement, finance and accounting, and transformation outsourcing, and supplier involvement in business transformation projects – it becomes very clear that, in modern outsourcing adaptive challenges far outweigh technical ones. Thus leadership – the ability to shape the context for and mobilize adaptive work – becomes key. Consider the following experience outlined by a HR executive in the Xchanging/BAE Systems (2001 and ongoing) HR outsourcing arrangement:

> Major challenges include managing change amongst the new role people, managing change within BAE Systems and particularly within

my peer group within the company. The change management is not something you sub-contract because it is policy strategy, it is DNA, for want of a better expression, and the business is about judgment, it is about relationships and it is also about managing the service provider. Managing the customer's perception of what has happened to their HR service is becoming the biggest challenge. TM was a particularly powerful figure in the business predominantly and he actually managed to drive this thing through. Thereafter, leadership was required to bring the HR people and the line managers on board. The line managers were more difficult than the people to be honest!

This outsourcing required the centralization of the HR service based on a new technology platform to be run by the new supplier. All parties experienced considerable adaptive challenges over nearly two years, requiring leadership at executive, management, and operational levels in the retained HR function, the business units and the supplier. We will develop this theme further, with examples, in Chapter 5.

The role of retained capabilities and the high-performance team

Each outsourcing arrangement possesses its own distinctive blend of technical and adaptive challenges. The most common mistake has been to pre-define outsourcing as a technical challenge requiring technical work, for which, largely, you hire suppliers to accomplish. Consider the following from an IT executive at a bank then four years into a major single supplier outsourcing arrangement:

> Before the outsourcing, and even now during it, there has been very little engagement from the business. Senior business management didn't see technology as something that was their problem. Let's get the best technical people, and let them get on with it. Indeed I think that state of mind, and dissatisfaction with internal IT, was what led to outsourcing in the first place. The result is problems get fixed now, but the outcome is rarely what they wanted.

The second mistake is to be faced with adaptive problems as they arise during the performance of the contract, and treat them as ones amenable to technical fixes. The same IT executive:

> We never resolve the issues. It's unresolvable because the bank still doesn't lead on or own the outcome. So while they continue to blame the

outsourcer for not delivering something which they can neither describe nor write down or articulate or agree on, it's just not going to work.

Unfortunately, these two species of mistakes, in different forms, pretty much describe the root of the problem in all the failed or deeply disappointing outsourcing deals we have encountered in our research and advisory work.

Leadership has to be provided on a 'whole organization' basis within the context of a sourcing strategy consistent with long- and short-term business direction and ambition. These issues are dealt with in Chapters 1 and 5. Chapter 3 also demonstrated that, for effective outsourcing, supplier leadership was needed in up to 12 capabilities. With such a leadership context in place, retained core IS capabilities operate much more effectively than if an isolated leadership source. In IT outsourcing, the core team's leadership role then resides in retaining control of the IT destiny, developing creative responses to issues, achieving superior performance, and keeping the innovation agenda alive. This means dealing with the mix of technical and adaptive challenges facing the business units, external and internal suppliers, that is leading in business, technical supply and governance competencies (see Figure 4.1). This means teaming across the business units and supplier(s) as well as within the IT function. As one financial services CIO put it: 'Across the parties there's got to be a tight link, a kind of family-type link.'

In the core capabilities team, leadership is most obviously found in the role of CIO: 'How important do I think leadership skills, relationship building skills and influencing skills are in my role? That is the job isn't it? (CIO of a media company).

However, leadership, with or without authority, will be needed in each role in order to identify and deal with adaptive challenges as they arise. Susan Mazur, deputy CIO, described this through two generations of DuPont's multiple supplier outsourcing arrangements:

> Every problem we have is a leadership problem...Leadership is extremely key, it's key at making anything work at any level. I guess some of that is relationships, but it's trust, it's credibility and part of credibility is making things work...I think making technology work, beginning well and then having the credibility to be able to make decisions and make things happen go hand in hand...I think that's relationship building, it's leadership and we're also learning from the suppliers.

Looking at Figure 4.1, clearly the other eight roles are set up to provide leadership in distinctive areas, whether at strategic, managerial, or operational levels. But the fundamental task of leadership in outsourcing is delivered through the synergies of operating as a high-performance team.

Leading through the high-performance team

The nine roles form a team in two senses: the roles are complementary and interdependent; secondly, the role holders need to be able to work together interpersonally. The roles require high performers, that is, people who outperform others by a considerable margin. Chris Rawson at Lloyds of London described his people thus: 'I've de-layered the structure ... the staff have to be self-managing and self-motivated and deal with issues themselves rather than historically moving up the hierarchy of control to get the answer ... it's much flatter and definitely more flexible. More responsive'.

Our research shows these high performers sharing three characteristics. First, they are achievers with a projects/results orientation. They tend to set high standards for themselves, are decisive and tough-minded, with good communication/influencing skills. Secondly, they have a learning orientation. They are motivated by change, have a high learning capability, are imaginative and enjoy experimenting. Finally, they are adaptable with flexibility in their management style profile, and a networking/partnership orientation.

Given that these high performers have distinctive styles and motivations, there is a potential threat to the teamwork in the high performance IT function. However, looking across 35 companies with extensive outsourcing arrangements that have adopted aspects of the core IS capabilities model, mutual respect for ability, together with the network orientation of most role holders does allows creative rather than destructive tension.

Beyond the quick fix: Evolving to lead and innovate in outsourcing

In the history of outsourcing many organizations outsourced as a quick fix to dealing with the 'necessary evil' of IT – needed but a commodity – or out of dissatisfaction with the internal IT function's cost and service performance. They got rid of some problems, but others persisted, and the act of outsourcing introduced all too many new ones – for which it was all too easy to blame the supplier. Senior executives need to change their mode of management if they are to leverage outsourcing successfully. This in itself is a major adaptive challenge. The learning has been slow, frequently painful, but, when it comes to outsourcing, to get really strategic benefits, organizations need to evolve their ability to lead and innovate.

Our work distills four rules for this.

1. Diagnose your position: Learn to be smart about your ignorance

To pinpoint where you are look at Figure 4.3. If at the question mark stage, you really are having trouble. IT proliferates, costs are not under control, internal IT service is inadequate, business users are seeking alternative suppliers and looking to their own IT needs, there are no IT synergies and economies of scale across the organization. Is outsourcing a solution? It could be, in part, but do you have the ability to manage anything other than very small-scale contracts, or a few independent contractors? Almost definitely not. Outsourcing may be a quick, but it is unlikely to be a lasting fix.

A better move is to shift into a *Delivery* phase of developing internal capability. At this stage, an IT executive will need to be appointed to focus on building the reality of technical and service competence, while ensuring that business managers gain a correct perception of improvements in IT performance. Building internal IT know-how and capability is vital during this stage.

With the Delivery phase accomplished and providing a reliable platform, a *Reorientation* phase sees the business units needing to become more pro-active in leveraging IT strategically for business purpose, while the IT staff need to become more business-focused. The CIO, with the help of senior business executives will need to provide active leadership to achieve these objectives. The adaptive challenges involved in this, and the lack of internal capability to manage large-scale outsourcing point to incremental use of the external IT services market. Reorientation is a crucial phase and many organizations who get disappointed by lack of strategic payoffs from

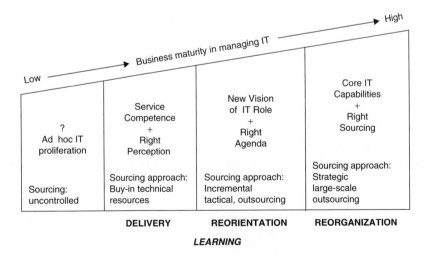

Figure 4.3 Growth stages and sourcing for the IT function

the outsourcing they have done will diagnose themselves as somewhere early in the Reorientation phase.

With Delivery and Reorientation accomplished, the organization can now embark on *Reorganization*. With IT and business strategy closely aligned, and business managers mature in their ability to fulfill their roles in leveraging IT for strategic purpose, many IT responsibilities can be devolved to the business units, as we found was increasingly the case at DuPont and CBA, for example. Meanwhile the IT function can complete its move to a high performing, core capabilities model. Large-scale outsourcing becomes much less risky, and the strategic payoffs more likely.

2. Prioritize the development of retained core capabilities: There is no quick fix

Across the organizations that implement our core capabilities framework, we can discern a common pattern and timing to the building and usage of specific capabilities (Figure 4.4). We have seen organizations starting in the Delivery stage take between three and five years to evolve through to Reorganization.

In the first stage – Delivery – organizations focus on Contract Facilitation, Making Technology Work and Architecture Planning. The CIO, as leader, often has a strong technical and service track record. These capabilities ensure effective delivery of services to meet business needs, and that 'fire-fighting' does not impede the development of the longer term capabilities. At the same time Architecture Planning ensures the development of a coherent blue print for the present and future technical platform.

Reorientation can only be begun once the Delivery stage has been accomplished and remains in place. Reorientation requires much adaptive learning by both IT and business staff. To support this, within the IT function, priority will be given to developing Business Systems Thinking and Relationship Building capabilities, while the CIO will be more focused on, and need the skills for, working with senior executives and the Board. At this stage, we often see the CIO repositioned as a direct report to the CEO.

Reorientation is a crucial phase. Once an organization has the right IT and business capabilities in place and orientated toward leveraging IT strategically for business purpose, then effective IT-enabled business transformation becomes feasible, as we found in two major outsourcing deals at DuPont and CBA across the 1997–2007 period.[9] But only providing the business has also developed and can apply core organizational capabilities in program, project, and change management (even if these are first developed within the IT function). IT leadership is no longer just the preserve of IT but spreads also into the business units and Board.

During Reorganization the core capabilities model can be fully staffed, and its leadership potential harnessed to superior IT performance. The CIO will focus on strengthening considerably its Contract Monitoring, Informed Buying, and Vendor Development capabilities. This allows the internal high-performance team to leverage multiple suppliers and the external services market more extensively and on a more long-term, collaborative basis.

3. Use the external services market selectively: Timing is everything

The evolution of core IS capabilities shown in Figure 4.4 has strong implications for how to mitigate the risks inherent in using the external IT services market. At the Delivery stage the IT function is often not good at managing outsourcing; and its main priority should be building up internal technical and service capability. Where external resources are needed, they should be contracted for on a 'buy-in' basis, whereby the organization pays for external resources that remain under internal management control (Figure 4.4).

At the Reorientation phase selective outsourcing – typically 15–35 percent of the IT budget's handed over to third party service provider management becomes a low-risk option. There is an IT strategy in place, technical service is understood and measured, and low value IT work can be passed on so that new development and work of higher business value can be prioritized by the internal IT workforce. To assist this approach, typically some contract monitoring capability is needed.

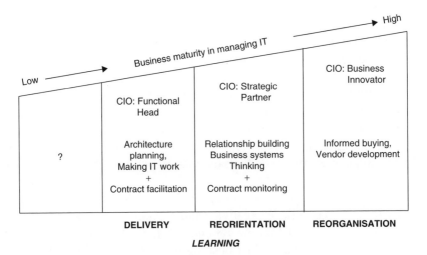

Figure 4.4 Evolving core back-office capabilities

For the organization to move to the Reorganization phase, the IT organization must be positioned to add value to the business through both its internal capabilities and by leveraging the external IT services market – not by just cost cutting. At this stage apposite vendor development and informed buying must be built to match the degree of outsourcing to be undertaken.

In our experience large-scale outsourcing is highly risky unless an organization has moved its IT function and its business management practices well into the Reorganization phase. Thus both CBA and DuPont only fully came to terms with their capability problems some three years into their respective large-scale outsourcing deals. They then had to play catch-up – implementing core IS capabilities that really needed to have been in place before contract signing.

4. Develop and apply creative and flexible leadership: Attend to the adaptive challenges

Leaders operate in conditions of uncertainty, complexity, dynamic contexts, and ever changing business requirements. In such circumstances rational planning can only get you so far. But how to respond to short-term crises and needs while preserving future business direction and differentiation? A key component of the work of leadership is shaping the context in which desired futures become possible. This applies as much to outsourcing as any other business strategy.

A core component of leadership is then mobilizing people to achieve adaptive work. In our research we found senior executives shaping contexts in ways in which more outsourcing was not only possible, but was much more likely to succeed. We also found leaders able to grab diagnostic tools and apply them to solve specific problems in distinctive contexts, while preserving the future IT platform and how it could be leveraged for business advantage. We also found leadership at executive, managerial, and operational levels, spread among people both people with and people without authority, in IT, functions, Boards, suppliers, and business units alike. We found such leadership vital because to succeed in outsourcing it is not enough to deal with the technical challenges it presents. The payoffs come from surfacing and dealing with the hidden, adaptive challenges.

In many firms and public sector agencies we also saw senior executive demonstrating considerable creativity and flexibility in developing core capabilities. In terms of Figures 4.3 and 4.4, they all started at different points, but creatively went about pushing their core capabilities forward, within the resource constraints pertaining, dealing with urgent issues, while always having in mind the end point of the evolutionary process. Such characteristics helped them play and deliver on the vital game of 'catch-up', and endorse why evolving core IS capabilities will continue to be perennially powerful in contemporary organizations.

Conclusion – lessons on keeping control through core retained capabilities

Core retained capabilities emerge from our research as the single most effective means by which to leverage an outsourcing arrangement while mitigating the risks of using external service suppliers. Adoption requires senior executives to accept that outsourcing is not business as usual but about managing in a different way. Adoption also requires senior executives to bite the bullet on 'spending to save' while at the same time looking to achieve sustained cost containment or reduction through outsourcing. This chapter suggests the following lessons:

1. Getting innovation and business value-added from outsourcing requires pro-active business leadership, alignment of business and sourcing strategies, and organized, in-house core IS capabilities being applied to the task.
2. Nine retained capabilities are required to provide leadership, governance and control, elicit and deliver on business requirements, retain control over technical direction and manage external supply. Underresource these capabilities at your peril.
3. Organizations need to develop long-term strategic focus through applying all nine capabilities rather than being drawn into fire-fighting and focusing only on the shorter term capabilities in the core capabilities framework.
4. High performers with distinctive skills, capabilities, orientations need to be developed or appointed. This should be embedded in Human Resource policies. These performers need to be welded into a high-performance team.
5. Core IS capabilities success levels are related to other mitigating factors, namely governance mechanisms in place, inflexibility of outsourcing contracts and deals, the level of resourcing (numbers of staff), supplier capabilities and its responsiveness to new demands.
6. Project management and security are being increasingly regarded as core retained IS capabilities.
7. In modern outsourcing adaptive challenges far outweigh technical ones. Thus leadership – the ability to shape the context for and mobilize adaptive work – becomes critical.

8. Selecting and leveraging the right supplier is made possible through developing leadership capability for outsourcing. The Leadership Payoff is control, flexibility, governance, leveraging the relationship, and innovation.

9. Look to be smart in your ignorance. Evolve capabilities and outsourcing incrementally at a pace of change and learning you can absorb. This means diagnosing where you are and passing through up to three stages: delivery, reorientation, and reorganization.

10. Bring IT all together by diagnosing your position, prioritizing the development of retained core capabilities, using the external services market selectively and developing and applying creative and flexible leadership.

11. The high-performance retained capabilities model has been applied to other major back-office functions, and continues to demonstrate their relevance and significant impact.

Notes

1. The importance of such capabilities is established in the resource-based view of the firm (RBV), which argues that firm performance depends on the organization's ability to acquire, deploy, and maintain a set of advantageous 'resources' (or 'assets'). Extending RBV, the capability-based perspective, popularized through Prahalad and Hamel's landmark 1990 HBR article on core competencies, focuses on intangible resources, suggesting that a firm is a learning organization that builds and deploys assets, capabilities and skills in order to achieve strategic goals.

2. Described in detail in Willcocks, L., Petherbridge, P. and Olson, N. (2003) *Making IT Count: Strategy, Delivery and Infrastructure*. Butterworth, Oxford.

3. See Reynolds, P. and Willcocks, L. (2008) 'Building and integrating core IS capabilities in alignment with the business: lessons from the Commonwealth Bank 1997–2007', *MISQ Executive*, 6, 3, pp. 127–45.

4. See Oshri, I., Kotlaskry, J. and Willcocks, L. (2007) 'Managing dispersed expertise in IT offshore outsourcing: lessons from Tata Consultancy services', *MISQ Executive*, 6, 2, pp. 53–64.

5. See 'The Promise of Enterprise Partnership', in Lacity, M. and Willcocks, L. (2009) *Information Systems and Outsourcing; Studies In Theory and Practice*. Palgrave, London.

6. See Lacity, M. and Willcocks, L. (2009) *Information Systems and Outsourcing: Studies in Theory and Practice*. Palgrave, London, chapter 15.

7. BP tried this in its 1993–98 outsourcing with three suppliers but found they had to do a lot of unanticipated refereeing and management. Other deals have seen the primary contractor model experience mixed outcomes. Lacity and Willcocks (2001) op. cit. concluded that the risk mitigating approach was

to deal directly with each supplier and manage pro-actively the boundaries between suppliers.

8. Heifetz, R. (1994) *Leadership Without Easy Answers*. The Belknap Press, Cambridge, MA.

9. See Willcocks, L., Reynolds, P. and Feeny, D. (2007) 'Evolving core IS capabilities to leverage the external IT services market', *MISQE*, 6, 3, pp. 1–25

CHAPTER 5

Collaborating to innovate: The next phase

The future is already here – it is just unevenly distributed.

– William Gibson[1]

We are only the facilitator. We bring together those technologies in IT and in our network and take the products to the customers. We are not the most innovative party. We have to challenge the suppliers for innovation.

– Hans Wijins, Director of Innovation KPN

Innovation, for me is, twofold. One is the ability to wake up one morning and realize there is a different and better way of doing something. Secondly, combining that with an ability to deliver.

– Damian Bunyan E.ON

Introduction

Our research has been tracking the evolution of the outsourcing market since its modern beginnings in 1989 with the seminal Eastman Kodak deal in the US. Our four previous chapters provide the foundational lessons and practices that make for effective sourcing strategy and delivery. This chapter asks: what next?

The answer is to be found in the relatively few organizations that have matured their strategic ability to handle global sourcing to the degree that they have converted outsourcing's weak spots into opportunities and strengths. There is a great deal of research, including our own, to show that the key disappointments between 1989 and 2010 were twofold: variable quality of relationships, and all too little innovation experienced.[2] This has translated into good to strong success where limited objectives were pursued, but a patchy record when more transformative, multiple objectives have been attempted.

In practice, outsourcing so far has been *contract administration, contract management, or* at best *supplier management* (see Figure 5.1). Client and supplier organizations now need to consider how to make a step-change in their ability to lead outsourcing for strategic business purpose by collaborating to innovate. The 2007–10 economic downturn made this need more urgent, not less, especially as organizations needed to be fit for purpose both for the downswing and the subsequent upswing. Figure 5.1 captures the four phases we have observed client organizations pass through in their outsourcing management evolution. In looking at Figure 5.1, undue optimism in the earliest stage often results in a debased form of contract management we call 'contract administration'. In Phase 2 clients tend to get their act together on managing the contract (see also Chapter 7), but it is only in Phase 3 that they really begin to focus on how to leverage the supplier beyond the contract. In all this, most have learned the hard way, by making mistakes, finding out what works and what does not across two or three generations of outsourcing. The wise ones have been 'smart in their ignorance,' taking an incremental route into more and more outsourcing, learning as they go, limiting their risk exposure, building up their understanding, and also their retained capability to run a sourcing regime aligned with their business strategy and imperatives.

By 2010 a critical mass of organizations had reached, or were reaching for, Phase 3, at least in their management of information technology outsourcing (ITO). The shorter learning curve, from 1999–2010, meant they lagged behind this in their business process and offshore outsourcing practices. By 2009 all these organizations stood on a cusp of an outsourcing decision – whether to drive down a traditional cost-cutting route under recessionary conditions, with limited payoffs, or make a step-change and go for sustainable cost reduction and business-focused innovation.

On the basis of our research between 2008 and 2010 this chapter reports the research findings from studying how organizations can make this step-change toward what we call 'collaborative innovation,' and the practices on which it needs to be based. In particular, we show how collaborating creates the environment for innovation and thus enables organizations to expand their business priorities and outcomes. We suggest that this may be a sustainable way to manage both through economic downturns and in periods of economic growth, that is by leveraging a lot more of the potential value that resides in using external service suppliers.

We studied 26 organizations selected for their considerable outsourcing experience and relative sourcing management maturity. We also talked to highly experienced practitioners from both client and suppliers about alternative models, possibilities, and practices. Given the relative immaturity of the IT/BPO outsourcing industry, we also draw upon studying

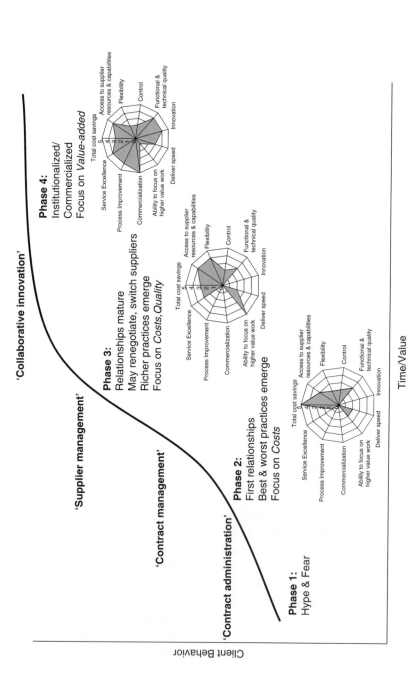

Figure 5.1 The global sourcing learning curve 1989–2010

collaborative practices in the construction industry, which has led the way, in some respects, in this field. The chapter proceeds first by getting our hands around what we mean by collaboration and innovation. We then detail transferable lessons from studying the construction industry's path to deeper collaboration, in particular focusing on the project to build Heathrow Terminal 5. Three illustrative case histories follow – KPN, StatoilHydro, and Spring Global Mail, each providing major insights into how to progress toward collaborative leadership. We then describe a four-phase framework for moving toward collaborating to innovate – leading, contracting, organizing, and behaving. Throughout we provide further examples drawn from our recent research and global research base.

Familiar ideas, new practices

The management world abounds with buzz words and fashions, so it is important to be clear that what we are dealing with here is an evolution of sourcing practices that have been in the making for some twenty years. Collaborating to innovate builds on the solid foundations detailed in previous chapters and takes them to a new level. The problem is that familiar ideas have all too often not been converted into new practices. Let us look more closely at what we understand collaboration and innovation to mean for the organizations we have been studying.

Collaboration

Collaboration is a co-operative arrangement in which two or more parties work jointly in a common enterprise toward a shared goal. In the context of business relationships the word collaboration signals close partnering behaviors developed over and for the long term, distinguished by the high trust, flexibility, reciprocity risk sharing, and investment of resources and time essential if high performance on individual and shared goals is to be achieved.[3]

As Chapter 2 made clear, all outsourcing requires a relationship to succeed. But what *kind* of relationship works? This depends on the activities being outsourced. Commodity services such as accounts payable processing, mainframe processing, or specialized repeatable processes like credit checks, unique technology services – these can be accomplished with relatively hands-off, contract-based relationships between a client and its supplier(s). But deeper, more trust-based relationships are required if external resources are to be used for more sophisticated, risk bearing, and critical services including large-scale IT development projects, business process changes, and technology innovations. Some sense of the difference is communicated by this comment on Suncorp's move into Agile methods and the change required in client and supplier behaviors:

> The standard behavior in an organization is everybody does their job, they deliver it and then somebody else goes and creates the same thing over and over again; but with collaboration comes leverage. In collaboration, you will be welcoming an advance from me to be able to find out how you did it and to share it with me. Partnering is an ongoing relationship where you are leveraging the skills that your partner has, and learn from them. Leadership is key in making progress in collaboration. (Senior executive, Suncorp Insurance Company)

Collaboration also has to stretch across suppliers, as the director of innovation at Dutch-based KPN makes clear:

> What we need is collaboration from our suppliers. If they are competitive then we have a very special meeting and say this behavior is unacceptable; you have to work together. Collaboration only happens if there is a higher level goal for everyone. We put in the necessary incentives for them to put their best people on it and they can't succeed without the help of the other suppliers.

As we shall see in the cases below, collaboration requires a different mindset toward other parties, underpinned by different forms of contracting and behaviors.

The role of suppliers

Clients see suppliers as having an integral pro-active role in collaborating to innovate:

> A pro-active partner is aligned in thinking with you and comes up with new ideas and innovation. *They think for me.* They say we can do it like this and it will cost you that and we can do it with these people in this time. They make a whole business case and I just have to say, okay, we do it or we don't do it. That's being very pro-active. (Senior contract manager, Aegon)

Rune Aase at StatoilHydro pointed out to us how innovation requires new ways of working together:

> We have established a road map to become world class within shared services. But of course, when we do that, we need to have sourcing

partners that are on the same road map and are willing and able to change and to be innovative.

While innovation executives from Logica gave us a supplier perspective:

> For us innovation is really the sum of technology, creativity and organization. The trick is to be really creative with existing technology and look for value-added services or products, rather than just applying state-of-the-art technology, without any link to where the value is for the end user. Creativity ... has to do with cross industry experience and expertise, knowing what you are doing. But innovation will only succeed if you are able to organize the whole process of innovation, knowing what the pitfalls are, and being able to really serve all the stakeholders in the value chain touched by innovation.

In earlier chapters we commented on the observable trend toward relationships becoming increasingly managed and leveraged as strategic assets. The indicators of this can be seen in our most recent research: more rigorous relationship planning and measurement, more contracting based on values and behavior, and, on client demand, suppliers becoming more entrenched in their client's business – including supporting the client's mainline services, becoming a client of the client, and identifying new sales opportunities. Collaboration sees added-value relationships as a norm, with clients looking for business ideas, innovation, and environmental scanning from their suppliers, and a much greater focus on business, not just technical outcomes. Collaboration in a strategic sourcing context, then, is pro-active working together and risk sharing, in flexible integrated ways, to achieve high performance on larger, mutually rewarding commercial goals.

So the challenging role for suppliers is to:

- Ensure they have the *key capabilities for collaboration*. This means that their planning and contracting, organizational design, governance, leadership, program management, and customer development capabilities must be strong (see Chapter 3). But *collaborative thinking and action* must be in the DNA of all managers and delivery staff.
- *Invest* significantly in innovation resources and capability.
- Be very *pro-active with clients* on how things can be done differently to joint advantage.
- Be capable of *working with and across other suppliers*, together with the client where there are adaptive challenges and innovation is required. As we shall see in a variety of cases, multi-vendor environments are typical rather than unusual and this is where collaborative innovation takes place.

Types of innovation

As will emerge, collaboration is the foundation for effective innovation. But what does innovation mean to clients, and what sort of innovation do they care about? For Damian Bunyan of E.ON:

> Innovation, for me is, twofold. One is the ability to wake up one morning and realize there is a different and better way of doing something. Secondly, combining that with an ability to deliver. My job is to get into supplier organizations and make sure that my company has a higher percentage of their innovators' and decision-makers' time than other companies.

For Wouter Hijzen at Spring Global Mail: 'Innovation to me is really simple…. It doesn't have to be a product or a new service. It's doing things differently for the better, that's innovation'. Clearly innovation does not have to be one big thing, and it is also in the eye of the beholder: 'Although it might be the twentieth time that we implement some sort of system or product or whatever, for our client, it's usually the first time, a one-off. For them it might be really innovative, while for us, it's just business as usual.' (Supplier innovation executive)

Essentially innovation is the introduction of something new which creates value for the organization that adopts it.[4] The general innovation literature talks of product, process, and organizational innovations, referring to new products (or services), new ways of doing things, and new ways of organizing and managing people. Innovations are also characterized as incremental (small series of changes), radical (large, transformative change), or revolutionary (game changing).[5] For our purposes we adapt Weeks and Feeny (2008) and use client-focused definitions more suited to what is trying to be achieved in their collaborative arrangements with business and IT service companies.[6] On this schema there are three types of innovation:

IT operational – technology and IT organizational, work and personnel changes that do not impact firm-specific business processes, for example, new email platforms, new operating systems, IT infrastructure remodeling, new IT staffing arrangements. These could lead to better business use of IT, for example, introducing agile systems development at Suncorp in 2008 led to IT being in place quicker to support the business. Was this innovation? Yes. According to one executive: 'There are no sacred cows, they've all got slaughtered.'

Business process – by contrast, this innovation changes the way the business operates in some important ways. In his study of the BAe Systems-CSC deal Michael Weeks found one such successful implementation – the development of a Product Data Management System for the Astute submarine program. This helped to implement computer-aided technology into the production process by documenting all of the parts and essential manu-facturing information (weld placements, wiring diagrams etc) used in the design and production of the final submarine.[7] He also notes a successful vendor-supported SAP implementation at Rolls Royce which helped the firm ride the 2000–03 downturn more effectively through better financial management and inventory control.

Strategic – these innovations significantly enhance the firm's product/service offerings for existing target customers, or enable the firm to enter new markets. In his 2004 outsourcing study Weeks notes that organiza-tions tended to be going predominantly for IT operational innovations. We have been finding much more ambition. In Asia Pacific we found Crown Casino introducing technology to automate (and thus speed up) roulette and so increase revenues from high rollers. Similarly, the CFO of Repco, a car parts distribution company commented:

> One of the things that we came down to very rapidly was, we wanted IT to be a competitive advantage. That sort of changes the focus from being reactive to being proactive. It's about delivering a *business* product that's new and innovative rather than just keep going with what you've got.

In 2009 Repco, with the aid of suppliers, operationalized remote computer-ized car monitoring to pre-empt mechanical breakdown and provide positive response in terms of spares and repair: 'For us, it's a different strain of busi-ness, but the key thing is, we can actually say, your car is due for service and these are the parts you need. Here's a suggested place to go and service it.'

Given these definitions, our research points to a new performance agenda for outsourcing practitioners to aim at over the next five years. Essentially, superior performance through innovation is now feasible in a maturing industry, but requires a step-change in objectives, relationships and behaviors. The messages of our findings are present in Figure 5.2, and can be summarized as:

1. In outsourcing, the collaborative capabilities of all parties determine the type and degree of innovation possible. Only deep collaboration makes large business process and strategic innovations feasible.
2. Without an innovation focus, outsourcing can achieve cost-cutting mostly of a one-off kind, or at best cost-efficiency – similar service at lower cost.
3. Focusing on innovations in IT operations can and does achieve larger, sustainable cost reductions.
4. The real performance impacts over time come from business process and business product/service innovations. Business process innova-tions create sustainable business improvements in areas much bigger than IT operations alone – a bigger target, a more impactful innovation.

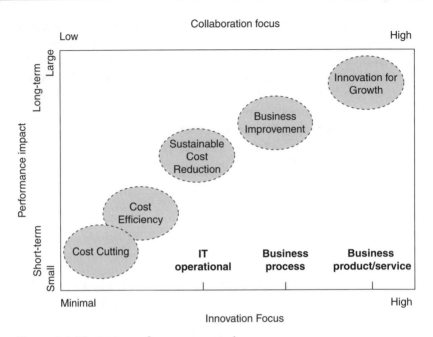

Figure 5.2 The new performance agenda

Business product/service innovations can, and do, support firms' revenue and profit growth targets.

5. Innovation is risky. Collaborative innovation finds ways of sharing and offsetting risk. It also galvanizes behavior toward lessening risk and achieving shared goals. Collaborative innovation definitely supports superior performance more realistically than more traditional outsourcing relationships.

This chapter discusses many examples of organizations that have successfully got on to the new performance agenda. As detailed illustrations, in the following sections we look at four initiatives, including one in the construction industry. From studying these and many other organizations, we then provide a fourfold framework for success on how to make the step-change to collaborative innovation. And as the case studies illustrate, in the future such collaborative innovation will usually take place in a multi-vendor environment.

Partnering and collaborating: Learning from construction

Background

The construction industry went through a number of crises in the 1990s, which the IT and business services industry can learn much from. The Latham Report of 1994 was sponsored by the Government and the Construction Industry following several poorly performing construction projects. The central message of this report, *'Constructing the Team'*, was that the client should be at the core of the construction process. The general route recommended to achieve client satisfaction was through team work and co-operation. One specific method was partnering. This message was strongly reinforced by the 1998 Egan Report, *'Rethinking Construction'*, that looked outside construction for lessons from other sectors like automotive, aerospace, and retail. It was distinguished by its higher level thinking, identifying five drivers of change:

- committed leadership
- focus on the customers
- integrated process and team around the product
- a quality driven agenda
- commitment to people

In 2002 the Strategic Forum for Construction, under Sir John Egan, published *'Accelerating Change'*. It identified the most important drivers as client leadership, integrated teams and the need to address people issues (especially, in construction, health and safety). In 2003 *Constructing Excellence* was formed to bring together all the government initiatives to provide a single interface with the industry.

The reviews by Latham and Egan emphasized the significant potential to increase the performance of the construction industry. But this would only be achieved if the industry and its clients changed their approaches and practices; clients they stressed, had a personal stake in this.

At the centre of this approach lies partnering and collaboration and great progress has been made in recent years. Some firms have led the way in best practice but others have preferred traditional procurements routes. Many clients still do not understand that fiercely competitive tenders accepting the lowest bid do not produce value for money in construction. 'Lowest price' tenders may well contain no margin of profit for the contractor, whose commercial response is then to try to claw back the margin which was not in the tender through variations, claims and 'Dutch auctioning' of sub-contractors and suppliers.[8] Such adversarial approaches have disfigured the construction industry over many years. They have produced high levels of litigation and conflict, low investment, inadequate research and development, negligible margins, and low level of esteem of the industry by the public in general and graduates or school leavers in particular.

Partnering and collaborating turns the process around. It assumes a win–win scenario for all parties. The stakeholders sign up to mutual objectives and agree on effective decision-making procedures. Problems are resolved collaboratively by the entire team with continuous improvement and benchmarking being crucial. Partnering can be for a specific project or on a longer term, strategic basis. It can achieve real cost savings and client satisfaction. But partnering does not mean that clients have a cozy relationship with contractors – thus increasing the risk of less value for money. Nevertheless, understanding this potential pitfall, clients are increasingly establishing long-term collaborative relationships or partnering with construction firms for the benefit of both parties – client and supplier. Even so, there are still many clients, consultants and constructors who see partnering as an alien or threatening process.

As Egan said:

'they could usefully reflect on how poorly they have been served by traditional methods'.

Building terminal 5: What really happened

Media focus on the fraught opening of Heathrow Terminal 5 (T5) in March 2008 and the Transport Select Committee's findings in November 2008 deflected attention from the subsequent turnaround, but, more seriously, from the project's real long-term achievements. The building of Terminal 5 is a good example of how the new initiatives in the Construction Industry were put into practice.[9] Sir John Egan was the CEO at British Airport Authority (BAA) from 1991 to 1999 and it was clear to him that the role of the client had to be fundamentally different. BAA needed to think differently about risk management and about long-term relationships with profitable suppliers. Together they worked to change the approach to the use of computer-based design for manufacture, supply change management, and safe and efficient processes, thus getting the best out of a well-trained workforce. The commitment to a ground-breaking contract – the T5 Agreement in which BAA held most of the risk – set a principle for the way of working. The right leadership, ongoing client involvement, and a focus on getting integrated teams to perform to a world-class standard have meant that the UK construction industry delivered a success story.

How it was done

British Airport Authority managed risk differently through the T5 Agreement (see Figure 5.3). This context allowed leaders to drive for success and trust differently while working with stakeholders and integrated teams. BAA was a committed, highly involved, intelligent client who over the years pioneered new thinking and different ways of operating in partnership with their supply chain:

> Understanding where value came from the supply chain was key and I guess understanding, ultimately the outsourcing model. Egan's mindset was, let's get to know our suppliers and let's work alongside them and let's understand how we get best value for everybody. (A. Wolstenholme, T5 Construction Director)

The T5 Agreement was a legally binding agreement that confirmed that, on a £4.3 billion program, the client BAA held most of the risk, with supplier exposure being loss of profit or insurance excess payments.

Suppliers would receive a guaranteed margin that ranged from 5–10 percent depending on trade for delivering at least industry best practice, and a team incentive plan was put in place, so that all the suppliers would have to succeed for additional bonuses to be paid where exceptional performance was achieved. Egan was clear that, given the long-term spend on construction, BAA needed to find the best suppliers, and work with them to try to develop best-in-class approaches to buying and building so that all organizations could create more value together over time.

The objective was to 'manage out risks' and 'manage in opportunity' (see Figure 5.3). The approach used at T5 focused on; empowering the project team to deliver and make their own decisions; enabling tradeoffs across projects; understanding the impact of one project on another; and accurately tracking the progress of each project within a consistent program

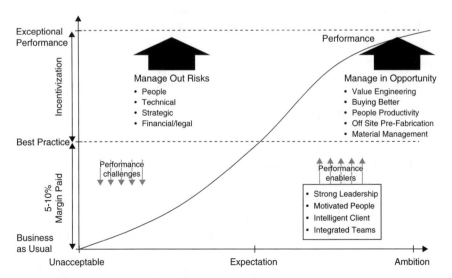

Figure 5.3 Heathrow Terminal 5 agreement approach

framework. Leaders had a great belief in the ability of the T5 team to solve any problem thrown at them and this was continually reinforced. Their belief spread into the teams, motivating them and encouraging every individual that they could personally make a difference. This leadership culture was meticulously implemented throughout the various management and governance forums. As Tony Douglas, T5 Managing Director said: 'Leadership made the difference on T5. The judgement, passion, determination with which we got the best out of the integrated teams and influenced the key stakeholders was second to none.'

According to Andrew Wolstenholme, the T5 Construction Director, those leaders who made a difference on and around T5 had five characteristics: thinking big picture, engendering and operating with vigilant trust, driving for success despite the odds, keeping stakeholders onside and aligned with objectives, and getting the best out of the integrated teams. Moreover, he notes that: 'At different phases of that project, it was right for different people to lead it.'

Working in integrated teams was one of the cornerstones of the T5 Agreement, and was a fundamental ingredient in the success of T5. Consultants and suppliers, in return for a guaranteed margin and access to an incentive scheme, committed to working in integrated teams alongside BAA. In practical terms the integrated teams approach included co-locating teams, and ensuring that they had the 'best person for the job'. This meant having people work in the spirit of problem solving, not protecting their company interest, as they tried to deliver, at a minimum, industry best practice while striving to achieve exceptional performance. The T5 Agreement was at the heart of the culture. This large document was digested and turned into a few simple pages, with teamwork, commitment, and trust as the values all needed to live by. T5 by no means got it right all the time in every team. What was critical was that leaders and the client understood that it was important to do everything possible to try to get teams working together and delivering.

Learning points for innovation

The Heathrow T5 experience would suggest a number of learning points for the IT/BPO outsourcing industry:

- focus on the customer's innovation needs
- the client role has to be fundamentally different
- think differently about risk management and about long-term relationships
- partnering and collaborating turns the process around; it assumes a win–win scenario for all parties.

- leaders make a difference
- integrated teams enable partnering and collaboration to lead to superior performance
- invest in people and in understanding relationships

Collaborating to innovate: Emerging blueprints

We noted in our research many other organizations pioneering the way toward collaborative leadership. In this section we focus on three of the more notable examples we found – KPN, StatoilHydro, and Spring Global Mail – and the blueprints they were working on.

KPN – 'challenging vendors for innovation'

KPN provides high-quality telephone, Internet, and television services and products and is an all-round provider of ICT services. Consumers in the Netherlands take fixed and mobile telephony, Internet, and TV from KPN. Business customers use an entire array of innovative and reliable services which include everything from telephony, Internet, and data traffic/management all the way through to the management of ICT services. In Germany, Belgium, and elsewhere in Western Europe, the services of the KPN group consist mainly of mobile telephony. KPN made a profit of €2.5 billion in 2007 on annual sales of €12.6 billion.

Between 2009 and 2010 the Netherlands business underwent a radical transformation. The All-IP network announced in March 2005 moved into its final phase with the implementation of a new access network. In addition, KPN will pursue a radical simplification of its business, both at the front-end in retail segments and at the back-end in network operations. The significant cost reductions that will be generated by this simplification will be used first for re-investment in revenue growth and secondly, will lead to margins improving.

Of nearly 60 interviews that we conducted for this chapter, only one client executive had innovation in their title. That person was Hans Wijins, the senior VP for Innovation at KPN. For Wijins, the maturing of the global outsourcing services market has now made it possible to do very large jobs and make large steps in innovation:

> You can't outsource innovation. Our responsibility is for time to market, for business development for innovation; we must have the architects. We don't outsource our vision. But we really do believe that innovation can only be done if we use a lot of capacity outside of the

company. I really believe that we have to use the knowledge and the power from places like India.

Hans Wijins saw the client as responsible for making the innovation plan for the next few years. He felt that a lot of sector-based innovation doesn't succeed any more and that KPN would have to find trans-sector innovation in the future. Requirements had to be very clear and this started at Board level. The first step is the strategy to market, and the next is the architecture:

> As an example, we put the designing teams from the several suppliers together in one building and in five months together they built the new IT solution. Designing, building, and testing their own part are the responsibilities of each supplier; we have the integration function and the architecture.

KPN use a lot of innovation power from their network of suppliers and not just IT: 'We are only the facilitators. We bring together those technologies in IT and in our network and take the products to the customers. We are not the most innovative party. We have to challenge the suppliers for innovation.' He stressed that KPN wanted to collaborate and not just contract manage. If the client only contract manages it makes it much more difficult to work with several suppliers:

> If they are competitive then we have a special meeting and say this behavior is unacceptable; you have to work together. Collaboration only happens if there is a higher level goal for everyone. We put in the necessary incentives for them to put their best people on it and they can't succeed without the help of the other suppliers.

The sourcing strategy, therefore, is long-term relationships with several partners focused on quality and delivery. KPN did not want to outsource all to one party and say, 'okay, we are not involved any more'. The Board wanted to be involved in its own destiny: 'I think that we have to co-create.'

For KPN innovation is related to what it brings in for the business. In outsourcing the network, cost cutting is not the main goal: 'We are looking to suppliers that can help us in transformation and not only in the existing network. It has to be a combination of cutting costs and innovation together.'

Learning points for innovation

- don't outsource innovation, but make an innovation plan
- trans-sector innovation will be the way forward
- use the innovation power from your network of suppliers

- suppliers need to collaborate with each other
- collaboration only happens if there is a higher level goal for everyone
- 'we have to co-create'

StatoilHydro – 'surprise me!'

StatoilHydro is an integrated oil and gas company based in Norway, the leading operator on the Norwegian continental shelf, and an expanding international company. It focuses on innovation in exploration and production to recover valuable resources that were previously thought unreachable. StatoilHydro's oil and gas portfolio ranges from development projects to mature fields. The group is the second biggest gas supplier in Europe and the sixth biggest in the world. StatoilHydro trades in petroleum products, methanol, power, and emission allowances and ranks as the world's third largest net seller of crude oil.

StatoilHydro is a mature organization, especially in ITO, with high value, multi-functional shared services since 1993. Its IT is divided into two – infrastructure and applications. It uses sourcing first of all to close capacity gaps and then to get additional competence into the organization. Perhaps surprisingly, costs have never been the driving mechanism for sourcing. Of course, cost is important but the capacity issue is their first priority. For IT outsourcing they do not have a single sourcing solution but look for, and expect, extra value from each supplier. One of those suppliers, Logica, has provided the Service Desk for IT since 2003. This supports IT and SAP in all geographies, is based in StatoilHydro premises and on their Service Management processes (ITIL-based) and is also integrated with other suppliers' processes. StatoilHydro is now looking at BPO concepts, on which, compared to ITO, they are immature.

In an extensive interview in 2009, Rune Aase, VP and Head of Service Delivery, described StatoilHydro's approach to sourcing. He said first of all, to be a sourcing partner you need to understand my business, which takes time, and you need to have competence within each area you are serving. Of course, relationships are also key in any partnership. If you go into partnership with an external supplier, you have to have a partner that is flexible and is looking for ways to improve both systems and processes throughout the contract period.

StatoilHydro has established a road map to become world class within shared services. But of course, in doing that, they need to have sourcing partners that are on the same road map and are willing and able to change and to be innovative:

> What we often see is that the way you establish your contracts with sourcing companies can be so stringent that it does not give them or

you any flexibility. If you don't have flexibility and there are no gains for suppliers in doing innovation then you have a problem.

Rune Aase stressed the importance of a partner that has the same culture and has the same understanding of where you are going. Partners need to be flexible and solution orientated. Moreover:

> We use our sourcing partners in innovation, but not necessarily as part of the existing contract. Innovation comes from a supplier that surprises me! I always say to my people and to our suppliers 'surprise me'. I want them to be proactive. They do it before you ask them. My job is to advise my customers and give them what they need, and I expect the same from my sourcing partners.

Learning points for innovation

- understand my business and bring competence/capability to each area
- establish and get on the same road map – understand where we are going
- don't make the contract too stringent and squeeze out any chance of innovation
- be flexible and continually look at ways to improve systems and processes
- surprise me! Do it before I ask – be innovative.

Spring Global Mail – 'outsourcing to make ourselves better'

Spring Global Mail is a world leader in the provision of international mail services to businesses. It is a joint venture company, formed in 2001 by three of the world's most dynamic and respected postal organizations: TNT of the Netherlands, Royal Mail of the United Kingdom, and Singapore Post. It employs 1100 people in 25 countries and its headquarters are located in Amsterdam, the Netherlands. Spring Global Mail has become the world's largest independent cross-border mail distribution company. It uses its creativity and experience to find solutions to the most complex of cross-border mail requirements. Their customers include some of the world's largest senders of cross-border mail.

We interviewed the CFO, Wouter Hijzen, who gave us his views on outsourcing and innovation. He started by saying that Spring Global Mail is an outsourcing company! It takes over all the mail and postal responsibility from its customers. It's a technical thing. Spring buy and sell mail. Clients choose Spring to operate their businesses more efficiently and cost effectively.

As one example, Spring set up Expert Terrestrial Offices of Exchange (ETOEs). A small part of New Zealand is in the sorting centre, which is also New Zealand post owned. It's like an embassy, but you can't recognize it because it's only a stamp. Spring send mail from Belgium to the Netherlands as if it had been posted via New Zealand. That's its traditional business. It's what is called the remail business in Europe. It's a really big business and Spring are the biggest doing it. Its role as an outsourcer has given Spring major insights into its expectations about suppliers.

In its own outsourcing, it used to do the Finance function in-house but outsourced it in September 2008. Spring have also outsourced all its IT services across the world to a TNT company. For finance it has a nine-year contract with Logica. All back offices with APAR credit control to certain countries are outsourced to Logica:

> When we were contracting for this we explicitly said, we are not going to outsource to a company that's only based in India. We want to outsource to a local company, local meaning European. This is because of language, time difference, and mentality issues. We don't outsource credit control to India; it remains in the Netherlands, somewhere close.

For Wouter Hijzen innovation is just looking at, and doing things differently. It doesn't have to be a product or a new service. On the finance side the fact that this is the core business of Logica and the fact that Spring's IT is the core business of the people they outsource to for IT makes a huge difference:

> We have outsourced to make ourselves better; that's the main thing that triggers innovation. As an example, we didn't have an electronic system to approve invoices. We couldn't afford it. It was just too expensive to build it for ourselves, Logica had one. We now make use of Logica's. I don't think it's innovation for them but it is for us.

For Wouter, trust is most important; without it there can be no innovation. Trust is built by letting some things go. Once you go back to the contract you are in a fight and trust is lost. That's why the general outline of the contract is more important because Spring knows that suppliers can't make money if they don't innovate. So it is not important to have innovation explicitly in the contract, because he knows *his* suppliers will seek innovation. He has suppliers that are really good in the contract and that's why he trusts them. They write down what they will do and then they deliver.

It is leadership that creates trust:

> We always thought that, together we would be more cost effective as a whole – that was active collaboration. In Spring, we always say it's a team. It's not a family. You have to work together, but you don't have to sleep together. You establish trust through delivery but when it goes wrong you have to show leadership.

Spring had already squeezed out all the money from their back office functions. The big reason for outsourcing was because they couldn't make it better. Outsourcing wasn't about cost savings or making it more efficient, but to make IT and finance better and to make the people better. Like at KPN, Spring see themselves as having a facilitator role with outsourcing:

> If my company wants to continue to make the same kind of money now we need to innovate. We don't do anything ourselves. We are just the brains and not the hands. We need suppliers for everything we do. We only put together suppliers and customers and hopefully, we can make money out of it.

Learning points for innovation

- innovation is really simple, it's about doing things differently
- it may not be innovation for the supplier but it is for us
- without trust there can be no innovation
- you establish trust through delivery
- when things go wrong you have to show leadership

Collaborative innovation: The framework for success

Our case studies make very clear the critical success factors that drive collaborating to innovate. In the rest of this chapter we consolidate our learning into four fundamental shapers and components of effective collaborative innovation. These are leading, contracting, organizing, and behaving. Of these, leadership is primary (see Figure 5.4). Leadership *shapes and conditions* the environment in which requisite contracting, organizing, and behaving can occur. The right kind of contract supports collaborating and is an incentive for the right behavior. The right kind of organization supports teaming among the parties and enables high performance. Let us look at this process in its four phases.

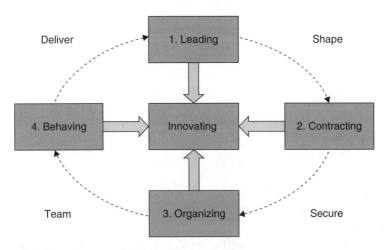

Figure 5.4 The process of collaborative innovation
Source: Willcocks and Craig 2009

Phase 1: Innovation's open secret – leadership for collaboration

In Chapter 4 we met the work of Ronald Heifetz. His excellent book *Leadership Without Easy Answers* makes an important distinction between technical and adaptive work. Here, with the help of Figure 5.5, we reprise and develop the implications of this distinction. It will be recalled that technical problems are rarely trivial but what makes them technical is that the solution, in the form of specialist know-how, techniques, and routine processes, already exists within the organization's (or a supplier's) repertoire. Managers can delegate such work to specialists and monitor the outcomes.

By contrast, leadership deals with adaptive challenges. In fact, Heifetz defines leadership as shaping and mobilizing adaptive work, that is, engaging people to make progress on the adaptive problems they face. He suggests five strategic principles of leadership:

1. identify the adaptive challenge
2. keep the level of distress within a tolerable range for doing adaptive work
3. focus attention on ripening issues and not on stress-reducing distractions
4. give the work back to the people, but at a rate they can stand
5. protect voices of leadership without authority

For him, the hardest and most valuable task of leadership is advancing goals and designing strategy that promote adaptive work. An adaptive

Challenge	Type of Work	Done By
Technical	Apply current know-how techniques, processes	Specialists
Adaptive	Learn new ways	The people with the problem

Figure 5.5 The leadership challenge: Technical versus adaptive work

challenge is a particular problem, often difficult to specify precisely, where the gap between values and aspirations on the one hand, and circumstances on the other, cannot be closed by the application of current technical know-how and routine behavior. Adaptive challenges require experiments, discoveries, and adjustments from many parts of an organization. When is it an adaptive challenge? When peoples' hearts and minds have to change; when all technical fixes fail; when conflict persists despite all remedial action; when a crisis arises, indicating that an adaptive challenge has been festering. As we have seen, modern outsourcing is full of adaptive challenges and work that cry out for leadership and learning strategies. And innovation is essentially an adaptive challenge.

As we saw in the four previous chapters, the CEO and senior executives, including the CIO, lead in outsourcing firstly by shaping its context. This involves:

- Formulating and monitoring the sourcing strategy that fits with dynamically changing strategic and operational business needs over the next five years.
- Ensuring the organization can buy in an informed way through understanding the external services market, supplier strategies, capabilities and weaknesses, and what a good deal with each supplier would look like.
- Shaping relationships and putting in place a process for managing outsourcing across the lifecycle of a deal.
- Shaping the conditions for a contract that delivers what is expected and needed without sustaining hidden or switching costs.
- Developing and sustaining a post-contract management capability that retains control of the IT destiny and leverages supplier capabilities and performance to mutual advantage.
- Facilitating the maturing of business managers' ability to manage and own IT as a strategic resource, including stepping up to roles as sponsors and champions of major IT-enabled business projects.

The case studies of collaborative innovation detailed above are saturated with leadership challenges and responses. In Chapter 4 we considered Xchanging/BAE Systems (2001 and ongoing) HR outsourcing arrangement. A similar pattern, though with many more major adaptive challenges, can be seen in the 1999–2006 $US600 million HR outsourcing deal between BP and Exult. Here the complexity of taking over an 'As-Is' HR function covering 56,000 employees, and centralizing and standardizing the service, was greatly underestimated. Moreover, the supplier was a start-up, and the premise that its superior technical web expertise would take BP's HR to a new level greatly underplayed the risks and adaptive challenges. Much leadership at all levels within BP and the supplier was needed over four years to put this deal on an even keel. Even so, Exult lost the rebid for this contract.[11]

As Wouter Hijzen told us: 'You establish trust through delivery but when it goes wrong you have to show leadership. Taking responsibility is the beginning of leadership. If you keep telling people what to do they will never become leaders.'

In our experience, leadership begins in the Boardroom with the CEO and key executives. In their study, Earl and Feeny [12] found that the CEOs who leveraged IT the best had a vision that IT could transform their business, and demonstrated their belief by their own behaviors. This CEO transformation agenda is also what is needed to achieve innovation with outsourcing collaborators. It also needs a top management team process designed to achieve new things, the relevant CXO (whether IT, HR, procurement etc) as a member of the top team, and a CXO tied and capable of delivering on an innovation agenda. Gooding's work on CIO innovators[13] applies to other CXOs. He found the major attributes being business visionary, member of the 'inner circle', communicator of direction, external, and internal networker, purposeful change agent, holistic implementation champion and creator of agile IT. The payoff from leadership is indicated by Andrew Wolstenholme, the T5 construction director: 'We set up an environment within which innovation could flourish; I didn't come up with all the clever ideas. We created a place where people could innovate and that's the act of good leadership; making it safe for people to stick their necks out.'

Phase 2: Contracting for collaborative innovation – making the game change

Leadership, then, creates the environment for innovation. In earlier IT outsourcing deals, especially the long-term 'strategic alliances' signed in the 1990s – for example, EDS-Xerox, IBM-Lend Lease, BAE-CSC,

UBS-Perot Systems – invariably innovation was cited as something the customer expected, and the 'world class' supplier could and would deliver. In study after study we found such innovation not forthcoming. For example, even in what is considered a relatively successful finance and accounting outsourcing deal at an oil major, an IT executive reported: 'We are not getting dynamic innovation, to say the least, on a continuing basis. After the initial burst of creativity, it went flat.'

One response is to create an innovation fund for suppliers to bid for. According to one public sector IT manager: 'In the previous contract we never asked for their strategic view, so that was half our fault. But equally, they didn't come up with a lot of innovation. Lesson learned: for the 2008 round we are putting in a formal mechanism to encourage innovation.'

Our experience is that even large innovation funds have rarely produced lasting, important innovations. The same applies to many joint venture and equity share initiatives designed partly to stimulate innovation. They disappoint invariably because they are mere add-ons in mainly fee-for service deals where, in practice, both clients and/or suppliers prioritize service and cost issues well above innovation issues. Let us pursue this issue further.

In practice, senior executives' organizations have available four main approaches to achieving innovation, each with a distinctive knowledge objective and approach (see Figure 5.6).

In Figure 5.6 we summarize our research findings on the suitability, benefits, and risks of each innovation option[14] 'Do-It-Yourself' scores highly on retaining control and keeping the value of transformation within the company. But to succeed, it requires both funding and appropriate skills which may be lacking. It is also the option most likely to encounter internal resistance if senior management does not give a clear signal

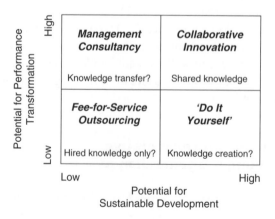

Figure 5.6 Options for back-office innovation

of its importance. An example of success we have previously cited is Commonwealth Bank Australia. Despite having two major outsourcing deals, between 2003 and 2005 it achieved a major CRM implementation largely through using internal resources, and has further extended its internal development capability since. The *'Management Consultancy'* route brings in external energy, gives a clear signal of commitment to major change by bringing in outsiders, and reduces political resistance. The most significant risks we have seen are cost escalation, lack of sustainability, and little knowledge transfer.

'Fee-For-Service Outsourcing' – whether ITO or BPO – can see limited, usually 'one-off', innovations through reforming inherited back-office management practices, streamlining business processes, and fresh investment in new technology, but even where these are forthcoming, our research shows that the innovation zeal is rarely sustained. The contract is structured around cost/service issues and does not incent the supplier to innovate. There is an over-reliance on the supplier to innovate in business areas where innovation should be primarily an in-house concern. The supplier gets focused on selling extra services to make further margins, and also gets imbedded in solving today's pressing crises and operational problems. The employer does not develop or employ people capable of innovating. The customer loses interest in joint boards and often downplays the in-house responsibility to leverage the relationship further. As one energy company IT executive put it: 'the relationship gets stale, and an outcome is lack of innovation and creative thinking.'

Some form of *'Collaborative Innovation'* is required if sustained, significant IT or back-office and business innovations are to be achieved. The greater the innovation ambition the more this is likely to have a risk-reward component in the contracting arrangement – as we saw in the T5 case. Collaborative innovation may also take the form of a formal joint venture as in the case of Xchanging's back-office deal with the London Insurance Market (2001 and ongoing). In that case a jointly resourced and owned third entity was created to deliver service and innovation to the client. The third entity had the competencies detailed in Chapter 3 including the transformational capabilities of reengineering, technology exploitation, leadership, customer development, program management, sourcing and behavior management. However the approach to innovation has been incremental rather than 'big bang'. As one executive we talked to put it: 'Innovation does not need to be a big idea – it can be lots of little things'.

But there are real dangers in relying overmuch on the supplier for technical and business innovation, even where this has been explicitly contracted for. This can be most dramatically observed in examples of transformation outsourcing. The problem here is when transformation is treated largely as a supplier responsibility. Transformation, as the word suggests, can rarely be merely a technical matter, and invariably involves behavioral, organizational, social, and political issues. Nor is it easy to define precisely the outcomes, what work is to be carried out, by whom and how. This means transformation is about learning, experimentation, and bringing many different forms of know-how together to deal with adaptive challenges. This immediately means it requires primary leadership and learning by the client organization.

These considerations probably help to explain some of the extreme difficulties the Sainsburys-Accenture IT and logistics transformation outsourcing program experienced, as mentioned in Chapter 1. The US$ 3.25 billion deal was signed in 2000. By late 2004 the deal had been renegotiated twice, and Sainsbury had announced a 2004–05 write-off of $254 million of IT assets and a further write-off of automated depot and supply chain IT. In October 2005 Sainsbury announced that it was terminating the Accenture relationship and bringing IT back in-house. In practice, the transformation was driven essentially by the supplier, more along 'management consultancy' lines, and the massive adaptive challenges received insufficient leadership attention.

In terms of contracting for innovation, it is salutary to reflect upon the different contracting assumptions underlying the Heathrow Terminal 5 project as shown in Figure 5.7.

Andrew Wolstenholme, T5 construction director said: 'We did not simply rely on a contract that identifies culpability when something goes wrong, but a contract that encourages people to get it right before it goes wrong.'

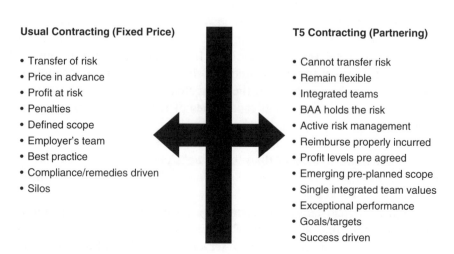

Usual Contracting (Fixed Price)

- Transfer of risk
- Price in advance
- Profit at risk
- Penalties
- Defined scope
- Employer's team
- Best practice
- Compliance/remedies driven
- Silos

T5 Contracting (Partnering)

- Cannot transfer risk
- Remain flexible
- Integrated teams
- BAA holds the risk
- Active risk management
- Reimburse properly incurred
- Profit levels pre agreed
- Emerging pre-planned scope
- Single integrated team values
- Exceptional performance
- Goals/targets
- Success driven

Figure 5.7 Heathrow T5 contracting assumptions

What is also particularly interesting in Figure 5.7 is the approach to risk. Traditionally both clients and suppliers look to transfer as much risk as possible to the other party. The actual distribution of risk depends on negotiating power, but, if skewed to the detriment of one party, can damage both the relationship and performance and curtail innovation severely. The T5 contract was a cost-plus contract, with a contractor receiving actual cost, plus a fixed fee, overheads, and profit. Additional incentivization existed for exceptional performance (see Figure 5.3). Here, operational risk is shared, but the client, BAA, holds the main risk, and together with its suppliers actively manages risk. A range of practices and behaviors surrounded cost-plus contracting to convert performance into partnering and collaborative innovation.

Phase 3: Organizing and teaming – the process of innovation

Let us distill from this study the learning on organizing and teaming. Our framework is shown in Figure 5.8. Technical work requiring the application of existing specialist know-how and techniques can be outsourced relatively safely, assuming competent specialists can be hired. The more work becomes adaptive the more leadership is required and the more multiple stakeholders need to be engaged with defining the problem, and working together on arriving at and implementing a solution. Adaptive challenges represent situations where problems and solutions are unclear, a multi-functional team is needed, learning is vital, innovation is usually necessary, and a general business goal rather than precise metrics point the way forward. The role of leadership is to maintain direction and shape the context and process by which all this can happen. Moreover, the more radical and business focused the innovation required, the more that leadership should be primarily by the client.

In practice, in-house leadership is vital to large-scale IT and back-office innovation and transformation because these inherently comprise predominantly adaptive challenges for the organization. But, as described above, even fee-for-service outsourcing has some adaptive challenges mixed in with, and often mistaken for technical challenges. For example, tried and tested technology introduced into a new client environment impacts on existing technical and social systems and presents adaptive challenges. The specialist will need to collaborate with business users and in-house IT people to get it to work. We have found this time and again with implementing ERP and HR systems, for example.[15]

Looking at Figure 5.8, technical work requiring the application of existing specialist know-how and techniques can be outsourced relatively

Issue	APPROACH		
	Technical	Techno/Adaptive	Adaptive/Innovative
Problem Definition	Clear	Clear	Unclear; Requires learning
Solution and Implementation	Clear	Requires learning	Requires much all-party learning
Primary Responsibility	Specialists	Specialists and User; Participatory	User with specialists; Multi-functional teams
Type of Problem-solving	Technical	Technical-adaptive	Adaptive-innoative
Contract with External Services	Outsource	Time/materials Resource-based	Shared Risk-reward Outcomes-based
Objective	Efficient use of existing technical know-how	Effective implementation of existing solution in new setting	Effective business solution
Primary Leadership	Specialist	Collaborative	Business Sponsor/ Champion

Figure 5.8 Technical, adaptive and innovative work in outsourcing

safely, assuming competent specialists can be hired. The more work becomes adaptive the more leadership and teaming is required and the more multiple stakeholders need to be engaged with defining the problem, and working together on arriving at and implementing a solution. The role of leadership is to maintain direction and shape the context and process by which this can happen. Moreover, the more radical and business focused the innovation required, the more that leadership should be primarily by the client.

Figure 5.8 makes clear that teaming across organizational boundaries and functional silos is vital for adaptive-innovative work. All our respondent organizations looking for innovation had this understanding and were actively putting it into practice. As two examples:

> We got sufficient leverage and sufficient buy-in and understanding from all the senior executives in the supply chain to say, we are prepared to sign up to this. This is about behaviors. This is about how we work together in this unit that we call integrated teams and it appears

that you are going to take off our shoulders the traditional commercial risk that we'd otherwise be carrying. In response to that, we need to give you our best people and we need to make sure their reputation is high. This is a very different sort of commercial leverage. (Andrew Wolstenholme, T5 Construction Director)

Tom Lamming was the vice-president of Transformation at Telstra and oversaw the IT-enabling component of its $A 20 billion transformation program. He commented:

We have 12 strategic technology suppliers.... 'I think a lot about the people and the chemistry and it's not about uniformity and unilateral decision making. We have multiple suppliers, and it's about the ability to team and work together for the outcome.

Phase 4: Behavior change – key to innovation payoff

Leadership, creative contracting and organizing, and teaming in new ways build the fundamental behavior changes needed to undertake collaborative innovation. The partnering behaviors required for innovation are summarized in Figure 5.9.

Building on the discussion in Chapter 2, the behaviors represented on the left side of Figure 5.9 are very limiting in terms of what can be achieved by either client or supplier. They are essentially tied to an adversarial game, with no 'third corner' to move to. Unfortunately, recessionary conditions often pressure organizations to regress to this default position. But as Max

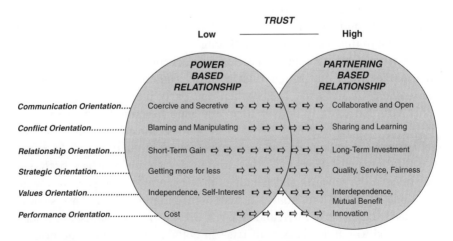

Figure 5.9 Power and partnering-based relationships

McKeown suggests, a crisis is a terrible thing to waste, and the best way to deal with a recession may just well be to innovate your way out of it.[16] Behavior change can come about as a result of a crisis, but lasting collaborative innovation is shaped in the context of prior work on leadership, contracting, and organizing, which creates rising levels of trust, teaming, and performance:

> There was a mindset change at the centre of T5. It was not a perfect project, but one where people woke up in the morning thinking, I know what the directives are and I'm part of a single team and I'm going to make this work. I think we'd worked with each other for sufficiently long enough that we had a level of trust. We actually had to spend a lot of time and investment in people and in understanding relationships. (Andrew Wolstenholme, T5 Construction Director)

As Figure 5.9 illustrates, trust is a key component in partnering. As we have noted in other studies,[17] there is no such thing as instant trust in outsourcing. It is built over time through demonstrable performance:

> You build trust by spending time together. You need to have capacity within the organization to do that and to build competence and business understanding. You can't just outsource things and then think that everything is going to go well; you need to invest in the relationship. (Rune Aase, StatoilHydro)

Weekes and Feeny have developed a useful three-pronged model of trust that reflected the complexities of the outsourcing environment.[18] *Personal trust* refers to the confidence one has that another person will work for the good of the relationship based on their integrity and adherence to moral norms. The high uncertainty associated with innovation adds another dimension to this, but one can see through all our case histories how high personal trust means that all parties will accept responsibility for risks that do not work out, rather than pointing fingers or deflecting blame. *Competence-based trust* exists when one party has confidence that the other will successfully deliver their allocated tasks and responsibilities. This may well include innovation. Successful completion of projects and achievement of joint goals enhances competence-based trust, while operational failures will degrade it. *Motivational trust* refers to where both parties believe the rewards and penalties they experience are geared toward the achievement of joint goals – a 'win–win' situation. As we have seen in our cases, bonus structures and risk-reward sharing mechanisms are elements used to build this type of trust in collaborative innovation efforts. Ultimately all three types of trust have to be present across all parties for success. Our evidence suggests that that is true whether the goal is IT operational, business process, or strategic innovation.

Finally, organizations do not deliver collaboration and innovation, people do. The importance of the behavior change exhibited in Figure 5.9 becoming part of the DNA of *individual actions* is captured well by Damian Bunyan, the MD of the company E.ON IS – an internal IT provider for the E.ON Group:

> Being a strategic partner, as a supplier, means that if I tell you to come and visit me because I've got a problem, you will come and visit me. I always make sure I get more of the time of both decision makers and the innovators in those supplier organizations. It's only the people in that company that can be innovative, and innovative (as opposed to inventive) people back up words with actions.

Toward third corner thinking

Successful collaboration and innovation share what we call 'third corner thinking'. In traditional outsourcing, problems are dealt with largely as a contest between the two parties with different vested interests to protect. For example, the client wants more service at lower cost, while the supplier wants to make margins and lower the costs it bears on service delivery. Third corner thinking sees both parties finding a larger, overriding mutual objective they can aim at.

Relatedly, innovation is at its best when it overcomes some contradiction between conflicting objectives. The most successful products deliver two benefits that contradict each other – for example, Linux challenges Windows because it is free and open. Such innovation attempts to reconcile the irreconcilable. Third corner thinking is unwilling to accept the compromise between two opposing characteristics, or the adversarial needs of two opposing parties.

In effect, our overall research in these first five chapters has documented the 20-year rise to globalism of IT and business services outsourcing. The key quest for clients has been how to leverage the ever expanding services market for significant business advantage. The common denominator in the findings: we have uncovered no quick fix. Most have learned the hard way, by making mistakes, finding out what works, and what does not, across two or three generations of outsourcing. The wise ones have been 'smart in their ignorance,' taking an incremental route into more and more outsourcing, learning as they go, limiting their risk exposure, building up their understanding and also their retained capability to run a sourcing regime aligned with their business strategy and imperatives. Suppliers have also faced learning curves in their attempts to differentiate their services, find new markets, and deal with new competition from potentially anywhere in the world. The 2008–10 economic downturn made their capabilities and suppliers' abilities to leverage them ever more critical.

Clients and suppliers now need to consider carefully the role of third corner thinking and leadership for their sourcing strategies. Leadership is about shaping the context and mobilizing resources to deal with the adaptive challenges organizations face. Leadership is also about transforming how things are done, and leveraging techniques and capabilities in new ways. Leadership therefore, is essentially about third corner thinking, innovation, and its delivery.

Conclusion – lessons on collaborating to innovate

This chapter makes clear that changing business needs, recession, the globalizing and technologizing of the supply of business services, and the much greater use of outsourcing, will provide challenges that will require many more organizations to make a step-change from outsourcing management to collaborative leadership – if governance, control, flexibility, innovation, and superior business outcomes are to be outsourcing's consequences. This chapter suggests the following lessons:

1. Innovation is even more important in economic recessions. Innovations can be changes in IT operations, business processes, or in products and services offered, or in the business model of how the firm competes. To survive and thrive through a recession requires sustainable change. A focus on cost-cutting alone, or even cost-efficiency solves short-term problems, at the expense of building the future business.
2. Innovation using the external services market is increasingly realistic as both clients and suppliers are maturing their ability to go beyond traditional outsourcing relationships and build the collaborative arrangements necessary for innovating. This means clients can move from contract administration and outsourcing management to a new phase of collaborative leadership. They can also develop a new performance agenda.
3. Innovation with large-scale, long-term impact requires deep collaboration within clients, and with and across their external suppliers. Without this, innovation, and the consequent high performance, cannot be delivered.
4. Collaborating to innovate requires a step-change in objectives pursued, relationships with suppliers, and how work and innovation is conducted. Our study of effective practitioners suggests distinctive practices for

success. These can be classified into a fourfold framework – leading, contracting, organizing, and behaving.

5. Leadership shapes the context for collaboration, innovation and high performance and is primary. Leadership deals with adaptive challenges, and must be at all levels in each of the collaborating parties. Leadership also changes the approach to risk in order to share and manage down risk and manage in opportunity.

6. New forms of contracting are required for collaborative innovation to succeed. Such contracts share risk and reward in ways that incent innovation, collaboration and high performance to achieve common goals.

7. Organizing for innovation requires more co-managed governance structures and greater multi-functional teaming across those organizations and people responsible for delivering results. Teaming now requires the ability to collaborate within a client organization, between client and supplier and between suppliers in multi-vendor environments.

8. Leading, contracting, and organizing in these ways incents behavior and enables collective delivery of superior business performance. Collaborative innovation is most effective when it generates high personal, competence-based and motivational trust among the parties. High trust is a key component and shaper of the collaborative, open, learning, adaptive, flexible, and interdependent behaviors required.

Notes

1. A quote from William Gibson who wrote *Neuromancer* in 1984, a novel in which the concept of cyberspace was first introduced.
2. Our own work over this period is collected in two volumes Lacity, M. and Willcocks, L. (2009) *Information Systems and Outsourcing: Studies in Theory and Practice*. Palgrave, London, and Willcocks, L. and Lacity, M. (2009) *The Practice of Outsourcing: From IT to BPO and Offshoring*. Palgrave, London) See also Ross, J. and Beath, C. (2005) *Sustainable Value From Outsourcing: Finding The Sweet Spot*. Centre for Information Systems Research paper vol. 5, 1a MIT, Boston. Also Hirschheim. R. Heinzl, A. and Dibbern, J. (2009) *Information Systems Outsourcing: Enduring Themes, Global Challenges and Process Opportunities*. Springer, North Holland.
3. Our definition, but backed by a significant literature in the strategy, but not in the outsourcing literature. See Kern, T. and Willcocks, L. (2000) *The Relationship Advantage: Information Technologies. Sourcing and Management*. Oxford University Press, Oxford.
4. The definition was developed for use at Intel. See Westerman G. and Curley, M. (2008) 'Building IT-enabled Capabilities at Intel', *MIS Quarterly Executive*, 7, 1, pp. 33–48.

5. Davenport, T., Leibold, M. and Voelpel, S. (2006) *Strategic Management in the Innovation Economy*. Wiley, New York. Westland, J. (2008) *Global Innovation Management*. Palgrave, London. McKeown, M. (2008) *The Truth About Innovation*. Pearson, London.

6. Weeks, M. and Feeny, D. (2008) 'Outsourcing: from cost management to innovation and business value', *California Management Review*, 50, 4, pp. 127–47.

7. Weeks, M. (2004) 'Information Technology Outsourcing and Business Innovation: An Exploratory Study of a Conceptual Framework', PHD thesis, Oxford University, Oxford.

8. For an outsourcing parallel see our paper Kern, T., Willcocks, L. and van Heck, E. (2002) 'The winner's curse in IT outsourcing: strategies for avoiding relational trauma', *California Management Review*, 44, 2, pp. 47–69. Also Willcocks, L., Cullen, S. and Lacity, M. (2007) *The Outsourcing Enterprises – The CEO Guide to Selecting Effective Suppliers*. Logica, London.

9. A good account up to mid-2008 is provided by Doherty, S. (2008) *Heathrow's T5 – History in the Making*. Wiley, Chichester.

10. See Heifetz, R. (1994) *Leadership Without Easy Answers*. The Belknap Press, Cambridge, MA. Also Heifetz, R. and Linsky, M. (2002) *Leadership on the Line*. Harvard Business Press, Boston.

11. A detailed account appears in Willcocks, L. and Lacity, M. (2006) *Global Sourcing of Business and IT Services*. Palgrave, London.

12. Earl, M. and Feeny, D. (2000) 'How To Be A CEO In An Information Age', *Sloan Management Review*, Winter, pp. 11–23.

13. Gooding, G. (2002) *The Contribution of the CIO To Business Innovation*. PhD Thesis, Oxford University, Oxford.

14. These findings are based on the present research and earlier studies detailed in Willcocks and Lacity (2006) and (2009) ops. cit.

15. Examples appear in Willcocks, L. Petherbridge, P. and Olson, N. (2003) *Making IT Count: Strategy, Delivery and Infrastructure*. Butterworth, Oxford.

16. McKeown, M. (2008) *The Truth About Innovation*. Pearson, London.

17. See Lacity and Willcocks (2009) and Willcocks and Lacity (2006, 2009) ops. cit.

18. Weekes and Feeny (2008) op. cit.

Key Practices

CHAPTER 6

The Governance Charter: Overseeing the outsourcing arrangement

Introduction

Successful outsourcing arrangements cannot be guaranteed by virtue of having a signed contract alone. The contract is a necessary but insufficient governance tool for outsourcing. That said, however, poorly constructed contracts, based on faulty cost service analyses, and containing ambiguities, loopholes, and incomplete terms, can seriously damage outsourcing health.

Contracts do not manage themselves, and good management of an outsourcing deal does not happen by accident. This Key Practice chapter shows you how to prepare a Governance Charter – a key document in promoting good governance of a contract. It defines the management roles and responsibilities of each party, the meetings and reviews, and the processes surrounding issue, dispute, and variation management – all critical to the success of outsourcing.

Why governance is important

Good governance has been a topic of great interest in business in recent years. This is not only because of recent corporate governance failures and corporate scandals including Enron, Tyco, and WorldCom which gave rise to the Sarbanes Oxley Act of 2002 (also known as the Public Company Accounting Reform and Investor Protection Act). There have also been numerous contract governance problems, reported all over the world, which have blown out costs and resulted in inadequate work quality.[1]

A decade of in-depth studies demonstrates that outsourcing cannot be contracted for and then not managed if an organization desires its deals to be successful.[2] An indicative economic study conducted in 2002[3] found that the quality of services as assessed by the client is affected to a greater degree by the nature of the client and its management techniques than by economic factors such as competition. Failure to focus upon critical issues or adopt key processes has also been argued to lead inevitably to an adverse affect on the client organization realizing its objectives;[4] insufficient planning has also proved to be disastrous.[5]

As earlier chapters have established, outsourcing is neither good nor bad in itself. The outcome is determined by how it is managed, before and after the contract has been signed. For example, in a study of organizations seeking IT cost savings, it was found that management made a 40 percent increase in cost savings.[6] In a more recent study on IT governance in 256 enterprises, Weill found that firms with above-average governance had more than 20 percent higher profitability than those with poor governance following the same business strategy.[7]

It is easy to confuse good contract governance practices with good relationship practices, but they are not one and the same. As established in Chapter 2, the importance of the relationship is indisputable. Practitioners and researchers say that a key to success in outsourcing is good working relationships, and some argue that outsourcing relationships replace many of an organization's traditional assets (people, technologies, facilities, methods, and know-how), and becomes an asset itself requiring ongoing investment.

As important as the relationship is, it should not be relied upon in lieu of having proper governance in place. This is because relationships are between people, not organizations, and people sometimes, for example, get promoted, or leave to join a new company. If there is no proper governance structure and procedures that exist independent of the relationship, far too much reliance can be placed on the 'unwritten understanding' which is difficult to evidence, and also has a habit of changing over time, as different people become involved with the deal.

Governance is about establishing a constitution, the rules of the game, if you like, in terms of establishing how decisions get made, and who is responsible for what decisions, actions, and outcomes. An important part of this in outsourcing is establishing a Governance Charter.

A form of governance agreement – the Governance Charter

A Governance Charter imposes a commitment on both sides to manage the deal in a diligent and agreed manner, thereby ensuring strong controls as well as facilitating an efficient working relationship. Typically it comprises the following six main areas:

1. relationship structure and roles – who in each party is responsible for what;
2. meetings – who will get together about what, and how often;
3. reviews – who will assess what, and how often;
4. issue management – how problems and ideas for improvements will be raised, tracked, and resolved;
5. dispute management – how 'difference of opinion' will be raised, tracked, and resolved; and
6. variation management – how amendments, modifications, and corrections will be raised, tracked, and accepted or rejected.

While you may find in your contracts that some of these matters have been addressed in some capacity, rarely will you find them all readily accessible in one spot in an easy to understand format. When good governance needs to be an ongoing process, that process is not assisted by having the odd clause scattered throughout the contract. Rather, the Governance Charter provides the 'one-stop-shop' document providing the agreed governance mechanisms.

Nevertheless, not all outsourcing arrangements warrant a Governance Charter. If the outsourcing deal is short term, once-off transaction, and/ or is of low risk and low value, the cost of preparing and complying with a Governance Charter may outweigh the benefits.

Typical reasons to consider the use of a Governance Charter include:

- **Importance** – if the outsourcing arrangement encompasses services that are important to the organization, if the commercial relationship will be long term, or the outsourcing deal is high value or high risk;
- **Complexity** – if the management activities involve a number of personnel in either or both organizations, or the tasks are complicated or extensive;
- **Clarity and accountability** – to ensure everyone in both parties understands their roles and the roles of others;
- **Conflict resolution mechanism** – to provide agreed processes and records for resolving issues and disputes; and
- **User-friendly contract document** – to have the management-related part of the deal in a useable form, easily understood, easily referenced – all of which makes the deal easier to manage.

The rest of this chapter discusses each section of the Governance Charter, and provides details on preparing and managing it, including its place in the contractual documents; the point in the outsourcing lifecycle (see Chapter 1) in which to prepare the document; planning the preparation effort; and ongoing management.

Sections of the Governance Charter

This section provides information and examples about each of the sections in the Governance Charter.

1. About this Governance Charter

Good practice in contract writing suggests that all contract schedules begin with an introduction so the reader knows the intention and function of the schedule. Accordingly, this section provides the reader with the purpose of the Governance Charter and a bit of background (if useful to their understanding).

2. Relationship structure and roles

As we pointed out in Chapter 1, outsourcing is not a fad, but a substantial part of corporate and government expenditure, needing top team oversight and management. This section provides an organization chart regarding the management of the contract. It is followed by a table depicting the accountabilities of the roles in the structure.

For the inter-party organization chart, a simple diagram such as that shown in Figure 6.1, can provide much needed clarity in and control over relationships.

Figure 6.1 Example of a governance structure

Once the structure has been planned, the responsibilities of each role is defined. Table 6.1 provides an example of this, using the inter-party organization charter depicted in Figure 6.1.

It is important that the accountabilities are mutually exclusive, that is – two people within the same organization should not have the same job. The table also often has sign-off authorities such as monetary amounts and/or document approvals (i.e., reports, variation requests, etc).

All of this goes a long way towards clarifying roles, and in doing so provides proper control over relationships, to say nothing about saving an organization a great deal of frustration, as the following case helps to illustrate.

Table 6.1 Example of accountabilities

Client	Provider
CEO	Managing Director
• Resolve disputes with Managing Director • Planning and strategic relationship management	• Resolve disputes with CEO • Planning and strategic • Relationship management
General Manager	Account Manager
• Liaise with Account Manager to resolve escalated issues • Conduct annual strategic reviews	• Liaise with General Manager to resolve escalated issues • Conduct account planning
Contract Manager	Service Delivery Manager
• Liaise with Service Delivery Manager • Manage client's day-to-day responsibilities • Approve invoices, resolutions, and variations or escalate • Conduct performance reviews	• Liaise with Contract Manager • Manage provider's day-to-day responsibilities • Prepare reports and meeting information • Conduct audits
Team Leaders	Service Leads
• Liaise with Service Leads to resolve issues • Attend fortnightly operations meetings	• Liaise with Team Leaders to resolve issues • Supervise workforce • Lead operations meetings

Case: Lack of control resulted in high costs

A state-based insurance provider had its costs blow out 500 percent in the first year of outsourcing. After a brief analysis, the root cause was determined to be due to the lack of control over the relationship. Anyone in either organization could contact anyone in the other party, since responsibilities and authorities were widely disregarded. Thus, the insurance company staff were requesting and getting many more services than were provided for in the contract, and the service provider never said no. In fact, the service provider quickly realized it could offer many more services and the organization's staff would never turn them down. It was not until rules governing out-of-scope work were put in place by the accounting department that the finances were brought back under control.

3. Meetings

Face-to-face contact is critical in any successful relationship, and a partnership-style relationship cannot occur without this. If the parties are not meeting regularly, they may not be talking enough. Meetings are an important part of governance, and these are detailed in this section.

There are a variety of meetings that may be conducted throughout the life of an outsourcing arrangement. Strategic meetings such as assessing the overall success of the contract, the contract scorecard, or the relationship values charter (see Chapter 2) as well as the strategic planning and benchmarking of costs and service levels have tended to occur annually, but are getting more frequent. Technology forums, where new products and technologies are presented and improvement opportunities are identified, also tend to occur annually.

Performance-related meetings such as the review of the Key Performance Indicators (KPIs), audit findings, technology refresh and consolidation initiatives, milestone progress, and variation patterns should occur more frequently.

Monthly service meetings are the norm, where the service provider typically presents a number of reports, like performance over the month and any resultant KPI recourse/reward effect, and service plans for the upcoming month, and staffing moves and changes.

The most frequent type of meetings are those concerning operational matters, covering the current day-to-day operational issues requiring attention of both parties, the raising of variation requests and either approval or rejection, and update of procedures and documentation.

At a minimum, consider:

- strategic planning meetings in line with business planning cycle
- performance meetings in line with the timing of the performance reporting
- pre-invoice meetings if invoices might vary from period to period and the amounts could be subject to debate, and
- more frequent operational meetings

Rather than have everyone go to a massive monthly meeting whether they need to be there or not, experienced managers have found it more efficient to only have those people at the meetings (or the part of the meeting) specifically connected to their role in the deal. The frequency of meetings and seniority of attendees can depend on the maturity and stability of the arrangement, the degree of potential changes to either party's business or the work, whether KPIs are being met, the nature, number and importance of projects in process, and how close the contract is up for renewal.

Some meetings are not just to solve issues but also to forge a 'partnering' style relationship, such as regular 'partnering' workshops and continuous improvement meetings where shared goals, visions, and values are developed, partnering principles are reinforced, and business opportunities are thrashed out (see also Chapters 2 and 5 for examples).

Most organizations by 2010 had adopted the concept of continuous improvement in their outsourcing arrangements. This applies not only to the performance of suppliers but also to the performance of the organization itself. In line with this concept, both parties' staff are expected to find ways to improve the performance of the activities they perform. Good governance allows the flexibility, opportunity, and scope for the supplier to be smart and improve the way the work is being done; but at the same time ensuring that it does what it has contractually agreed to do. This has become of such importance that many organizations make it a contractual requirement over the supplier to put forward regular new work practice concepts complete with accompanying risk assessment and business case and dedicate regular special meetings to present and consider adoption. The following case gives real-life example of what could happen if this is not done.

Case: A deal motivating the supplier not to improve

An insurance company found out that suppliers might not routinely put in a continuous improvement process, particularly when under a fixed price with little margin. In this case, by the end of the seven-year contract, the entire IT infrastructure and related practices were obsolete and effectively not supported anywhere in the industry (i.e., the desktop fleet had not been changed in the seven years). The contract had a 12.5 percent mandated annual cost reduction, capped profit and capped labor – all driving the supplier to retain obsolete technology and prevented any improvement.

It is worth noting that the Governance Charter also gives the rules around these meetings. For example, only the specified individuals are permitted at a particular meeting, unless notified in advance to the other party. This avoids any perceptions of being ambushed with 'surprise guests'. And to ensure the specified people actually do attend, some organizations have made attendance at meetings a KPI, when there is concern that individuals from the parties might be haphazard with their attendance.

The chairing and minuting responsibilities are described as well because in many cases, merely specifying that meetings are to be held is not to enough to ensure these actually take place. One must also ensure specifications are carried out, as the following case exemplifies.

Case: The meeting plan stays unimplemented

A government agency had put substantial effort into defining the meetings that would take place. However, there was one oversight. No party was assigned the role of organizing the meetings – therefore, both parties expected the other party to do it. Neither did. As a result, the meetings were not held. It was not until an independent government auditor wanted to see the minutes of meetings that the current contract manager for the client, the third in three years, even knew the meetings were detailed in the contract.

The section of the Governance Charter pertaining to meetings can be as simple as shown in Table 6.2. However, some organizations have found they need to specify meetings in more detail than bullet points in tables allow. This ensures that the meeting accomplish what the stakeholders expect, and avoids ambiguity about the nature of the meeting, information required by the parties prior to the meeting, and expected decisions resulting from the meeting. An example of this more detailed specification is in Figure 6.2.

4. Reviews, audits, and assessments

Compliance with a contract is never guaranteed by virtue of a contract alone; the contract merely provided recourse or remedy in the event of failure. The evaluation of the supplier's performance is critical in ensuring the organization is obtaining what it paid for, particularly because as the planning and evaluation function of management replaces the direct control over the staff the organization had under in-house sourcing. The role of the contract management staff is not to interfere in the work method practices the provider adopts, but to measure and assess whether it produced and complied with the requirements in the contract. Failure to establish compliance can have interesting consequences, as the following case demonstrates.

Table 6.2 Illustrative meetings schedule

Frequency	Meeting	Attendees		Topics
		Client	**Provider**	
Annually	1. Executive meeting	• CEO • General Manager	• Managing Director • Account Manager	• Future strategies • Review overall performance
	2. Partnering workshop	• General Manager • Contract Manager	• Account Manager • Service Delivery Manager	• Develop shared goals, vision, values • Develop partnering principles • Strategic planning for the forthcoming year • Business opportunity development
Quarterly	1. Technology forum	• Contract Manager • Team Leaders	• Service Delivery Manager • Service leads	• Presentation of new product releases/new technologies • Discussions relating to technology trials
	2. Capacity planning meeting	• Contract Manager	• Service Delivery Manager	• Review capacity report and recommendations
Monthly	1. Service meeting	• Contract Manager • Team Leaders	• Service Delivery Manager • Service leads	• Present reports listed • Planning for upcoming month • Staff moves and changes • Upcoming projects • Update of asset register, documentation, and schedules
	2. Pre-invoice meeting	• Contract Manager	• Service Delivery Manager	• Review proposed invoice

Purpose	Review performance, provide improvement directions, and approve plans for the upcoming year

Authority	The Annual Review will have authority to
	  a. Approve contractor bonus
	  b. Recommend variations and changes in contract operations
	  c. Set contract outcomes for the following year
	  d. Approve the management plans

Attendees	Client
	  a. Contract Executive
	  b. Contract Manager
	  c. Finance Manager
	
	Contractor
	  a. Account Executive
	  b. Account Manager
	  c. Finance Manger
	
	Other personnel as required

Chair	Client Contract Executive – Agenda to be distributed at least five days prior to the Annual Review
Minutes	Contractor – Minutes to be distributed within 48 hr of the Annual Review

Key topics	Quality of performance and delivery against KPIs over the previous 12 months
	Achievement of strategic objectives set in previous Management Plans
	  a. Performance against contract outcomes
	  b. Regulatory and contract compliance
	  c. Fees and charges
	  d. Management plan approvals
	  e. Other issues relevant to the performance of the services as the client determines

Timing	Within 60 days of each anniversary of the Commencement Date

Reports required prior to the Annual Review	Two weeks prior to the Annual Review, the Contractor to distribute the Management Plan results for the year and the updated Management Plans including:
	  a. Workforce Management Plan
	  b. Strategic Management Plan
	  c. Disengagement Plan
	  d. Risk Management Plan
	  e. Technology Upgrade Plan
	One week prior to the Annual Review, the Contractor to distribute the updated schedules including:
	  a. Key Personnel Register
	  b. Subcontractors Register
	  c. Other schedules which may have been varied, or require variation
	One week prior to the Annual Review, the Contractor to distribute the
	  a. Issues Register summary report (high priority only)
	  b. Variations summary report (major variations only)

Figure 6.2 Sample detailed meeting specification

Case: No oversight affects compliance

A government organization assumed that compliance with the contract was a foregone conclusion, so it believed no oversight of the outsourcing contract was required. As a consequence, it handed oversight over to a low-level contract administrator and did not perform any compliance reviews until four years into the five-year contract. At that point, it hired an independent audit firm to evaluate the situation.

After an extensive process, the auditors determined that the supplier was only 40 percent compliant with the contract but that the client was negligent in its governance processes. Pre-paid work totaling $200,000 a year had not been performed, because the contract required the client to issue work orders against it, which it had not done. Many KPIs were not being reported, let alone being complied with. However, the client did not follow up on KPIs and did nothing whether KPIs were met or not. Many required reports were not being generated by the service provider, but again the client did not make any requests for reports that were missing. Furthermore, the client did not perform performance reviews, conduct any form of planning forums, and so on. The key finding of the audit report was that the client did not install any governance over the contract, so the supplier was allowed almost complete discretion in what it did.

As a result of this audit, and to better manage its next-generation deal, the organization put in place a seven-person contract management team, led by a senior contract manager. This contract-management function cost $360,000 a year, but it saved $830,000 a year through specific contract-management activities, experienced personnel, and pro-active management.

Audits of the supplier's operations can be complicated by the presence of other clients and their privacy rights, and the complexity of the supplier's environment/s. Furthermore, depending upon the specific audit rights agreed to in the contract, some organizations are not able to obtain unrestricted access, not able to conduct surprise audits, and many need to negotiate the degree of assistance the supplier must provide (some being required to pay for such assistance). For this reason, the type of reviews and audits are specified in the Governance Charter to ensure the organization will have unfettered access and no surprise charges.

Reviews focused on the service provider include, but are by no means limited to:

- compliance with the contract, SLA, and other governing documents;
- cost and service performance relative to the agreement, but also relative to industry norms;
- source data and calculations of KPIs and any other information for which the organization is relying upon the supplier to accurately generate;

- degree the supplier's obligations to the organization meet current needs and expectations;
- the supplier's risk management and controls over service operations and costs;
- improvement initiatives implemented; and
- user and other stakeholder satisfaction with services.

Governance involves reviewing not only the service provider's performance but also the organization's own management effectiveness. The uneconomic, inefficient, and ineffective use of services, whether the services are provided internally or otherwise, will inhibit an organization's ability to achieve its objectives. The greatest efficiency and effectiveness gains are often in how the organization plans for and uses the provider's services. Consider the following case.

Case: Outsourcing resulted in duplicate systems

For example, a stockbroker outsourced all of its IT operations as part of an automation, 'paperless office', initiative. It was assumed that once the technology was in place staff would merely disregard the old way of doing things and move right into the new. What happened, however, was that staff just added the new processes to the old rather than create new, more efficient processes, thus ending up with two systems – one paper based, and one electronic. This was discovered 18 months into the contract when internal audit was performing a review. They discovered that neither system was functioning effectively, and the hybrid created was exceedingly time consuming. As a result, a specific 'no paper' policy was implemented.

Internally focused reviews should include:

- the degree the organization is meeting its obligations to the supplier;
- progress toward the achievement of the objectives/business case for the outsourcing initiative;
- determination of ongoing value for money;
- efficient use of the supplier's resources (i.e., use of non-peak windows, extraneous labor);
- effectiveness of the contract management function; and
- improvement initiatives implemented.

Each review, the scope of the review, which party is to conduct it, who it is to be presented to, and how frequently the review is to be conducted are all detailed in this section of the Governance Charter as shown in Table 6.3.

Table 6.3 Example of a reviews table

Frequency	Review	Presented to:	Conducted by:	Scope of review
Annually	1. Governance review	Client • CEO • General Manager	Provider • Managing Director • Account Manager	• Analyze the parties' compliance with obligations • Recommend better ways of working together • Prepare actions and variations required
	2. Agreement Review Meeting	Provider • Account Manager • Service Delivery Manager	Client • General Manager • Contract Manager	• Review of audit findings • Variations • Review and updating of documentation • Cost and service level benchmarking
	3. Quality audit	Client • Contract Manager	Provider • Service Delivery Manager	• Compliance with the Quality Plan • Quality Plan improvement actions
Quarterly	1. SLA/ Contract Review	Client • General Manager • Contract Manager	Provider • Account Manager • Service Delivery Manager	• Review of KPIs • Variations • Milestone planning • Identification of improvement opportunities, technology refresh, and consolidation
	2. Efficiency and cost reduction review	Client • Contract Manager	Provider • Account Manager • Service Delivery Manager	• Identification of operational efficiencies • Identification of cost reduction opportunities
Monthly	1. SLA performance review	Client • Contract Manager	Provider • Service Delivery Manager	• Analyze overall performance of SLA • Analyze performance against KPIs • Prepare actions and variations required

continued

Table 6.3 *continued*

Frequency	Review	Presented to:	Conducted by:	Scope of review
As directed by the client	1. KPI calculation audit	Provider • Service Delivery Manager	Client • Contract Manager	• Determine correct KPI calculations and source data of calculations
	2. Other	As directed by Client	As directed by Client	• As directed by Client

5. Issue management

Neither party needs to, nor should, solve problems alone. Unresolved issues are disputes waiting to happen, thus sound issue management can make or break an outsourcing deal. This includes how issues can be raised by either party, how issues will be logged and tracked, and what approvals are required for issue resolution – all of which are defined in this section.

Good issue management in outsourcing is very similar to that for good project management. That is, there is a formal process for raising, recording, and resolving issues that arise and these are logged and tracked. It is not unusual to find, in moderately large or complex outsourcing deal, at least 300 live issues on any given day in a reasonable complex outsourcing operations. Effective issue management allows for a visible decision-making process, typically by using some form of an issue sheet. An example of an issue sheet used in many contracts to record and resolve issues is given in Figure 6.3.

6. Dispute resolution

Should an issue not be able to be resolved, then dispute resolution is likely to come into play. Generally speaking, disputes are not often arguments over fact, but rather are over interpretation and perceptions (different understandings on what was agreed or done) or philosophical differences (contrasting opinions where there is no 'right' answer). These can take a considerable amount of time to resolve.

Both parties are best served if disputes can be resolved using the inter-party structure described earlier in this section. Once third parties are involved (be they mediators, arbitrators, courts, and/or the legal profession), a costly war that neither party 'wins' is typically the result, and a mutually agreed compromise is generally harder to arrive at. As an example, consider the dispute about project completion described here.

Issue Sheet		
Issue Sheet ID:	Raised by:	Date submitted: ____/____/____
Issue title:	Priority: High Medium Low	Governing documents affected: ☐ Conditions of Contract ☐ SLA ☐ Price Schedule
Assigned to:	Priority rationale:	☐ Other Schedule: _____ ☐ Procedure: _____ ☐ Other _____
Description of Issue:		
Proposed resolution:		
Implication of not resolving Issue:		
Related Issues:		Information/background attachments:
Investigation/further work required:		Investigation assigned to:
Description of resolution:		
Resolution approved by: Client: _____, Date: ____/____/____ Provider: _____, Date: ____/____/____ (name, signature)		
Comments:		

Figure 6.3 Sample issue sheet

Case: A dispute about project completion

This case concerns a university and shows the need for clear acceptance criteria of deliverables. The parties could not agree as to whether a software development project was completed as there was no acceptance criteria on which to form an objective assessment. The provider believed it had completed the project and had already suffered a huge loss. The client believed many of the functions it was seeking were not present in the way that they were supposed to operate.

The parties hired a consulting firm who reviewed the bid, the development processes, and the understandings that were evidenced during the project. The documentation able to be provided by the parties was neither thorough nor did it appear complete. Numerous documents that could be reasonably expected to be available for observation and confirmation by the review team were unable to be provided by either party. After six months, the advisor resolved that the university should withhold payment only for items not delivered that were specifically identified as a function in the original request for tender, but the client had to pay for those functions that had been delivered but for which the quality was under dispute. There was no evidence supporting a specification of 'quality'.

Later the consulting firm and the university had their own dispute over the cost of the review. The bill exceeded the $200,000 quote due to extra work performed by the firm. Because of the lack of evidence the parties had to support their arguments and the university refused to pay.

Dispute management is very similar to issue management. That is, there is a formal process for raising, recording, and resolving disputes that arise, and these are logged and tracked through the use of dispute notices. An example of a dispute notice form used in many contracts is given in Figure 6.4.

7. Variation management

Variations are a natural occurrence in outsourcing contracts. An example of variation request appears in Figure 6.5. Variations do not need to be just about price – all the contractual documents should be 'living' and reflect the current practices. Not only does this serve to keep the documents reflective of the current agreement in practice, it also ensures that the next generation deal will be based on and operating with current information.

There are a raft of variations that can take place during the life on any outsourcing deal, including:

- a change in the IT systems – a rationalization, new platform/s, new enterprise software, formation of a standard operating environment, etc;
- a change services levels – either appreciably upgrade or downgrade based on the supplier's performance or the organization's business requirements;
- the desire by the organization to backsource certain services – either because the supplier has not been performing those services adequately and the organization does not believe an emergency step-in will solve

DISPUTE NOTICE FORM		
Dispute ID:	Raised by:	Date submitted: ____/____/____
Dispute title:		Dispute to be resolved by:
Assigned to: Client:_____ Service Provider:_____		☐ Independent expert ☐ Mediation ☐ Arbitration ☐ Court ☐ Other _____
Description of dispute:		
Previous resolution attempts:		
Related Issues Sheets (attach copies):	Information/background attachments:	
Investigation/further work required:	Investigation assigned to:	
Description of dispute resolution:		
Approved by: Client: _____, Date: ____/____/____ Provider: _____, Date: ____/____/____ (name, signature)		
Comments:		

Figure 6.4 Example of a dispute notice

it, the organization wishes to rebuild the competence, or believes the services should be performed internally in hindsight;

- a change in expected demand levels – either to a much larger or smaller extent;
- the need to incorporate further services – that were not foreseen or are currently out-of-scope but have been purchased repeatedly;
- the need to rectify defects or omissions – including accountability concerns (if actual operations have lead to resources or activities being duplicated or omitted), poor or ambiguous specifications, or inclusion of schedules to form part of the legal framework;
- a desire to refresh the entirety of the agreement – either because there have been extensive variations or the agreement is not meeting the needs of either or both parties or to introduce good outsourcing practice deemed necessary (i.e., KPIs, incentives, etc);
- a desire to revise the pricing arrangement – to variabilize prices that were fixed but should not have been, to change variable unit prices into

fixed lump sums where demand is now predictable and stable, clarify the reimbursables, etc; or

- a change in the organization itself – merger, acquisition, divestment, reorganization, expansion, etc; necessitating a contract overhaul.
- A formal process for issuing and tracking variation requests and resolutions is a core component of good governance. Without it, things can go awry very quickly, as the following case illustrates.

Variation Request		
Variation Request ID #: Variation Request title:	Raised by: Name of Representative Signature_____	Date submitted: ___/___/___ Date Variation is to take effect:___/___/___
Priority: High Medium Low Priority rationale:	Documents to be varied: ☐ Contract ☐ SLA ☐ Price schedule ☐ Other document _____ ☐ Procedure _____	
Description of proposed Variation:		
Business Case for the Variation		
Benefit:	Risk:	Cost:
Implication of not making a Variation:		
Related Variation Requests (if applicable):	Information/background attachments	
Investigation/further work required:		
Approved for investigation (Y/N) Investigation assigned to:_____ Investigation due date: _____	Investigation results:	
Variation resolution: Rejected Deferred – until ___/___/___ Approved	Signatures: Client representative name _____ Signature _____, Date ___/___/___ Provider representative name _____ Signature _____, Date ___/___/___	
Description of approved Variation resolution (attach implementation schedule, if applicable):		

Figure 6.5 Example of a variation request

Case: Undocumented undertakings

This case, involving an international airline, highlights a common problem when documentation is scarce. In this instance, stakeholder satisfaction surveys were yielding poor results and there was a general feeling of adversity with the supplier of the IT support services (LANs, desktop fleet management, and help desk). Yet, the KPIs were showing reasonable performance, certainly of a standard that did not warrant the animosity exhibited. A root cause analysis determined that the major contributing factor was that both the supplier's sales staff and the operational staff were making unwritten 'promises' to various client personnel, few of which were being followed up on. Neither party maintained records of the discussions and correspondence leading to the client now having certain expectations (access to global research, technical briefings, facilitation of special interest groups, to name a few). Once the supplier harvested all the unrecorded expectations, it realized it could not meet these expectations and keep within its profit margins. It instituted a 'no promises unless supported with a variation' procedure instead.

Preparing and managing the Governance Charter

Place in the contract documents

An outsourcing contract typically comprises the terms and conditions (the 'legals'), which make up the body of the contract, and many schedules. For example, key schedules present in nearly every significant outsourcing arrangement include the Service Level Agreement (SLA) that provides the definition of successful work including the work responsibility matrix, work specifications, KPIs, and reporting and the Price Schedule that specifies the manner in which the work will be billed.

The Governance Charter is another key schedule that oversees the way the deal will be managed between the parties. Although the Governance Charter is a schedule to the contract, and hence part of the legal framework, it is crucial that it be written in management language, rather than 'legalese'. This is because it is an often used and referenced document within the entirety of the governing documents.

Point in the outsourcing lifecycle

As we have seen in earlier chapters, the outsourcing lifecycle consists of nine building blocks representing best practice in forming and managing outsourcing arrangements. As shown in Figure 6.6, the Governance Charter is prepared by the client organization in the design building block 4 and issued with any competitive tender process to the prospective bidders. This is because the contents of the Governance Charter must be detailed at some point. Leaving it until later means that the service provider would have made incorrect assumptions about how the deal is to be managed, and thus would not have made the appropriate costing, and not provided for the right people and processes. Outsourcing arrangements not only require a work specification (the SLA), a legal specification (the body of the contract), and a pricing model specification (the price schedule), but also a governance specification – because all ultimately affect the price on offer. Otherwise, the bidders may not include the cost of the governance specification in their bid.

Planning the effort

Before beginning a Governance Charter there are two key preparatory steps that would have taken place if the outsourcing lifecycle has been followed:

- Building block 1: Investigate – research has been conducted into how other organizations govern deals of this nature and what worked well and did not work in practice.
- Building block 2: Target – the seven profiles (service, cost, staff, balance sheet, commercial relationships, stakeholders, and governance) regarding the scope of work to be outsourced have been detailed. The Governance Profile provides much of the research information required to draft the Governance Charter because it provides the details over the current state and future desired state.

A first-time Governance Charter, given the previous steps in the outsourcing lifecycle, is likely to take a few weeks to prepare. However, an experienced Governance Charter writer can draft one in only days (even hours!). If these early steps have not been complete, you will be in a significantly inferior position for drafting the Governance Charter – effectively beginning with little information. This will at least double the standard drafting time.

The client writes the Governance Charter because the initial version is released with any request for tender, proposal, or offer. The provider

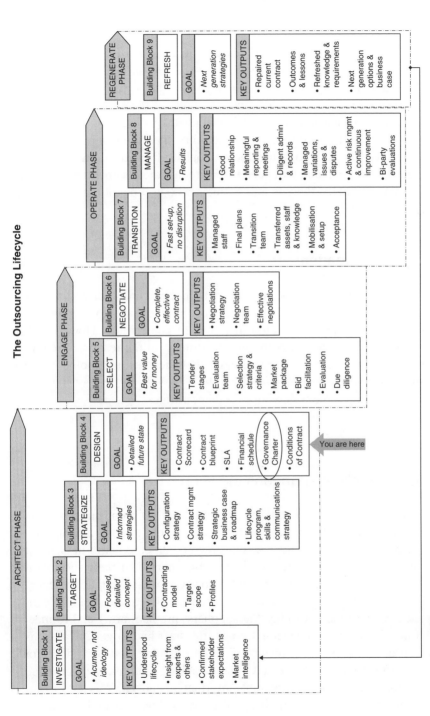

The Outsourcing Lifecycle

ARCHITECT PHASE

Building Block 1
INVESTIGATE

GOAL
• *Acumen, not ideology*

KEY OUTPUTS
• Understood lifecycle
• Insight from experts & others
• Confirmed stakeholder expectations
• Market intelligence

Building Block 2
TARGET

GOAL
• *Focused, detailed concept*

KEY OUTPUTS
• Contracting model
• Target scope
• Profiles

Building Block 3
STRATEGIZE

GOAL
• *Informed strategies*

KEY OUTPUTS
• Configuration strategy
• Contract mgmt strategy
• Strategic business case & roadmap
• Lifecycle program, skills & communications strategy

Building Block 4
DESIGN

GOAL
• *Detailed future state*

KEY OUTPUTS
• Contract Scorecard
• Contract blueprint
• SLA
• Financial schedule
• Governance Charter
• Conditions of Contract

You are here

ENGAGE PHASE

Building Block 5
SELECT

GOAL
• *Best value for money*

KEY OUTPUTS
• Tender stages
• Evaluation team
• Selection strategy & criteria
• Market package
• Bid facilitation
• Evaluation
• Due diligence

Building Block 6
NEGOTIATE

GOAL
• *Complete, effective contract*

KEY OUTPUTS
• Negotiation strategy
• Negotiation team
• Effective negotiations

OPERATE PHASE

Building Block 7
TRANSITION

GOAL
• *Fast set-up, no disruption*

KEY OUTPUTS
• Managed staff
• Final plans
• Transition team
• Transferred assets, staff & knowledge
• Mobilisation & setup
• Acceptance

Building Block 8
MANAGE

GOAL
• *Results*

KEY OUTPUTS
• Good relationship
• Meaningful reporting & meetings
• Diligent admin & records
• Managed variations, issues & disputes
• Active risk mgmt & continuous improvement
• Bi-party evaluations

REGENERATE PHASE

Building Block 9
REFRESH

GOAL
• *Next generation strategies*

KEY OUTPUTS
• Repaired current contract
• Outcomes & lessons
• Refreshed knowledge & requirements
• Next generation options & business case

Figure 6.6 Timing in the lifecycle

can always suggest modifications, of course, but the Governance Charter describes how you want the deal to be managed; do not let other parties decide what that will be.

Governance Charters require reviews by a number of individuals prior to release to potential providers. The first review should be by the evaluation team. This is because the Governance Charter will be bid upon by the potential service providers and the scope of the Governance Charter contributes to the evaluation criteria that the team develops. Second in line to review the Governance Charter should be the individuals who will fill the positions noted in it, since these people will need to manage various aspects of the deal, and will need to ensure that the document will actually assist them. Finally, there is management who will be ultimately accountable for the deal.

Ongoing management

Good governance requires an investment in the people that will deliver it. Such people will have the skills, experience, and outlook along with enough time, resources, and support to fulfill their responsibilities. However, if the parties have not made appropriate investments in the resources required, then the Governance Charter will most likely become just another piece of paper made with good intentions, but that is quietly filed away and forgotten ... or worse, as the following case demonstrates.

Case: A client abandons the shop

A federal government department conducted its first business process outsourcing (BPO) initiative as part of a whole-of-government mandate. The service provider was awarded contract to begin in October and had planned a three-week transition period in their successful bid. Unbeknownst to the provider however, was fact that the client had made all but three staff redundant in June. Management considered the function to be 'the suppliers' problem now' and to meet financial year-end headcount goals 'the staff had to go ... now'. This caused a number of problems. First, no regular work was done for three months, which created a huge backlog, and many disgruntled customers. Second, considerable information and data was left incomplete, inaccurate, and missing. Third, no staff were available to assist with the transition or manage the contract. It was well known in the industry as a 'total disaster' in the first year. The client, in this case, had assumed no responsibility for any contribution to the relationship, governance, or operations. It resulted in costing the organization significantly more than the bid price, and the quality of services espoused in the original business case to award the contract was never able to be achieved.

The continued usefulness of the Governance Charter document itself over the term of the contract depends on how up-to-date it is kept. If there are additional meetings that have been found to be appropriate, then add them to the document. If there are process improvements over dispute resolution, make sure you reflect them in the document. If a role has been added to a party, add it to the inter-party organization chart and specify the role's accountabilities. In this manner, the Governance Charter acts as a systematic understanding that can survive any turnover of the personnel involved.

Conclusion

Outsourcing inevitably creates a partnering relationship (albeit rarely in the legal sense), as the organization and its suppliers acknowledge greater levels of interdependence. The parties need to be acting in concert, as running and maintaining the arrangement, as an ongoing collaborative process requires that everyone works as a team. Of course, this is easy to say, but much harder to do. However, the Governance Charter is a relatively simple tool that facilitates successful management of the deal for both parties because it forces the parties to think about and agree how they will work together. Good governance is not an inherent attribute of a contract, but is only operationalized by design. Forethought and action on governance has been demonstrated in our work to prevent issues becoming major roadblocks, and can lead to clearer, more efficient relationships and more effective performance.

Notes

1. See 'U.S. failing to monitor millions spent on contract labour', 04 Nov 2005, www.management-issues.com; 'Review of the Whole of Government Information Technology Outsourcing Initiative' Richard Humphry, Audit of Contract Management Practices in the Common Administrative Services

Directorate, May 2004, www.nserc.ca/about/PIR/cmp/cmp_e.pdf; 'Accenture contract review', www.window.state.tx.us/comptrol/letters/accenture.
2. Study findings are summarized in Cullen, S., Seddon, P. and Willcocks, L. (2005) 'Managing outsourcing: the lifecycle imperative', *MIS Quarterly Executive*, 4, 1, March, pp. 229–46. Detailed studies appear in Willcocks, L. and Lacity (2009) *The Practice of Outsourcing: From Information Systems to BPO and Offshoring*. Palgrave, London; also Lacity, M. and Willcocks, L. (2009) *Information Systems and Outsourcing: Studies in Theory and Practice*, Palgrave, London.
3. Domberger, S., Fernandez, P. and Fiebeg, D. (2002) 'Modelling the price, performance and contract characteristics of IT Outsourcing', *Journal of Information Technology*, 15, pp. 107–18.
4. Nagel, T.W. and Murphy, M. T. (1996) 'Structuring technology outsourcing relationships: customer concerns, strategies and processes', *International Journal of Law and Information Technology*, 4, 2, pp. 151–75.
5. Martinsons, M. G. (1993) 'Outsourcing information systems: a strategic partnership with risks', *Long Range Planning*, 26, 3, pp.18–25.
6. Willcocks, L. P. and Fitzgerald, G. (1994) *A Business Guide to Information Technology Outsourcing*. London: Business Intelligence. See also Willcocks and Lacity (2009) op.cit.
7. Weill, P. (2004). 'Don't just lead, govern: how top performing firms govern IT', *MISQ Executive*, 3, 1, pp. 1–17.

CHAPTER 7

Contract management strategy

Introduction

There are many different ways in which internal service provision (known as in-house sourcing or 'insourcing') and market provision of services (outsourcing) operate. Depending on the degree of outsourcing performed in an organization, outsourcing can entail a profound change in strategic and operational mechanisms. As earlier chapters established, especially Chapter 4, the use of outsourcing does not imply less effort in managing IT, only a different emphasis. Outsourcing changes, or should change, the emphasis from managing day-to-day operations to a focus on specifications of service delivery and from staff management to planning, evaluating, and relationship management.

Specifications and Key Performance Indicators (KPIs) replace job descriptions and internal performance metrics. Negotiation with the provider replaces command over internal staff. Control via contracts replaces control via employment. Invoices are paid, rather than salaries. Reviewing providers' outputs replaces managing the former inputs and processes.

One way to look at this is through W. Edwards Deming's PDCA model, one that has been around for decades.[1] In Deming's work with quality management, he put forward the landmark PDCA (Plan, Do, Check, Act) continuous feedback loop model for successful business processes (Figure 7.1).

Bearing in mind Chapter 4, and looking at this very simplistically, after outsourcing, the client organization is no longer primarily the 'doer' – the provider becomes the main 'doer'. The client organization's primary job then is to *plan* the outsourcing arrangement (and future generations of it), *check* compliance with the contract and performance measures, and *act* on changes need to improve results and/or correct deficiencies. The provider *does* (most of) the work. Of course, this cycle continues after the contract is in place with the client continuously planning, checking, and acting.

As organizations increasingly move toward contracting for the provision of services, contract management is becoming one of the core activities of overall business management. Furthermore, the same documents used in contracts are also being increasingly used to manage internal service

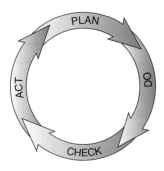

Figure 7.1 Deming's PDCA model

provision through the use of service level agreements or the award of in-house bids – making the skills and strategies of contract management even more imperative.

The time to decide what needs to be done and by whom is not after the deal has been signed and everyone has either left, or transferred to the provider. It is tempting to wait and try to 'make a go of it', but this approach assumes a level of effortlessness regarding contract management that rarely exists. This fatal flaw has left some organizations with out-of-control costs, inadequate monitoring, and poor results, as the following case illustrates.

Case: An insurance company puts the provider in charge

A state-based insurance company had entered into a 'strategic partnership' with an IT organization. The board, believing that the provider was now its official IT department and would act accordingly, saw no need to retain any IT capability. Accordingly, it outsourced the entirety of its IT people, processes, technology, and strategy to the provider. After the transition was completed, the soon-to-be-exiting CIO realized that no thinking had taken place regarding managing the provider, let alone managing the utilization of IT in the company. He commissioned a study to determine what prudent management should be in place and was startled with the level of basic management required alone. He proposed the resultant IT and contract management strategy to the board, but was overruled. Instead, board put the provider in charge of its own contract on behalf of the insurer. Five years later, IT strategy was non-existent and IT costs were demonstrably higher than the market. The organization has now started to rebuild its IT organization again, beginning with the hiring of a CIO.

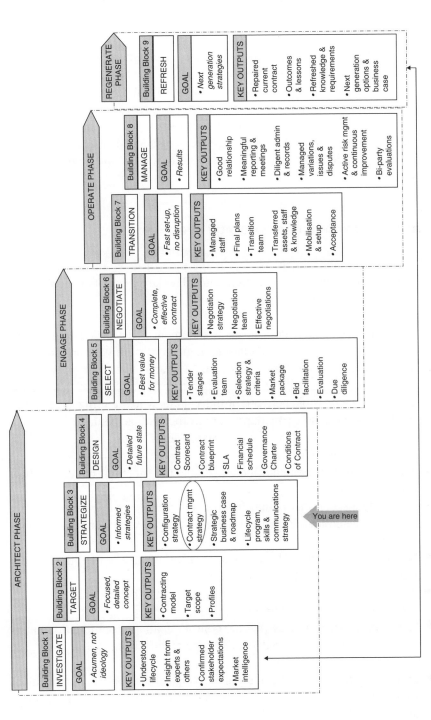

Figure 7.2 The outsourcing lifecycle

Any organization is in a superior position if it develops the contract/ provider management strategy early in the outsourcing lifecycle[2] as shown in Figure 7.2.

The greatest payoff from such contract management investment (note: contract management is an *investment* in getting the benefits sought from a contract while keeping the risks under control – not a *cost*), comes when a client prepare its contract management strategy prior, or as part of, preparing the contract as shown in Figure 7.2. In this way, as client, you are able to decide the way you want to manage the contract and design the contract accordingly, rather than hoping whatever is written is able to be managed effectively.

Contract management strategy overview

The contract management strategy is the plan of how you as client want to manage your outsourcing agreement/s. The key elements which will be discussed in this chapter are:

- The contract management mission statement – the articulation of the ultimate goals of successful contract management in your organization.
- The contract management network – management of outsourcing arrangements is rarely the sole domain of one person, and this section discusses the possible network of individuals who are utilized as appropriate, based on the particular nature of the arrangement.
- The skills set – the diversity of competencies required to successfully manage the contract.
- The contract management function – what the function is to do and how it will be structured.
- The budget – contract management is an area that can be significantly under-budgeted for, so this section provides you with some useful planning data.
- Key protocols – internal protocols, or rules, involve notifications, communications, consultations, and approvals.
- Key dates and milestones – both parties must deliver things to each other and this section maps out these milestones.
- Reporting – the reporting that the contract management function needs to provide to its stakeholders (the reports due from the provider are specified in the contract).
- Meetings – focused on the internal meetings of the contract management function itself and those with the stakeholders (the inter-party meetings are specified in the contract).

- Auditing the provider – the approach to ensuring appropriate internal controls, compliance with the contract, and accuracy of key calculations.
- Reviewing performance of the provider – the approach and topics used to determine how well they are performing.
- Internal reviews – the approach and topics used to determine how well your organization is performing.
- Administration, documentation, and recordkeeping – specifying the evidential requirements of your arrangement.
- Planning and continuous improvement – identifying how you will keep the deal evolving.
- Ongoing risk assessment – the process for reviewing and updating the initial risk assessment and mitigation strategies.
- Relationship management – deciding if you will be power-orientated or partnering-orientated.
- Rights plan – the confidential plan regarding your rights that you really intend to use.

Contract management mission (or purpose) statement

A contract management strategy needs to identify firstly the ultimate aims of contract management in the client organization. Then, as client, your entire strategy can be built around these core 'values'. Examples of goals in a mission or purpose statement include:

- appropriate processes and skills are in place;
- both parties fulfill their obligations;
- the desired outcomes of the deal are met;
- value for money is continuously demonstrated;
- risks are identified and mitigated (e.g., financial, legal, technical, operational, reputational); and
- the deal and contractual documents are amended as the requirements and/or practices evolve.

Contract management network

Participation in the management of outsourcing arrangements is rarely the sole domain of one person. There is a network of individuals who are utilized as appropriate, based on the particular nature of the arrangement and the skills present in your organization.

Figure 7.3 provides an example of a contract management network that had a single contract manager reporting to a management steering

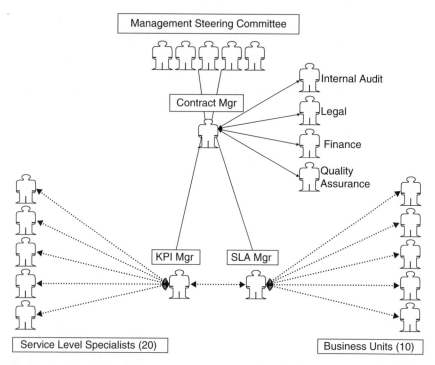

Figure 7.3 Example of a contract management network

committee. The contract manager had two direct reports, an SLA manager who managed the individual business units' SLAs, and a KPI manager that managed the KPI specialists, who in turn managed the portfolio of KPIs across all the business units. The contract manager was also the liaison with head office functions including audit, legal, finance, and quality.

Organizations tend to have their own titles for jobs within such a network particular to each organization. The key to a successful contract management in a network lies first within defining the boundaries and scope of each role, and then for each individual to conduct their responsibilities prudently. The point here is that the capability to fulfill these responsibilities should exist whatever titles are used, otherwise problems set in. There is no 'best' structure for a contract management network – each network is unique to each organization,

The contract management skill set

As Chapter 4 demonstrated, the changes required in the core competencies of the IT organization and the ability to manage outsourcing arrangements should not be underestimated. Organizational inexperience in outsourcing is the most significant problem witnessed by organizations. From then on, the majority of significant problems are usually attributed by the client to the provider (see Table 7.1 as one illustrative research finding).[3] If one thinks a little harder here, though, it just might be that indifferent provider performance is a product of poor in-house management. Too often client organizations expect too much from the provider, and not enough from themselves. In fact quite often we find that in problematic outsourcing engagements, the client will see blame lying 60–70 percent with the supplier, but when walked through events and causes, will come to recognize that the blame is more often something like 40 percent supplier and 60 percent client. What makes a significant difference is the quality of in-house contract management.

The skill set required in the contract management network to perform effective and efficient contract management can include, but is certainly not limited to:

Financial skills:

- **Accounting** – specifying financial reports, and the accounting procedures to be used by the provider, general ledger coding of goods/services, accruals for work-in-process but not yet billed, etc.
- **Cost management** – tracking, trend analyses, forecasting benchmarking, variation management, etc.
- **Pricing** – to determine the appropriate pricing model to be used, the detailed specification of each, and the request management techniques

Table 7.1 Problems in outsourcing arrangements

Most significant problems experienced	Caused by	
	Supplier (%)	Customer (%)
1 Lack of experience with outsourcing arrangements	19	60
2 Lack of understanding of your business	59	10
3 Lack of pro-activity	59	8
4 Lack of responsiveness	45	8
5 Staff expertise	42	26
6 Communication	41	33
7 Inflexibility	36	12
8 Getting different suppliers to work together	32	9
9 Staff turnover	28	9
10 Failure to meet responsibilities	27	14
11 Unreliability	14	0
12 Difficulty in applying contract penalties or sanctions	10	15
13 Distrust	10	12
14 Lack of cooperation	10	8
15 Lack of fairness	6	3

Source: Cullen et al. (2001), 78 responses

to be employed by your organization, as well as price sensitivity analysis (modeling changing scenarios and the impact on prices).

- **Invoicing and payment** – specification of invoice formats and payment terms, electronic invoicing and payment, matching of invoices to the contract, etc.
- **Tax** – to ensure the most tax effective approach to sale of assets, pricing, and billing of goods and services.
- **Insurances formation** – to ensure your organization, the contractor, and subcontractors (where applicable) have the appropriate insurances (type, coverage, amounts).
- People skills:
- **Collaborative negotiation** – creating win–win situations and solutions as opposed to win–lose styles of negotiation and blame displacement.
- **Formal communications** – strategy, techniques, and conduct within your organization and between the parties.
- **Inter-party relationship management** – to transcend adversarial styles and move toward a partnering style.
- **Interpersonal skills** – informal communications which garner mutual respect and trust.
- **Liaison/networking** – with stakeholders (internal and external).
- **Organizational behavior and change management** – planning and directing behaviors to achieve objectives.
- Process skills:
- **Administrative** – recordkeeping and control, approval processes, information distribution.
- **Performance management** – specification of KPIs and measurement formulas/data, risk/reward options, reporting, and benchmarking.
- **Planning and forecasting** – future requirements and demand scenarios, business change impacts, budgeting, etc, as well as the next generation deal.
- **Problem/issue management** – identification, tracking, and resolution.
- **Project management** – setting in place and monitoring the tasks, resourcing, and timing required to accomplish all the activities required within the contract.
- **Quality management** – industry standards, quality processes, best practices, etc.
- **Re-engineering** – restructuring internal processes and accountabilities, and if need be also those of the provider to ensure your organization's needs are met.
- **Reporting** – specification of performance, operating, and strategic reports by the provider, as well as internal reports needed by internal stakeholders.

Specialist skills:

- **Auditing** – contractual compliance, internal controls, accuracy of reporting/information/systems of both parties.
- **Commercial and legal negotiation** – strategy, conduct, and administration.
- **Contract law** – a working knowledge of all key areas including formation, estoppel, remedy, and termination.
- **Risk management** – identification, probability/impact determinations, mitigation strategies, and monitoring.
- **Technical skills** – in the goods and/or services being provided to scope and accept work/products.

The skills your organization will need are probably much greater than originally envisioned when signing a deal. Chapter 4 delineated nine key retained capabilities, and one danger is to believe that these can be performed by one person called a 'contract manager' or a small group of people called a contract management function. While this may work in a small outsourcing arrangement, it is clear in outsourcing arrangements that the nine retained capabilities represent the minimum requirement if the client is going to maintain control over outsourcing direction and performance. Many 'first generation' (first time outsourcing) organizations assume that once the contract is signed, all the hard work is done. As Chapter 4 detailed, it is actually when the hard work starts. The important thing is to identify what skills your organization will need and when, and develop the contract management network so that these skills are present. In terms of Chapter 4 what we are here calling contract management will lie mainly within the informed buying and contract monitoring capabilities.

The contract management function

The only consistency between organizations regarding the contract management network is to have an individual accountable for the success of each contract. This person often carries the title of contract manager, but other terms such as contract officer, contract superintendent, and contract supervisor are also common. The contract manager (or equivalent) is the hub of the contract management network for the contracts under his/her control.

Accordingly, the contract management function should act with:

- a working knowledge of the multitude of skills required to manage the arrangement in totality, then utilize other's skills as appropriate;

- due care and diligence – never leave your organization exposed;
- authority that is clear to all relevant stakeholders;
- a strategic and holistic perspective – outsourcing is a means to achieve goals, not an end itself; and
- detailed understanding of how the provider operates.

The contract manager role, itself, involves much more than merely administering the contract – it must ensure the arrangement achieves its strategic, financial, and tactical objectives while minimizing risks. The basic responsibility is to manage the efficiency and effectiveness of the relationship, processes, and performance in a systematic manner while ensuring your organization is prepared for and protected against unforeseen circumstances.

Accordingly, the contract manager should be appointed to manage all aspects of the arrangement, be involved as early as possible in the outsourcing lifecycle, and must be appropriately trained, empowered, and briefed in regards to her/his obligations. However, this is not always the case, particularly if such responsibilities are not part of their job description, is not part of their performance reviews, or if they do not have the skills or understanding necessary as illustrated by the following case.

Case: A hospital plans well, but drops the ball after contract signed

The outsourcing contract was thoughtfully prepared with ongoing contract management requirements in mind. It had clear responsibilities and performance measures, specified a variety of regular meetings with respective attendees and agendas, and detailed a comprehensive reporting regime. After the contract was signed by the parties, management assigned it to an employee who had no job specifications, training, or experience in contract management with the instructions to 'administer this'. She diligently rubber-stamped every invoice. Not one performance review took place, or meeting, and contractor reports were never opened, let alone reviewed, as she did not know what to review for.

In many cases, the contract manager handles the strategic and administrative aspects of the arrangement while utilizing others as part of the contract management network such as technical experts and lead users to perform distinct tasks. The appropriate processes and people depend

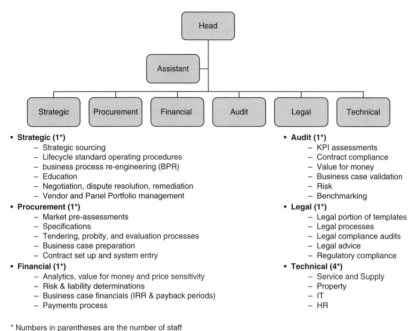

Figure 7.4 Sample contract management function

on the skill set available within your organization, compared to what is required, and the cost/benefit of using external experts.

In a complex environment, the contract management responsibilities might be spread among a dedicated group as opposed to residing with an individual. An example of a small function of this type is shown in Figure 7.4. In this example, an 11-person contract management function managed the whole-of-organization contracts, while the business units managed the individual contracts that pertained only to that business unit.

Contract management budget

Contract management is an area that can be significantly under-budgeted for, particularly when the organization cuts too deeply into its skilled work-force as a result of outsourcing. Managing contract arrangements often does not lessen the management effort required, merely changes the emphasis.

A Cutter Consortium study of 73 organizations in 26 countries across the globe representing 877 outsourcing contracts indicated that, on average, 12.5 percent of the per annum value of the contract is spent on managing the contract.[4] However, this figure does not take into account whether the contract is being managed effectively. Even though there were large standard deviations with regard to the sample, this average is a reasonable starting point for a client's budget. Interestingly, this cost shows no correlation to the number of contracts or the number of suppliers. Accordingly, one should not suppose that more contracts mean a higher overall level management costs. The true cost driver is the total amount of expenditure outsourced, not the number of contracts.

Key protocols

The purpose of this activity is to outline how the internal stakeholders within your organization are to be involved, and in what capacity, under what processes. This provides much needed clarity in and control over accountabilities, without which events, like that detailed in the example of an insurance company below, become more likely.

Case: An insurance company – lack of control resulted in high costs

A state-based insurance company that outsourced had its costs significantly blow out from the previous year. After a brief analysis, the root cause was determined to be the lack of control over the relationship. Anyone in either organization could contact anyone in the other party. Thus, staff were requesting and getting many more services than were provided for in the contract and the provider never said no. In fact, the provider quickly realized it could offer many services and the organization's staff would never say no.

Internal protocols, or rules, involve notifications, communications, consultations, and approvals. There are many items requiring various internal protocols including:

- **Payments** – approvals of invoices, treatment of financial recourse/ reward, and the supporting detail required for payment.
- **Work requests** – particularly for 'out-of-scope' work in order to manage uncontrolled scope creep (as demonstrated by the previous case).
- **Deliverable acceptance** – who needs to be involved in testing/inspection, who approves, and the documentation process to be followed.

- **Notifications** – who needs to be notified of what (i.e., legal if there is a request to vary the conditions of contract)
- **Disputes** – who needs to be involved (in a consultation and/or escalation capacity), as well as the documentation process.
- **Variations** – who needs to be involved (in a consultation and/or approval capacity) in approving variation direction/requests to and from the provider, as well as the documentation process. These were all missing in the case shown below.

Case: Unmanaged 'scope creep' in a bank

As can be typical in a major ERP implementation, a bank suffered immeasurable scope creep driven by the numerous variations raised nearly daily. Eventually, the ERP project blew out from AUD$200 million to $800 million with only one module implemented in a test site. The bank called in an independent party to review how this was allowed to occur. At the end of the day, the bank's personnel did request the changes, formally and informally, and the provider put them into the project, with neither party acting as a 'devil's advocate'. Eventually the project was brought back in-house and scaled down after both parties filed suits and the media generated much negative publicity.

Key dates and milestones

Imagine that you are the provider. You walk into the client's contract management office and there is a very large Gantt chart on the back wall. In that Gantt chart, all the deliverables due from the provider throughout the initial term of the contract are marked as red milestones and all those due from the client to the provider as blue milestones. This is obviously a diligent client who knows what is due to whom and when. The team is going to have to work harder and it is probably worthwhile to ask for a copy.

Accordingly, while mapping the key dates and milestones has a direct benefit to you in that you know what is due to whom and when, it also often provokes more conscientious behavior from your providers. Of course, these items must be specified in your contract, or neither party is legally obligated to comply. While there is some software available for this, you probably already have what you need on your computer (either MS Project™ or MS Excel™)·

The type of key dates and milestones to consider putting in your contract Gantt chart includes the due dates for:

- annual certificates (i.e., ISO, insurances, etc)
- audits
- forecasts and budgets
- key meetings
- reports
- reviews
- update of plans (i.e., asset refresh, annual work program, exit plan, etc), and
- work deliverables.

Reporting

Reports serve as analysis summary tools, evidencing the degree of success of the arrangement, providing key performance and operational indices, and identifying areas for improvement. There are a variety of reports prepared throughout the life of an outsourcing arrangement. The ones that the provider is to prepare are typically specified in the SLA. The contract management function will undoubtedly need to prepare numerous internal reports as well.

The main categories of reports and examples of the type of information presented include:

- **Strategic reports** – trend analysis regarding performance, capacity, volumes, etc;
- **Financial reports** – past and projected spend (both capital and operating), allocation to business units (chargeback), analysis of general ledger codes, and variations;
- **Performance reports** – each KPI agreed, the actual level achieved, the variance between them, and any resultant recourse/reward;
- **Operating reports** – the statistics necessary to keep abreast of what is happening operationally, for example, in workload, volumes of transactions, number of hours worked, etc;
- **Progress reports** – updating your organization on the status of work in progress, projects, the continuous improvement agenda, etc.

The design of the reporting framework is part of the contract management strategy, as the client organization is in the best position to establish the reporting mechanisms before outsourcing, not after. In many cases, needed reports require information that neither the organization nor the provider currently collect data for. Or worse still, the required reports never make it into the specification, as in the case below.

Case: No reports specified, so none provided

A law enforcement agency wanted to re-tender its helpdesk. The contract was only a one-year deal created to reduce head count (staff numbers) at the force. No reporting was specified in the agreement, thus none was done. When the client requested detailed operational reports with which to go to market, the provider stated it was not obligated to provide such reports, and in any event, because the helpdesk did not use an IVR system to save money, such information was not available.

Meetings

Receiving and reviewing reports are not sufficient in themselves. Face-to-face communication with stakeholders (as well as the provider, however this is specified in the contract) is required of any reasonably large, complex, or strategic outsourcing deal. The meetings framework is part of the contract management strategy to establish the interpersonal communication and problem-solving mechanisms and the required participation of the contract management network before outsourcing, not as an afterthought. Of course, specifying meetings is not enough, as one must also ensure specifications are carried out, as the following case exemplifies.

Case: The meeting plan stays unimplemented

A government agency had put substantial effort into defining the meetings that would take place. However, there was one oversight. No party was assigned the role of organizing the meetings – therefore, both parties expected the other party to do it. Neither did. As a result, the meetings were not held. It was not until an independent government auditor wanted to see the minutes of meetings that the current contract manager at the client, the third in three years, even knew the meetings were detailed in the contract.

The inter-party meetings are specified in the Governance Charter. Thus, what the contract management strategy focuses on are the internal meetings which may include:

- **With internal clients** – capacity/requirements planning, satisfaction assessments, process improvement brainstorming;
- **With management** – financial and performance results and plans;
- **With finance** – budgeting, chargeback review, satisfaction with invoicing;
- **With human resources** – team education and development planning, individual performance reviews; and
- **Within the contract management function** – health of interpersonal relationship assessment with colleagues at the provider, development goals, process improvements, period Strengths, Weaknesses, Opportunities, and Threats (SWOTs).

While a structured communication and meeting approach will serve any organization well, the degree of communication, frequency of meetings, and seniority of attendees that will be required to successfully manage the client-provider arrangements will ultimately depend on:

- the maturity of the arrangement;
- whether KPIs are being met;
- the commercial value of arrangement;
- how close the contract is up for renewal;
- the degree of potential changes to either party's business;
- the degree of proposed changes to the services; and
- the nature, number, and importance of projects in process.

Auditing the provider

The auditing role of the contract management function is not to supervise directly the provider's work or to interfere in the work method practices it adopts, but to assess whether it produced and complied with the requirements in the contract. Actual practice is never guaranteed by virtue of a contract alone as the following case highlights. It is important to understand the contract might merely provide some recourse or remedy in the event of failure (assuming your organization is not in breach as well – then the result is simply a mud fight).

Case: No oversight affects compliance

A government organization assumed that compliance with the contract was a foregone conclusion, so no oversight of the outsourcing contract was required. Thus, it handed oversight over to a low-level contract administrator and did not perform any compliance reviews until four years into the five-year contract. At that point, it hired an independent audit firm to evaluate the situation.

After an extensive process, the auditors determined that the provider was only 40 percent compliant with the contract. Work totaling $200,000 a year had not been performed, many KPIs were not being reported, many reports were not being generated, and the list went on. The provider noted that it had not done the work because the contract required the client to request the work, which it had not done (even though it paid for the work). Furthermore, the client did not follow up on KPIs or request missing reports, did not ask for performance review or planning forums, and so on. The key finding of the audit report was that the client did not install any governance over the contract, so the provider was allowed almost complete discretion in what it did.

As a result of this audit, and to better manage its next-generation deal, the government organization put in place a seven-person contract management team, led by a senior contract manager. This contract-management function cost $360,000 a year, but it was required to ensure savings of $830,000 a year through specific contract-management activities, experienced personnel, and pro-active management.

Audits over a provider's operations can be complicated by the presence of other customers and their privacy rights, the complexity of the provider's environment(s), and your audit rights (or lack thereof) in the contract.

For example, if you want to conduct surprise audits, you will need to have that right specified in the contract. If you want access to the provider's site and your records, you will need that right. If you want assistance at no additional charge, or for a specific charge, that will need to be specified. If you expect the provider to conduct audits, you will need to specific what audits, how often, the scope, and audit techniques (i.e., sampling). Until you plan your audit approach here in the contract management strategy, it is unlikely that you have really thought about it, which also makes it unlikely that the contract has the 'right rights' in it.

Many of the audit tasks are similar across organizations and having each client organization perform its own audits is expensive for everyone involved, and can be quite disruptive to the provider's operations.

For this reason, many providers commission an independent auditor to prepare an audit report for their clients. However, caution is required when using these reports. Many state that 'nothing came to our attention' during the auditor's review, but do not state what was actually audited. You should not derive any comfort from an external financial audit (which is designed to test compliance with accounting rules) that a data centre is secure. Inevitably, nothing you care about would come under the review. This is why the *US Statement of Auditing Standards (SAS) 70* is the de facto global standard regarding independent audits on internal controls at service organization. A SAS70 compliant audit is the minimum audit that should be done in instances where the provider is engaging the auditors. Nonetheless, make sure you get the audit objectives and program to ensure it meets your organizations expectations and requirements.[5]

Alternatively, you may want the provider to facilitate the formation of a 'User Group Auditing Authority' comprising representatives from participating organizations, the provider and all the parties' auditors (internal and external auditors). This Authority establishes audit priorities and programs, and employs independent auditors to conduct one audit on behalf of all the participating organizations. In addition to the economies of scale this provides, it also provides economies of scope in that specialist expertise can be obtained which may not have been cost-effective for each organization acting on its own.

There are two types of audits that you will need to do yourself: (1) compliance with your contract and (2) calculations of invoices and KPIs.

1. Compliance – Compliance audits of the provider's performance are critical to ensuring your organization is obtaining what it is paying for, particularly because the 'check and act' function of contract management replaces the direct control over staff that your organization had under insourcing.

Many organizations assume that if an obligation has been stated in a contract, that the provider will comply with it and no further work needs to be done. However, astute organizations do not assume compliance, they ensure it. The time to discover the provider has not done so is not when your organization is seeking to invoke the clause, as the next case illustrates.

Case: An applications contractor goes under

An application development and support contractor went bankrupt and discontinued operations. Under its standard outsourcing agreement signed with a number of customers, it was required to maintain source code and documentation in escrow. Furthermore it was to ensure that its software licenses were transferable in the event of insolvency. It had done none of these things. Development customers had to start applications over from scratch and support customers were forced to run applications that could not be modified without unacceptable risk.

Typical clauses that require periodic compliance audits to ensure the obligation is being done include (and this is only an indicative list of items, a comprehensive list can be 20 pages long):

- bank financial guarantees – existence, amounts, and provisions;
- confidentiality and security procedures – comply with the contract and/ or ISO or other standards;
- data backup and storage – are conducted as specified;
- disaster recovery planning and testing – includes the client's data, not just sample data from other clients;
- employment conditions for transferred staff – match the requirements specified in any negotiated transfer conditions;
- escrow – the items to be placed in escrow have been done so and the escrow agreement is one that reflects the requirements specified in the outsourcing contract;
- insurance – public liability, professional indemnity, occupational health and safety, and others is in effect for the period, amounts, and conditions meets the requirements specified;
- license transfer options – that any software and hardware licenses have novation and assignment, in particular related to termination of the outsourcing agreement;
- performance guarantees – that the guarantee has been signed by the appropriate parties and has the terms and conditions reflecting the specification in the outsourcing contract;
- recordkeeping – checking that whatever is supposed to have been kept has been;
- staff certifications, qualifications, and training – ensuring appropriate staff are doing the work;

- subcontractor agreements – including ensuring the back-to-back provisions (the clauses that are supposed to be carried into subcontracts such as intellectual property rights, insurances, confidentiality, etc) and additional provisions (such as seeking redress from only the contractor and not the client, allowing assignment to the client, and having a expiry date the same as the head contract) have in fact been put into subcontractor contracts;

The timing of the compliance audits is also important. If an audit is done at the end of the contract, there will be little you can do in terms of corrective action that yields a good return on your audit investment – as the following case illustrates.

Case: A homewares' manufacturer leaves it too late

In this case, like most outsourcing arrangements, performance reports were to be provided by the provider and the detailed reporting requirements were specified in the SLA. An end-of-contract audit found that the provider was only reporting two-thirds of what they had agreed to. Unfortunately, this reconciliation of actual practice to contractual requirements took place near the end of the contract and the data had never been collected by the provider, thus the information was unattainable. The provider agreed to report in full compliance for the remaining six months of the contract, a poor substitute for full compliance.

---

2. Calculations of charges and KPIs by the provider.

Verifying that charges are valid is another core function of contract management. While each invoice is typically reviewed by the contract manager or designated personnel prior to payment, the source data used to bill should be audited periodically or assessed prior to payment by an appropriately skilled person. The more complex and variable the price structure is, the more auditing that may need to be performed. The following case illustrates the importance of checking calculation of charges.

Case: An insurance company checks the bills

Just for assurance, a Contract Manager decided to use a redeployed systems programmer, who had a bit of spare time on his hands, to review mainframe CPU processing consumption and related billing. The programmer obtained recent source data and discovered two very costly practices had been allowed to occur. First, the wrong times for peak and off peak usage were being used by the provider, and second batch programs were being run at more expensive peak times if the provider had spare capacity during those times (rather than at the specified non-peak periods). How long this had been occurring was anyone's guess – old source data had long been deleted.

Regarding KPIs, the provider typically prepares performance reports. Beyond the fact that providers have an inherent aim to present results in the most favorable light; reports can be in error accidentally or produced from inappropriate sources. Periodic audits of the source data used in performance reporting will insure that your organization is obtaining the levels it purchased.

How often you might need to perform compliance and/or calculations audits will depend, of course, on the complexity, value, and significance of your contract. However, you certainly need to perform your first ones as early in the first term as practical.

Evaluating performance of the provider

Reviews focused on the provider include, but are by no means limited to:

- financial and service performance relative to the agreement, but also relative to industry norms;
- continuous improvement initiatives implemented; and
- user and other stakeholder satisfaction with services.

Performance reviews are often subjective, and that is perfectly fine when given in the spirit of helping the provider to improve as opposed to inflicting punitive damages. If the intent is to penalize the provider, the performance assessment needs to be objective, detailed, have supporting evidence, and allow for the provider to give rebuttal evidence as well. Performance reviews of the latter nature tend to quickly move away from performance and focus on the nature of the evidence, and this can give rise to disputes. For this reason, an 'observations and suggestions for improvement' oriented process yields better operational results.

In addition, while most organizations perform some form of benchmarking as part of the letting of a contract, prudent contract management continues this process throughout the life of the agreement, comparing what you are getting to what others are getting in terms of performance and value for money. Benchmarking can be a difficult and expensive process regardless of how services are sourced, internally or externally.

Internal reviews

Contract management involves reviewing not only the provider's performance but also your own client organization's management effectiveness. The uneconomic, inefficient, and ineffective use of IT, whether the service is provided internally or otherwise, will inhibit an organization's ability to achieve its objectives. The greatest efficiency and effectiveness gains are often in how your organization plans for and uses the provider's resources.

Internally focused reviews include:

- progress toward the achievement of contract objectives;
- the degree to which your organization is meeting its obligations to the provider;
- efficient use of the provider's resources (i.e., use of non-peak windows, extraneous labor, ad hoc services);
- the effectiveness of the contract management function and network; and
- improvement initiatives implemented.

In our audits of contract management functions, we have found some alarming issues. A very common finding is that the majority of contract managers had never read the contracts they are managing, preferring to merely react to operational issues. This was typically because they did not have the time to do so, or felt that 'that's the lawyer's job'. Even more disturbing findings include a contract management function that believed they needed to 'earn' penalties from the providers at least equal to the group's salary to justify their existence and be 'self-funding'; a contract manager that did not know what her role was and didn't understand the contract, thus rubber-stamped the invoices without any verification; a contract manager that never reviewed any of the KPIs and by contract end only 40 percent were being reported upon; a contract management function that delighted in the provider's failings, (and called themselves the 'toe-cutters'), and would celebrate when a supplier went bust under their contracts because 'getting a price under cost is what we're all about'. All of these result in higher prices, higher risks, and worse results.

Administration, documentation, and record-keeping

One of the main functions of contract administration is to have a systematic repository and log of records and decisions. Maintaining diligent administration provides an efficient reference system and audit trail should any aspect of the arrangement be called into question by either party or an external body (i.e., a regulator).

Examples of the items requiring such diligent control include:

- agendas and minutes of meetings – particularly where decisions have been reached or implied agreements may have been made;
- all financial data – including bills and quotes;
- approvals and signoffs – as evidence that it actually occurred;
- audit reports and findings – noting compliance, defects, and proposed rectification;
- correspondence and discussions between the parties – particularly where decisions have been reached or implied agreements may have been made;
- customer satisfaction surveys – particularly to track history and provide information for improvement initiatives;
- governing documents and variations – as the primary source of the parties' understandings;
- issue logs – to track the history of issues and the resolutions;
- precursor documents (request for tenders, bids, etc) – should the intent of aspects of the agreement need to be referred to; and
- reports – performance, progress, audit, etc.

One of the core document administration functions is to ensure that results of renegotiations, the outcomes of resolved issues, and current practices are reflected in the governing documents. Variations are a natural occurrence – taking place continuously in procedure manuals, frequently in SLAs and occasionally in the conditions of contract. A formal process for issuing and tracking variation requests and resolutions is a core component of good governance. The advantages of good documentation variations are illustrated in the two cases below.

Case: Change in account manager changes everything

The contract had been running for a year when the provider changed account managers. The new account manager immediately started to change services and cut some out entirely. All her actions were in complete alignment with the originally agreed contract. However, early discussions between the parties had developed and agreed to the current practices. The contract manager had documented all discussions and was able to produce evidence. All services were re-instated and both managers then made appropriate variations to the governing documents.

Case: Variations on variations become unmanageable

A fourth generation maintenance contract (that is, a contract in its fourth term) had one binder for the contract and three binders for the agreed variations. The variations evidence included in those three binders included copies of emails, correspondence, and on occasion, a signed variation agreement. However, it was nearly impossible to know the current state of the conditions of contract, as many of the variations related to previous variations, but none of the documents were cross-referenced. Inevitably, the parties agreed to re-write and sign the contract.

Documentation is critical in that it captures discussions, provides evidence of commitments and changes, assists in resolution of disputes, can be used as evidence during any legal proceedings, and captures the history of the arrangement. Undocumented undertakings become very difficult for either party to manage, as in the case below.

Case: Undocumented undertakings

This case, involving an international airline, highlights a common problem when documentation is scarce. In this case, stakeholder satisfaction surveys were yielding poor results and there was a general feeling of adversity with the provider of the IT support services (LANs, desktop fleet management, and help desk). Yet, the KPIs were showing reasonable performance, certainly of a standard that did not warrant the animosity exhibited. A root cause analysis determined that the major contributing factor was that both the provider's sales staff and the operational staff were making unwritten 'promises' to various client personnel, few of which were followed up on. Neither

party maintained records of the discussions and correspondence leading to the client now having certain expectations (access to global
research, technical briefings, facilitation of special interest groups, to
name a few). Once the provider harvested all the unrecorded expectations, it realized it could not meet these expectations and keep within
its profit margins. It instituted a 'no promises unless supported with a
variation' procedure instead.

Planning and continuous improvement

As mentioned in the Introduction, planning is an ongoing part of the
contract management function. Not only does the function need to constantly be forecasting the demand for the provider's goods and/or services and the capacity requirements, but also changes to the business
requirements that may impact the arrangement – increasing scope, reducing volumes, even requiring termination for convenience due to mergers
and acquisitions.

Most organizations adopt the concept of continuous improvement over
their outsourcing arrangements in the planning area. In line with this
concept, both parties' staff are expected to find ways to improve the performance of the activities they are responsible for. Good contract management allows for flexibility, opportunity, and scope for the provider to
be smart and improve the way the work is being done; but at the same
time ensuring that it does what it has contractually agreed to do. This
has become of such importance that many organizations now make it
a contractual requirement over the provider to put forward regular new
work practice concepts, complete with accompanying risk assessment and
business case.

Case: A deal motivating the provider not to improve

An insurance company found out that providers might not routinely
put in a continuous improvement process, particularly when under a
fixed price with little margin. In this case, by the end of the seven-year
contract, the entire IT infrastructure and related practices were obsolete and effectively not supported anywhere in the industry (i.e., the
desktop fleet had not been changed in the seven years). The contract
had a 12.5 percent mandated annual cost reduction, capped profit,

and capped labor – all driving the provider to retain obsolete technology and prevented any improvement. The lack of a planning function in the client meant this was not addressed until the client decided to re-tender the contract.

Ongoing risk assessment

Risk assessment is a vital process in the ongoing identification and minimization of risks. In following the recommended process model, however, initial risk assessment and mitigation design was part of the Architect Phase, because your organization is in the best position to establish the mitigation mechanisms and the required participation of both parties before outsourcing, not after. Nonetheless, the plan must be periodically reviewed to ensure that the mitigation strategies are working, to incorporate new risks, and to reassess previously identified risks. Such risk assessment procedures should:

- identify events that could lead to an undesired result and estimate the potential effect that could occur if the event should occur;
- quantify the risk through a formal assessment matrix or other means to ensure that control activities are addressed on a prioritized basis; and
- identify key activities and controls based on how the event can occur that will prevent the probability of occurrence and/or minimize the effect should the event occur.

If the only risk assessment ever perform was early in the lifecycle, typically, at the business case stage (which tend to be more hypothetical than realistic), you are in real danger of missing the real risk profile of the deal.

Case: Understanding the impact of force majeure

For example, in a stock-broking firm, the client had no understanding of standard force majeure provisions that release the provider from its obligations due to uncontrollable events such as fire, flood, etc, and thus assumed the services were 'guaranteed' no matter what. For this reason, the service scope did not include any disaster recovery provisions. An external audit discovered the missing scope and management requested the provider to quote on providing disaster recovery services. The provider quoted a price that was equal to the services contract price. The client chose, instead, to set up their own recovery plan at a fraction of the price. But the opportunistic behavior by the provider damaged the relationship irreparably.

Relationship management

Recall Chapters 2 and 5. In most cases, your organization will want a balance between the two extremes of a completely power-based relationship and one based solely on trust. Extremes of either are rarely adequate for either party. Whether the relationship exhibits more power-based characteristics or more trust-based characteristics, long-term success will be dependent upon how the relationship is managed. The best contract becomes merely a weapon in a poorly functioning relationship – to be used against the other party, rather than to guide successful outcomes.

As important as the relationship is, it should not be relied upon in lieu of having proper governance in place. Relationships are between people, not organizations, and people leave organizations. If there is not a proper governance structure and procedures which exist independent of the relationship, far too much reliance can be placed on the 'unwritten understanding'. This off-the-record understanding can be difficult to evidence and also has a habit of changing over time and with different people involved. The following case hints at the sort of difficulties that can emerge if personal relationships in outsourcing are over-depended on.

Case: Short on details, long on issues

An agreement was made between two top executives, one at the company and one at the provider. It was simple enough. The provider was to take over the operations of the call center, which was its core business and the transport company could focus on its core business, logistics. Since it was a 'strategic partnership', both parties felt a short memorandum of understanding (MOU) was really all that was required. The two individuals had worked together for decades and the trust was implicit. Years down the track, after both individuals had left their particular organizations, an internal audit came up in the normal course of business. The first finding was that there was not a contract. The second, and more telling finding, was that the provider had been double billing for years. Each business unit was being charged a price per call from a standard price schedule for the allocated volume of calls and full cost recovery was being billed via the centralized accounts payable section. Neither organization could determine why this disparate billing process had occurred and the remediation process was extensive, to say the least.

Rights plan

If you have prepared the contract management strategy in the Design Building Block as recommended in this chapter, you would have also changed the contract clauses to enable you to manage the contract in the way that you want it to be managed. However, if you did not, there will be many clauses in the contract which you are unlikely to ever use. And then there are some you may need to invoke.

Many times the rights in the contract do not provide useful guidance to contract managers regarding how the provisions can be invoked and what is to happen if they are invoked. For this reason, this part of the contract management strategy examines the clauses you believe you may wish to bring into play.

In order to do this, you go through the contract highlighting the key provisions. Now assume that you are going to invoke them. Your contract is likely to only require a notice to the provider. But this does not help you with your internal processes. Who has to be involved in the exercise of this provision? Does anyone need to approve the notice prior to you sending it out? Do people have to be notified in your own organization? It is these types of internal protocols that are outlined in a 'rights plan'.

The actual operation of the right is then outlined. For example, if you believe you may need to invoke your right of termination, the plan would address the disengagement process regarding the current provider, the selection of, and hand-over to, a new provider (or alternatively, the 'back-sourcing' of the work under the contract – see Chapter 9).

By planning out the termination, and subsequent handover or backsourcing, you will inevitably discover that the contract clauses are ambiguous and do not address your requirements. For example, does the contract:

- Require a disengagement, or exit, plan from the provider containing the details of the procedures, processes, responsibilities, and obligations that arise after you give a notice of termination?
- Allow you to buy assets in use at fair market value?

- Require the provider to conduct training of the successor as directed by you?
- Allow novation or assignment of subcontracts, licenses, or other agreements?
- Vacate any on-site premises, at no additional cost, leaving the site in no less condition than when it became occupied by the supplier's staff or equipment?

Once you actually walk through a provision intending to put it into effect, then your real requirements become known as opposed to a high-level abstract 'right' that you cannot actually use. If you are preparing the contract management in the Architect Phase as recommended earlier, you now can go back and change the contract to something that will really work. If you have already signed the contract, then you need to retrospectively fix the contract and a variation is in order.

Not only do you need to have a plan to invoke and exercise the rights you believe you may need to, but also a plan regarding the possibility of the provider invoking its rights. This is best explained with an example. Let's return in more detail to the case of the stock-broking firm that had outsourced its entire IT operations, and then found out it was not covered in the event of a disaster.

The client had originally gone to the provider to confirm that it had a 'hotsite' and operations would continue as normal in the event of a disaster. However, while the provider did have such a hotsite, the client would not be covered – it had not signed up to the disaster recovery service. In the event of a disaster, the provider would, as a matter of formality, invoke the 'force majeure' clause (an uncontrollable event that releases the provider of its obligations).

The force majeure clause defined a force majeure event as

> any cause outside the party's reasonable control, including but not limited to an act of nature, insurrection, government or quasi-government act or regulation, blockade, riot, civil insurgence, act of terrorism, war, fire, explosion, lightning, industrial disputes of any kind, and epidemics or any other risks to health or safety.

It then stated that failure to perform due to a force majeure event was not a breach, 'The failure by either party to observe or perform wholly or in part any obligation (other than an obligation to pay money) under this Agreement will not be a breach of this Agreement to the extent that the failure was caused by or arose as a result of a Force Majeure Event'.

The client had no further rights. Realizing that the business was now facing a serious threat, it asked for a quote regarding the disaster recovery service. The quote was equal to the monthly fees currently being charged to run the IT operations. The client chose, instead, to set up their own recovery plan at a fraction of the price.

Had a contract management strategy been prepared and incorporated the actual management requirements for the clauses in the contract, this situation would have been discovered far before the client was in a position whereby the provider could take advantage of its superior position.

Conclusion

The changing nature of contracting means that the responsibility or management transcends the more traditionally administrative role (see Chapter 5). To manage today's contracts, a direct role must be played at a strategic and operational level to ensure value for money is achieved and risks are minimized.

The contract management strategy helps to ensure your outsourcing arrangements are intended to be managed well, and as a result, if the strategy is written in the Architect Phase of the outsourcing lifecycle, the contract will also be written to be managed well (as opposed to be written only for the courts).

Notes

1. Deming, W. E. (1982) *Quality Productivity and Competitive Position.* Massachusetts Institute of Technology, Massachusetts.
2. Cullen, S., Seddon, P. B. and Willcocks, L. P. (2005), 'Managing outsourcing: the lifecycle imperative', *MIS Quarterly Executive,* 4, 1, pp. 229–46.
3. Cullen, S., Seddon, P. B. and Willcocks, L. P. (2001) *IT Outsourcing Practices in Australia.* Deloitte, Sydney.
4. Cullen, S. (2007) 'The configuration concept: financial scale', *Sourcing and Vendor Relationships Executive Update,* Cutter Consortium, 8. 1. This figure is not far away from our own findings, as described in Chapter 4. We are finding that the cost of retained management capability, into 2010, is rising, in fact, possibly as a function of clients investing more, the extra management costs of offshoring, and because of multi-sourcing management costs, though, on the latter, there has been a shift toward supplier consolidation between 2008 and 2010.
5. Search 'SAS 70' on www.aicpa.org for further information.

CHAPTER 8

The contract scorecard: Design and measurement

Introduction

Organizations that are veterans at outsourcing know that the success of an outsourcing deal is dependent on many factors. They know it is not just the cost, but also the quality of the service that matters. They also know it's more than just getting what you pay for; it's whether the relationship between the client and the provider is rewarding or dysfunctional. Furthermore, they know that outsourcing is not an end goal in itself; rather it is a way to achieve any number of strategic goals. How does one identify and track the myriad of outcomes sought from an outsourcing deal? Organizations are now recognizing the value of applying a balanced scorecard approach to outsourcing arrangements called the contract scorecard.[1]

The contract scorecard helps the parties not only establish how the quality of the service will be evaluated, but also what the financial outcomes will be judged by, how the relationship is conducted, and if the outsourcing deal is achieving its strategic aims – in sum defining and then measuring the overall success of the deal from an holistic perspective. The contract scorecard enunciates the goals of the deal in order to guide the parties to the desired outcomes. It further articulates these goals in a measurable form, providing clear expectations as to what is driving the deal. As such, the scorecard provides a key design mechanism for guiding the detail within key governing documents as well as for selecting the right provider. It then provides a key tool for tracking, assessing, and driving the results of the deal.

We met the concept of the scorecard briefly in Chapter 2, where the focus was on relationship metrics. To aid in understanding and using the contract scorecard more fully, this chapter is organized as follows:

- Background – provides a explanation of the origin of the concept
- Perspectives – offers various perspectives from which to view and adopt metrics

- The Four Quadrants – describes each of the four attributes
- Timing in the Outsourcing Lifecycle – discusses the contract scorecard development and use in the lifecycle.

Background

Roots of the concept – the balanced scorecard

The contract scorecard takes its conceptual origins from the balanced scorecard. The balanced scorecard hit the corporate scene in the early 1990s compliments of Kaplan and Norton in a study capturing the attributes of successful US companies.[2] The success attributes were categorized as financial, internal business processes, learning and growth of staff, and customers. The balanced scorecard has since proliferated in many forms and spawned an entire consulting industry. Today, a search on Google for 'balanced scorecard' will yield approximately 2,200,000 results!

If the organization is employing a form of the balanced scorecard for its internal operations, that is well and good – if implemented properly. However, if a large portion of the organization's expenditures are paid to external parties, it may be leaving a great deal of its structure 'unscored', as in the following case.

Case: A regional bank scores only part of the picture

A fast growing regional bank had a decentralized management style, empowering staff to contract with whom, and how, each staff member saw fit. These expenditures were not systematically tracked or controlled. An insightful manager, after gaining substantial cost savings from contracts in her area, thought the techniques she employed could be useful in other contracts. Her initial guess at external spend with suppliers was approximately 30 percent of the bank's outgoings. A brief assessment of the accounts payable ledger found that the actual spend was above 50 percent. This is an amount far less than the spend on human resources. Thus, although staff, and management, are subject to extensive scorecard assessments to ensure good performance; most of the bank's expenditures did not undergo any type of evaluation. An initiative has now begun to get a contract scorecard underway.

While the balanced scorecard is a useful tool for an organization's internal operations, a different scorecard is required for the organizations' outsourced operations as a method used to design and evaluate the success of outsourcing arrangements in a holistic and balanced manner, thus encouraging organizations to think more strategically about their outsourcing deals.

The contract scorecard we describe here was developed in the study of 100 outsourcing arrangements over the last decade which categorized the key attributes in which success was sought. The result was the four quadrants you will recall from Chapter 2 (see Figures 2.11) namely (1) quality, (2) finance, (3) relationship, and (4) strategy. The detail within these quadrants will be discussed shortly. However, for those familiar with Kaplan and Norton's Balanced Scorecard wishing to know how the adapted version maps, our application of the scorecard approach to an outsourcing deal is not a direct application, per se, but a complementary one, based on our research findings.

Mapping to the balanced scorecard

The only quadrant the contract scorecard retains from the balanced scorecard is the financial quadrant. The 'customers' and 'business processes' elements are incorporated into the quality quadrant. In that quadrant, stakeholder satisfaction (customer) and effectiveness (business processes) are two of the five types of metrics discussed later in the chapter, from which the client build its definition of what quality means to the organization.

The success of the mutual relationship replaces 'staff learning and growth' as it is the well-being of the relationship between the parties that affects success, rather than the well-being of production staff as it is with internal operations. An outsourcing relationship replaces many of an organization's traditional HR assets – people, and their know-how; and becomes an asset itself (see Chapter 2).

Lastly, a new quadrant is introduced – that of strategic goals which represent business outcomes resulting from, or aligned with, the commercial relationship. Strategic goals can take many forms ranging from risk minimization such as safety, to industry development such as the use of local suppliers, to obtaining a better core focus, and many others as will be discussed later in this chapter.

Scorecard perspectives

A useful way to think about the scorecard is through the use of perspectives and that each stakeholder to an outsourcing deal will value certain attributes more than others. There are four stakeholder perspectives that an organization may adopt when assessing success using a contract scorecard.

Looking at Figure 8.1, the two perspectives that will receive primary CEO attention are the contract context and contract agenda perspectives. The 'context' perspective represents the setting surrounding how the contract is delivered (relationship + strategic) regardless of what is delivered and how much it costs. Chapter 2 focuses in more detail on the relationship component of 'context'. The 'agenda' perspective represents how the contract fits in the bigger picture (financial + strategic). Ideally, the contract not only is financially effective, but is also achieving your wider corporate goals. These wider goals are of particular interest to the CEO and senior management.

At a more operational level, the 'value for money' perspective represents what you get for your money (service quality + financial). Ideally, an organization is getting the minimum service metrics agreed to in the contract at a price that meets its financial expectations. This is the base expectation for most stakeholders, but particularly for the user business groups that receive the service and end up paying for it. The 'operations' perspective represents how the contract is conducted in practice (service quality + relationship). Ideally, the contract is being conducted such that the service outcomes are being achieved in a way that strengthens the commercial relationship and interaction (non-adversarial). This is of particular interest to stakeholders directly involved with the supplier, either as service recipients (users), part of the contract management function, or part of the retained functional organization.

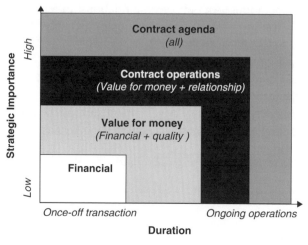

Figure 8.1 The contract scorecard: Four stakeholder perspectives

Once the decision to outsource has been made and the deal bedded down, it is easy for many to just let the deal run and manage it at a low level. However, such organizations will never know if they have gotten the outcomes and total value they wanted. For the CEO, a contract scorecard is one tool that that has proven successful, and is worth implementing. We see the scorecard concept being increasingly applied in outsourcing deals, and this growth will be accelerated with the ever developing focus on business analytics we are seeing in the organizations we research and advise.

As discussed in Chapter 2, whether an organization chooses to use a contract scorecard approach to evaluate the overall success of its outsourcing deal/s will depend upon: how actively it intends to ensure the myriad of desired outcomes are achieved and what the key stakeholders to the deal want to know on a regular basis. Figure 8.2 shows how one may choose to incrementally adopt the various perspectives depending on the strategic importance of the deal and whether it represents a single, isolated transaction or an ongoing, long-term service.

The choice of quadrants to employ in the organization's contract scorecard will be idiosyncratic to each organization and for each outsourcing deal it has. An organization can use as many or as few as are appropriate under the circumstances. For example, the only success criterion for infrequent transactions such as bulk equipment purchasing may be financial in the form of the price paid. However, as a deal becomes strategically more important and longer in duration, then one should consider using more of the scorecard incorporating speed and accuracy of equipment delivery. If the nature of the deal is to provide equipment over ten years and work with the client to specify the ongoing equipment needs of the organization, the strength of the relationship and the provider's ability to contribute to strategic goals will become increasingly important. The expectations for a

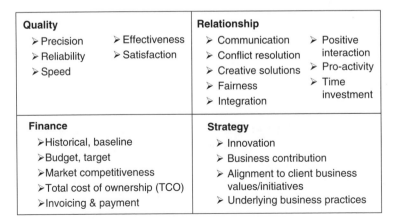

Figure 8.2 Contract scorecard – content

ten-year whole-of-IT deal, for example, will typically be more than purely financial, and success will be based on at least the value-for-money criterion if not the entire scorecard.

The four quadrants of the contract scorecard

In Chapter 2 we focused only on the relationship quadrant and its content. Figure 8.2 provides an overview of the possible contents of all four quadrants, which we will now discuss in detail.

Quality

Quality (the most frequent metric type in most outsourcing arrangements) is a key component, but not the only one of a holistic contract scorecard. Quality metrics are the operational metrics representing the key deliverables of the provider's services. The detail of the agreed quality metrics is most commonly articulated in the outsourcing arrangement's Service Level Agreement (SLA). The SLA is a schedule to the contract which is an evolved form of the more traditional statement of work or specification.

There are five types of quality metrics:

1. **Precision** – the degree to which work is error free and done in full.
2. **Reliability** – the degree to which the work is consistently dependable.
3. **Speed** – the swiftness in which the work is performed.
4. **Effectiveness** – the degree to which an end result is achieved that is outcome-focused as opposed to process-focused.
5. **Satisfaction** – the degree that users, customers, or other stakeholders are pleased with the work.

Table 8.1 gives examples of the Key Performance Indicators (KPIs) one might find in each of the five types of quality metrics.

Precision measurements seek to quantify the degree to which the work was performed accurately and in compliance with the rules set up under the contract. Specification-related performance measures typically begin with an assessment as to whether the work was conducted, or the product delivered, or the asset built, in accordance with the specification, statement of work, or to a specified standard.

Reliability measurements seek to quantify the degree to which you are able to rely on the work. The degree to which deadlines are met is important in many time-driven organizations that need certain things done by a certain time or date. For example, a program of work that has a series

Table 8.1 Quality KPI types

Precision	Reliability	Speed	Effectiveness	Satisfaction
• accuracy/ error rates • compliance to standards • fit to specification • completeness of work	• deadlines • availability • abandon rates • failure/fault rate • rework • shrinkage • recalls	• response rates • resolution/ rectification time • cycle time • queue time • processing time • volumes/ throughput • turnaround time • backlog clearing	• utilization • vacancy levels • call reduction • customer retention/ return rates • sales	• end users, • external customers • other stakeholders

of milestones would specify the due date of each and have a measurement regarding the percent of milestones meeting the due dates. Another common reliability-based KPI is an obligation regarding the minimum required availability of staff and/or systems, possibly with different availability requirements during working hours versus non-working hours. With regard to systems, this is measured in terms of *minimum scheduled uptime* (or the opposite, *maximum unscheduled downtime*).

Speed measurements seek to quantify how fast the provider does something for the client. As with all quality KPIs, this can be measured in many ways depending on what you want. In most contracts that have a service component, there would be a measurement regarding the response and resolution rates of the provider in responding to calls, faults, problems, and the like.

Effectiveness measurements seek to quantify an end-result that is important to the client's business. These measurements have a direct impact on the business activities. For example, two effectiveness measures of a help-desk are to record: (1) a reduction in repetitive/recurrent calls, and (2) the 'first-call resolution rate' (the percent of calls resolved by the helpdesk operator at the time of the call. In the case of the former, a business saves money if there are fewer calls to a helpdesk, thus requiring fewer operators. In the case of the latter, that of the first call resolution rate, it aims to minimize the total time that the caller needs to invest in getting the issue resolved and thus increase productivity.

Satisfaction is a 'soft' measurement of quality. This is because these are opinion-based measure (based on perceptions) as opposed to the earlier 'hard' measurements that are fact-based (based on systemic independent evidence). Any organization will find it quite insightful to examine the trend of perception versus fact with regards to their contracts, and to assure themselves that they are measuring what is important, that everyone has realistic expectations and that no tradeoffs are occurring that were not intended.

Financial

Financial metrics are the monetary metrics most commonly comparing amounts paid to the provider to different fiscal points or comparatives. These fiscal points can include past periods such as last month, baseline costs under previous service delivery regimes such as in-sourcing or to a previous supplier, and current market rates often established through benchmarking. Another type of financial metric can assess the impact of contract performance on the overall costs to the organization, known as total cost of ownership (TCO) or its variants (total cost of asset, total costs of supply/production, etc).

There are five types of financial metrics:

1. **Historical** – current cost compared to previous periods (i.e., last month, last year) or a baseline (typically against the cost when the services were in-sourced, or when performed by an earlier supplier).
2. **Budget/target** – current cost compared to planned or targeted expenditure (often both against the original budget as well as revised budgets as appropriate).
3. **Market** – current cost compared to current market rates (typically assessed through some form of benchmarking).
4. **TCO** – impact (either reducing or escalating) the entire supply chain, total asset or total technology costs.
5. **Invoicing and payment** – degree to which the payment cycle is effective.

Table 8.2 gives examples of the KPIs one might find in each of the types of financial metrics.

The financial metrics are also incorporated into the contract documents, most commonly as part of the pricing schedule. In that schedule, for example, an organization may, along with the quoted prices, set a KPI for reducing the level of reimbursable expenditures by 5 percent per annum or keeping to +/– 5 percent of the budget.

Should a market rate comparative be desired, it is most commonly performed through benchmarking. The processes around what metrics will be benchmarked, by whom, how, when, and what will be done with the results tends to be written up in the price schedule. However, it is quite

Table 8.2 Financial KPI types

Historical	Budget/ target	Market	TCO
Maintain costs to a percentage under historical baseline	Percentage goal under/over budget	• No less than a specified percent of agreed benchmark	• Portion of total cost represented by the contract
Ongoing reduction each year or a limited increase such as CPI (Consumer Price Index)	Within a percentage of agreed target figure	• Within a specified quartile of the benchmarking sample	• Impact of contract performance on downstream processes/ asset life

common for those that employ sophisticated benchmarking techniques to have benchmarking as a separate contract schedule so that it is easily distributed to those performing and evaluating the benchmarking. There is a cautionary note about benchmarking between contracts. It is a bit more difficult than benchmarking between internal operations, as one must consider unique constraints put over each contract that lessens benchmarking comparability (e.g., insurances, liability levels, warranties) to get at 'apples to apples' comparison.

Only a few organizations have sophisticated enough data collection to assess the impact of the contract on the total cost of ownership, supply chain, and/or asset. Those that do will often have the financial metrics, calculation techniques, and effect of results, specified in a separate contract schedule as well. Total cost to the organization, not just monies paid to the provider are well worth considering, as the following case highlights.

Case: A major retailer goes for lowest price/highest overall cost

The IT department of a retailing company had recently been transferred under the Corporate Services division that had a general manager with a background in procurement. It was her belief that commodity functions should be outsourced so that the division could focus on adding value to the operational business units. She targeted the 'commodity' IT services and went to tender for the IT data center operations, charging $500 to potential bidders to receive the RFT to 'weed out non-contenders'. The emphasis was placed on the price as she believed the services, and service providers themselves, were undifferentiated. Accordingly, the lowest priced bid was awarded the contract rather than any sort of total value for money assessment. This bid was 30 percent below the nearest bid.

Things began to go awry very quickly. Variations were the norm; in fact a person within the retailer had to be dedicated to variation management. Quality KPIs, set up as targets and not as minimum standards in the contract, were rarely achieved as there was no incentive to meet the targets, nor was there recourse if the targets were not met. In addition, the service provider had capped the number of resources they would provide in the contract and the general manager had to hire specialists to work in the data center to raise service levels back to what they had been. Within a year, the total costs were higher than the highest bid, higher than the in-house baseline and the division's remaining IT people were focused on firefighting, not adding value.

Invoicing and payment measurements are primarily designed to motivate the provider to bill accurately and on time. Contrary to the beliefs held in some quarters, client organizations really do want providers' invoices on time, so that their accounting staff can close out accounts and/or projects. Very few organizations actually look forward to receiving surprise invoices when the books have been closed. Many clients have reporting getting invoices years after the work has been performed. It is also imperative for all kinds of organizations that they get invoices on time for budget purposes.

Relationship

We have already met this part of the scorecard in Chapter 2. Getting the right values and cultures between the parties is often one of the most difficult aspects of an outsourcing agreement. One natural instinct is to make sure there is a watertight contract – so that the provider cannot re-interpret or escape; one that the organization intends to impose to every last detail.

One must, however, be clear that poor or onerous contracts can severely damage commercial relationships. The contract is a clear fail-safe device, there to be used, but one finds that in practice it cannot predict and cover every eventuality and that active relationship management on both sides is what sustains effective outsourcing performance. Poor contracts can make for poor relationships, if one is not careful.

Case: A manufacturer creates a lose–lose situation

One manufacturing client agreed to a contract clause stipulating that 'all costs of transfer of software licensing agreements will be borne by the client'. The first few transfers cost relatively little, but the next ten virtually eliminated the client's cost savings from the five-year deal. The service provider knew that it was a standard clause that he needed in the contract if he was to make any money at all. The client felt that he had been duped. The two sides then proceeded to beat each other up over every ambiguous clause they could find for the rest of the contract's duration in an attempt to claw money back from each other.

As established in Chapter 2, the contract is an important but relatively superficial driver of day-to-day behavior. The true behavior drivers are the underlying values held by the individual parties and the people involved in the agreement. Organizations that desire effective relationships set up and measure the relationship through KPIs representing the desired values.

In business-to-business arrangements, the well-being of the relationship between the parties has been shown in many studies to affect success.[3] A relationship need not be an inadvertent effect of a contract; rather, it can, and should, be a key part of the overall strategy.

Relationship KPIs measure behaviors exhibited by one party, in the eyes of the other. This is a 'soft' metric, in that the parties agree that the measurement is concerning the *opinion and perceptions* of the other party, and they are entitled to their opinion.

As discussed in Chapter 2, the typical types of relationship metrics include:

1. **Communication** – the degree that the parties communicate frequently and honestly.
2. **Creative solutions** – the degree that the parties continuously search for better ways of doing things.
3. **Conflict resolution** – the degree that the focus is on solving problems, not apportioning blame.
4. **Fairness** – the degree that the parties act fairly toward each other.
5. **Integration** – the degree that the services value chain appears seamless to the end customer.
6. **Positive interaction** – the degree that the parties enjoy working together and have respect for one another.
7. **Pro-activity** – the degree that the parties are pro-active to each other.
8. **Time investment** – the degree that the parties provide management time and focus for each other.

Table 8.3 gives more detailed examples of the KPIs one might find in each of the types of relationship metrics.

Table 8.3 Relationship KPI types

Communication	Conflict resolution	Creative solutions	Fairness
• Frequency • Openness • Correct method and protocol	• Problem solving focus • Collaborative style • No blaming, no abdication • Personality independent	• Idea generation • Continuous improvement mindset	• Empathy to other party • Win–win mentality

Integration	Interaction	Pro-activity	Time investment
• Seamless supply chain • End-to-end focus	• Enjoy working together • Display mutual respect • Strong interpersonal relationships	• Anticipate other's needs • Early notices and warnings	• Provision of management time • Demonstrated dedication • Appropriate prioritization

Like satisfaction (which was discussed in the quality section of this chapter), this is a 'soft' measurement, in that the parties agree that the measurement is concerning the *opinion* and *perceptions* of the other party. This contract scorecard quadrant differs from the others in that both parties provide their opinions. A commercial relationship results from the interactions of both parties, both parties need to exhibit the desired behaviors, not just the provider. Note that this approach is different from the one found in one-sided agreements, where only the provider's behavior is detailed and the client has no explicit obligations. The goal of the relationship quadrant of the contract scorecard is to identify which aspects of the relationship are working and which are not, and then agree on a process for fixing those areas that need improvement. In this sense, analogies that liken the contract to a marriage may be partly appropriate, and, as many of us know, it takes two to have a good marriage and to make it work.

Organizations that design and track the effectiveness of supplier relationships have adopted a form of agreement called a *Relationship Charter* or *Code of Conduct*. This is typically set out as a schedule to the contract and specifies the behaviors all parties are to exhibit during the course of the contract. A brief example, from a maintenance contract in the utility industry, of specified behaviors and the scoring system used to assess those behaviors has been included in Figure 8.3.

Strategic

Strategic KPIs measure results that often go beyond the letter of the agreement and represent more of an alliance-type situation. There is a wide

Code of Conduct

1. Overview

1.1 (**Purpose**) This Code of Conduct identifies the behavior that the parties agree to exhibit during the course of the Term of the Contract. The parties have agreed that if the Contract is to operate effectively, both parties must drive towards a "partnering" style of relationship. To achieve this, the parties have set out their common goals in this Code of Conduct that are to operate during the Contract and shall use this as a process for relationship review and improvement.

1.2 (**No effect on legal relationship**) The parties agree that their legal relationship must always be governed by the Contract. Nevertheless, the parties have identified that this process needs to be implemented to enable both parties to operate effectively without the Contract being relied on in every instance.

2. Conduct to be Demonstrated by the Parties

Conduct	Description
1. Accuracy	Information provided; reporting; and data entered will be accurate.
2. Communication	The parties shall communicate frequently, openly, and honestly with each other. An environment of "no surprises" shall be sought.
3. Continuous Improvement	The parties shall constantly search for better ways of doing things.
4. Meet Needs	The parties shall be both proactive and reactive to each other's needs.
5. Perform Responsibilities	Each party will perform its responsibilities to the standard expected by the other party.
6. Problem Solving	The parties shall focus on rapid solutions to the problem, not apportioning blame or responsibility. Issues shall be resolved at the lowest level appropriate.
7. Resource Reinvestment	The parties wish to have recognized leadership in the Services through continuous reinvestment in human and capital assets.
8. Site	The parties shall maintain a clean and orderly Site environment.

3. Scoring the Code of Conduct

3.1 (**Survey**) Each party will conduct a survey of 50% of its staff every six months. The 50% of staff not surveyed in the first survey shall be surveyed in the second survey. Each party shall conduct its survey at its expense.

3.2 (**Scoring**) The parties agree to score their perception of the other party according to the following.

1	2	3	4	5
Unacceptable	Below expectations	Adequate	Above expectations	Delighted

3.3 (**Target score**) The parties seek an average score for each party of at least "4" for each period.

3.4 (**Analysis**) Each party shall provide the other with a justification of each score given, improvements deemed desirable, and proposed solution for incorporation into the Improvement Agenda.

3.5 (**Report**) The Service Provider shall provide the combined trend analysis and report for each survey.

Figure 8.3 Example code of conduct/relationship charter

range of potential strategic metrics that an organization may apply, especially if the deal is more than a basic fee-for-service exchange.

Examples include:

1. **Innovation** – introduction of new technologies, business practices, and/or processes that add value to the client organization.
2. **Business contribution** – the parties have achieved more out of the deal beyond the fundamental exchange of money for services (e.g., joint product offerings to the market, R&D initiatives, knowledge transfer).
3. **Alignment with corporate initiatives or goals** – the extent to which the provider conducts business in line with your organization's broad corporate goals (e.g., the use of local companies, workforce gender balance, environment policies, philanthropic initiatives, etc.).
4. **Underlying business processes** – the management of the underlying resources and business practices of the provider used to fulfill the contract (e.g., workforce management and safety).

Table 8.4 gives examples of the KPIs one might find in each of the types of strategic metrics.

Most deals have some form of anticipated strategic goals, but leave these unarticulated, perhaps only mentioning them in background information contained in the tender documents. Strategic goals mentioned 'by-the-by' rarely have any chance of actually occurring. The strategic goals tend to be

Table 8.4 Strategic KPI types

Innovation	Business contribution	Alignment with corporate values and initiatives	Underlying business processes
• Improved practices • Enabling online applications • Research and development investment	• Greater focus on core business • Refocus internal staff on high value/ strategic activities • Level of knowledge transfer provided • Number of mutual business initiatives created and completed • Number of joint product offerings created, royalties earned	• Use of SMEs (small to medium enterprises) • Employment created (direct and indirect) • Positions filled by minorities • Environmental contribution • Societal contribution	• Safety (loss time injuries, workplace incidents) • Workforce management (turnover, replacement, etc) • Standardization

articulated in a number of places in the agreement depending upon what they are and how the organization wants to manage them.

All the organization's strategic goals are likely to have some mention in the main terms and conditions of the contract (typically in a recital clause or in a strategic intent clause), but these tend to be quite high level and are more to help a contract reader understand the context of the deal. Strategic goals that the client is serious about achieving are most often detailed in a separate contract schedule. For example, if the organization is in the public sector and has industry development requirements to be met by the provider, such as the development of a research facility or the use of regional contractors, the contract may have a separate schedule detailing those requirements.

Do consider having a separate schedule which articulates the strategic goals of the deal, and details the provider's obligations in assisting the organization achieve them. This makes it easier to manage as the contract manager (and all the stakeholders to the deal), will not need to wade through the contract to discover what strategic obligations the provider has.

Most client organizations expect that their providers will continually innovate on the work under contract, even if it is not a clearly articulated requirement within the contract. And most organizations are bitterly disappointed, when there is no innovation, feeling that the provider has misled them or let them down. But where was innovation specified? When was it agreed to be implemented?

As Chapter 5 made clear, if you want innovation, you must ensure it will occur, first by setting KPIs, and secondly by ensuring that other KPIs and the contract itself do not conflict with this goal. As an example of the former, having KPI regarding cost reductions that override any possibility of innovation. As an example of the latter, it is unreasonable to expect innovation to happen if the contract vests all created intellectual property rights to the client. If the client retains ownership of the created intellectual property, the provider is motivated to ensure no innovation occurs at all. This is because the ability of the provider to use the intellectual property in their business with other clients has been removed, thus it cannot gain efficiency or commercial benefits. Accordingly, such clauses act in direct conflict with any innovation expectations, unless of course, the provider has been adequately compensated.

Client organizations may want providers not only to do the work specified under the contract, but also to help improve the business, or contribute to business issues that the client believes they are capable at doing (see also Chapter 3 on suppliers' transformation and relationship competencies, and Chapter 5 on collaborating). The case shown below illustrates this very well.

Case: A logistics provider keeps adding value

A maintenance and logistics contract with a Pacific Rim client also had a requirement that the logistics provider seek tenants for vacant space at the client's premises. The provider was responsible for running all the facilities of the client, in addition to maintaining inventory of uniforms, equipment, materials, and supplies. The provider was able to decrease the scale of required real estate for warehousing and operations as part of its re-engineering process (driven by an innovation KPI). However, this left the client with 30 percent of its land and building holdings unutilized. As a result, the parties derived a gain-sharing arrangement whereby the provider was granted a 5 percent finder's fee for finding subtenants for the properties. The client had no staff available to manage the subtenant search and the provider was better placed with many possible contacts in the area.

You may want to ensure that the underlying business practices of your providers are sound before getting contractually committed, and not waiting until things go wrong, to find out that they are not. Merely having outcome-based KPIs, such as the quality measurements discussed earlier in this chapter, provide nothing in the way of ensuring that the way the work is performed is in accordance with your expectations – they merely ensure that the outcomes were achieved. Organizations have learnt (and some the hard way) that not only is achieving the outcomes important, but that the means used to achieve them can be just as, if not more important.

Most client organizations want providers to act in accordance with the organization's values and strategic initiatives. These can be in the form of environmental activities, social philanthropy, industry development and employment, and so on. The nature of the KPIs can be quite diverse between organizations and contracts, as the following two examples indicate:

- A state government legal panel (a panel of different firms that provided legal advice to the government as the need arose) set up a strategic KPI regarding the percent of women legal professionals used on work given to the panel members. This was part of an overall initiative to get more women into male-dominated professions within the state, including not only the legal profession but also engineering, construction, and technology.
- A global consulting firm wanted to demonstrate that it was actively reducing its carbon footprint. Accordingly, the firm required its new global technology provider to reduce its technology-based carbon

footprint. This was done by first requiring the provider to conduct a baseline footprint assessment to determine the current baseline and then agreeing on a reduction level per year (and the techniques that would be used to reduce the footprint). The KPI was merely that a reduction had occurred ever year as opposed to a set percentage reduction.

Timing in the outsourcing lifecycle

The contract scorecard activities are best begun in the lifecycle as soon as the organization believes a potential outsourcing initiative will begin. This is because the contract scorecard helps the organization direct its investment in the time and effort required for its desired outcomes, not least because of distraction that the day-to-day pressures of running the outsourcing initiative and later, running contract operations, cause. Nevertheless, no matter where the organization is in the lifecycle, it is never too soon or too late to implement the contract scorecard.

During the Architect Phase

It will be recalled that the Architect Phase is where the foundation for outsourcing is laid, consists of the first four building blocks – investigate, target, strategize, and design. At the end of this phase, the organization knows itself well enough to confidently publicize its needs.

During this phase, the contract scorecard is developed. Once created, the contract scorecard continues to evolve over the entire lifecycle as more information becomes known, when the goals of the deal evolve, and as the organization matures in its management of the deal.

As discussed throughout this chapter, various elements of the contract documents between the parties will need to be designed to ensure the detail underpins the scorecard. Otherwise, the scorecard becomes an afterthought to the deal, and more than likely, a nonessential overhead which loses its effect. The quality metrics are most commonly captured in the SLA schedule to the contract, the financial metrics captured in the contract's pricing schedule, the relationship metrics in the Relationship Charter/Code of Conduct. The Strategic metrics rarely have a single schedule; rather it is dependent upon the nature of metrics chosen. The appropriate location of strategic metrics depends highly upon what they are. For example, safety metrics can be defined in an OHS schedule, environmental metrics in an Environmental Management Plan, R&D commercialization in a Commercialization Investment and Royalty schedule, and so on.

Lastly, when one designs the contract management function, the nature of the functions activities and the individuals selected to make up the function must be aligned to the relationship behaviors the organization has committed to.

During the Engage Phase

It will be recalled that the Engage Phase is where one or more suppliers are selected and the deal is negotiated. It consists of the fifth and sixth building blocks – Select and Negotiate. The contract scorecard is very useful at this stage, to help form part of the evaluation criteria and selection process enabling the organization to select one that best demonstrates it has delivered the outcomes sought in the scorecard. Compliance, or proposed alternatives, with the KPIs submitted in the draft agreement is a key component. The specified behaviors in the Relationship Charter/Code of Conduct is effective, in particular, when used in conducting customer reference checks to ascertain whether the behaviors the organization wants are actually exhibited by that provider in other clients. Likewise, the strategic goal achievement is also assessed in reference checks, as well as forming part of the required vendor response.

During the Operate Phase

The Operate Phase, where the deal is put in place, operationalized, and managed through its term, is comprised of the seventh and eighth building blocks – transition and manage. The Operate Phase either proceeds smoothly as a result of the strategies, processes, documents, and relationship management designed in the earlier building blocks, or the phase suffers, due to misinterpretations, ambiguities, disagreements, and disputes. Regular scorecard assessments are a key feature of this phase, tracking progress and making refinements to the arrangement based on the results.

During the Regenerate Phase

The Regenerate Phase, where next-generation options are assessed, consists of one building block – refresh. Following this phase, the lifecycle begins anew, returning to the Architect Phase, where the organization prepares for its next-generation deal/s. Again, the contract scorecard is particularly valuable in assessing the overall performance of the deal, as well as determining the overall Strengths, Weaknesses, Opportunities, and Threats (SWOT) of the deal.

Conclusion

Outsourcing, whether of IT or business processes, onshore or offshore, continues to raise expectations and pose challenges for private and public sector organizations alike. Since outsourcing is rarely a reversible option, and can consume a large part of the operations budget, the ability to drive and demonstrate success will become more of a basic expectation of management.

Nonetheless, once the decision to outsource has been made and the deal signed, many organizations take a slapdash approach and just let the deal run, manage it at a low level, and never drive or ensure they have gotten the outcomes they had wanted – running in reactionary mode rather than a pro-active one.

A contract scorecard is one pro-active tool that has proven successful and is well worth adopting. The scorecard provides a key design mechanism for guiding the detail within the contract, as well as for selecting the right provider. It then provides a key tool for tracking, assessing, and driving the results of the deal.

Notes

1. A full treatment of the scorecard approach in the context of outsourcing appears in Cullen, S. (2009) *The Contract Scorecard*. Gower, London.
2. Kaplan, R. and Norton, D. (1992) 'The balanced scorecard: measures that drive performance', *Harvard Business Review*, Jan-Feb, 71–9.
3. Kern, T. and Willcocks, L.P. (2001) *The Relationship Advantage: Information Technologies, Sourcing and Management*. Oxford University Press, Oxford.

CHAPTER 9

Disengagement: Preparing for the next generation

Introduction

It is inevitable that an outsourcing contract will end – either by reaching the natural end of its term, the end of the specified extension periods, or through early termination. The end of the contract, in whatever manner, represents the completion of the lifecycle of the current outsourcing initiative and the start of the next generation.

After more than 20 years of growth in the outsourcing industry, most organizations of any scale in developed economies have experienced some degree of outsourcing of IT and business services. While statistics are not available on a global basis, empirical evidence shows that in the next few years we will start seeing far fewer first generation deals and the majority of new deals being next (second, third, or even fourth) generation ones. This chapter takes you through the considerations for ending a current deal and beginning the next generation.

The lifecycle anew

In the lifecycle, each phase, and its building blocks, prepares the way for the following phases and building blocks. Likewise, the success of each building block depends on the preceding ones, with the last phase, Regenerate, paving the way for the next-generation sourcing strategy and its lifecycle.

The last phase, Regenerate, the subject of this chapter, is where the future options are decided upon, the past and future assessed in order to go forward in an improved position – faster, better, and cheaper, or perhaps toward forms of collaborative innovation discussed in Chapter 5.

An organization must give itself plenty of time to conduct this phase. For example, in the UK the country's Inland Revenue gave itself nearly two and a half years to contemplate the end of its ten-year deal with EDS,

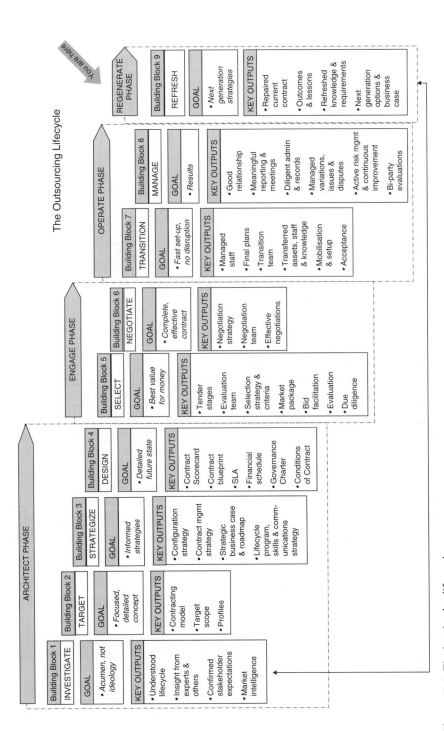

Figure 9.1 Timing in the lifecycle

as did BHP Billiton in Australia with its global CSC outsourcing arrangement. Consider the 'drop dead' date to be at least one year before the initial contract term expires, as any tendering activity usually requires at least six months. Even with starting at that time, an extension may still be necessary (but not for a full subsequent term). The goal is to have the next arrangement, if applicable, in place before the initial term expires and the handover date of the new arrangement either on, or before, the termination date of the previous arrangement.

The end of the contract, in whatever manner, represents the completion of the lifecycle of the current outsourcing initiative and the start of the next. Depending on how the organization chooses to progress, it could go through the outsourcing lifecycle in its entirety, should it wish to re-tender a much wider scope, or just continue with contract management if it decides to rollover on the same terms and conditions. All three options – re-tender, backsource, and retain – take a different path through the lifecycle once the first four building blocks have been conducted (see Figure 9.2).

If work is to be re-tendered, the lifecycle continues at building block 5 (Select) with the selection stages and strategy, albeit more efficiently, based on the lessons learnt from the previous arrangement.

If the incumbent is to be retained, the contract is typically renegotiated to reflect the organization's changed requirements and improvements in outsourcing practices – thus the lifecycle continues at building block 6 (Negotiate) with the negotiation strategy. However, if no major changes were required, the contract was often renewed following the standard contractual variation processes – thus the lifecycle continues at building block 8 (manage) with any required variations.

If work is to be brought in-house ('backsourced'), then the lifecycle continues at building block 7 (transition) with the transition strategy. Many organizations that backsource retain the Service level agreement (SLA) to guide and measure service delivery for that work. The contract is unlikely to be needed, unless the new supplier is a partially related entity, rather than an in-house service unit.

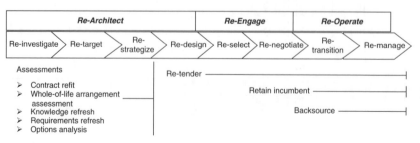

Figure 9.2 Options and the outsourcing lifecycle

Assessments

To be able to evaluate the best option for going forward and determining a new set of expectations, the organization will need to perform a number of assessments but now armed with the benefit of hindsight and experience.

But this only applies if the team in charge of planning the next generation is not a 'first generation team'. That is, they do not have the experience of multiple generations as did the case below.

Case: Next generation is not a cut-and-paste

In this case, the client organization decided to 'cut and paste' another organization's tender document and contract for its second generation re-tender. It did this because it had not retained any competence in the area and believed the quickest way to get the tender out was just to copy another organization's documents. However, during the tender evaluation period, the client quickly discovered that its needs were quite different from the organization from which it had copied. It had to issue months of clarifications changing its publicized requirements and conditions to its actual requirements. The final contract also took months of re-writing to get it right. The exercise ended up taking three times as long as it would have if the client did not try the 'cut and paste' shortcut.

The assessments that should be considered by any organization facing the end of a contract are as follows:

- **Contract assessment** – to ensure the current contract is ready for the next generation options.
- **Whole-of-life arrangement assessments** – to gather lessons and improvements.
- **Knowledge refreshment assessment** – to update understanding of best practices in the industry and to update understanding of the market.
- **New requirements assessment** – to update changed requirements.

Contract assessment

First in the series of assessments recommended for you to make is a review of the current contract to ensure all options are catered for. Of course, a much better time to do this was when the current contract had originally been drafted. However, such omissions still require fixing, albeit it might not come cheap, as the following case demonstrates.

Case: A late mop-up does not come free

In a recent next generation case, concerning the outsourcing of the HR function at a federal government department, no provisions had been made in the current contract to prepare for the end of the deal. The department was planning to re-tender and it was expecting the incumbent not to be successful due to inadequate past performance and a maturation of the marketplace. An urgent project was created to create a 'Deed of Disengagement' to put in the missing obligations of the supplier and rights of the client. The department did manage to obtain many of the needed provisions, as the incumbent did not want to adversely influence the relationship during the re-tender. But these did not come free, as the department was required to pay for all assistance required which would not have been the case if the original contract had catered for the exit, or unwinding, of the deal.

Below are the issues the current contract needs to address, prior to the next generation deal:

1. **Extension clauses** – short-term and longer term extension right and obligations. You do not want to be held to 'hostage rates' (prices far above the norm, because you have no alternatives). If your contract is silent on these, get a variation agreed now.

   - Are there agreed extension terms and conditions?
   - What are the obligations of the parties with regard to extensions? Is there a predefined extension period?
   - Is there a pre-agreed pricing provision or is it at the same pricing as normal operations?

2. **Termination and handover assistance clauses** – to ensure the next generation implementation goes smoothly. If your contract is silent, get a variation agreed before you announce any sort of next generation option decision, particularly if the decision is to backsource or handover to a new provider. Once the current provider has no motivation to continue creating goodwill, you have lost significant bargaining

power and all variations will come at a much higher cost (if you can get them at all).

- Are there agreed termination and handover terms and conditions?
- Are there predefined disengagement (process of unwinding) and handover (process of transferring to new provider or in-house) periods?
- Are the obligations of all the parties (new provider, former provider, and the client organization) with regard to termination and handover complete?
- Are there pre-agreed termination and handover pricing provisions or is it at the same pricing as normal operations?

3. **Post-termination assistance clauses** – to get help after the contract ends. Although you hope not to have to ask for help after the incumbent has left, inevitably you will need something from them. If your contract is silent, get a variation agreed now or you will not have any support after the contract finishes.

- Are there agreed post-termination terms and conditions?
- Are the obligations of the former suppler with regard to post-termination complete? Is there a predefined post-termination period?
- Are there pre-agreed post-termination pricing provisions or is it at the same pricing as normal operations?

4. **Staff and asset 'transfer' clauses and cost schedule** – for resources the incumbent provider has that the successor may want. If your contract is silent, get a variation agreed now or you will have to pay 'hostage rates' for equipment and will need to wait for until the 'non-poaching' period is over (the period in which the parties are not to make offers to each other's staff).

- Are there agreed transfer terms and conditions.
- Are the obligations of the incumbent with regard to transfer complete?
- Is there a predefined transfer offer period?
- Are there pre-agreed transfer cost provisions?

Whole-of-life arrangement assessment

The next series of assessments cover reviews over the whole-of-life arrangement and comprise:

1. **Assess the gap** between the contractual documents and actual operations – to determine what changes are needed to both.

2. **Audit compliance** of both parties with the contract – to determine if the contract is effective, or if improved contract management is required.
3. Determine the level of **stakeholder satisfaction** – with the incumbent provider as well as how the contract is being managed by the client organization.
4. Document **performance and cost trends** – to determine overall value for money since inception and establish a baseline for the next generation.
5. A **SWOT** – what the current deal has evolved to, what worked and did not, and what can be learnt from the earlier generation.
6. Determine the degree to which the **original objectives** for outsourcing were achieved – to understand what went wrong and needs to be improved, as well as what went right and needs to be continued.

1. Conduct a gap analysis between the governing documents and actual operations.

Unless the parties have been quite diligent in keeping the governing documents up-to-date, these documents are unlikely to be an accurate reflection of the current actual practices and informal agreements that have evolved over time. This can be seen in the following case of a government agency.

Case: A government agency expects a quick contract update

The agency was preparing to re-tender a contract near the end of its term. No major changes were believed to be necessary as the intent of the re-tender was for the same scope of services. The re-tender project manager reviewed the contract and SLA expecting that some minor changes might be required, but only gave himself a few days to finalize the new documents. However, he soon found that the contract bore little resemblance to the arrangement currently in operation. A pre-tender update project was required, delaying the tender by months.

Variation by conduct (otherwise known as estoppel) is a normal occurrence in outsourcing contracts. While the parties undoubtedly make every attempt to record and approve variations in a formal manner, most end up 'just happening'. If you send out the old contract documents for re-tender or just rollover the existing contract, the opportunity to have the contract documents reflect the actual current practice has been lost. While you are at it, take a look at the formal variations and their causes as well. This typically indicates problems with the original documents being ambiguous.

2. Audit compliance of both parties with the contract

Auditing outsourcing deals is not something every organization focuses on. There are usually so many operational fires to be fighting that the review process can be easily overlooked. While this should have been an ongoing contract management process, if it has not been done before now is the time to do it.

Undoubtedly you will find many areas where the provider, as well as your own organization, has been non-compliant. The point of doing this at near the end of the contract is not so much to determine who didn't do what (apportion blame), but to fix the contract and the contract management function for the future (fix the problem so it doesn't repeat).

3. Determine the level of stakeholder satisfaction with the incumbent provider.

This is more than a 'User Satisfaction Survey'. It includes all aspects of the provider's service delivery, contract, relationship, and cost management. Stakeholders are anyone that cares about the deal and can include end customers, contract managers, accounts payable, and business unit management to name a few. All of these will have different issues, different satisfaction drivers, and different ideas for the future. But first and foremost, determining your stakeholders 'satisfaction with the last deal establishes the baseline by which the next generation can be compared against.

4. Analyze performance and cost trends to determine overall value for money since inception

In addition to demonstrating the business case for the original outsourcing, the analysis provides the new base case for the future options. It also provides the data for benchmarking and for determining potential improvements in the value for money equation (better KPIs, lower costs).

5. Conduct a SWOT

The SWOT assesses all aspects of the past arrangement including the contract/ SLA, supplier, scope, the contract management function, and the retained organization – anything of potential relevance to the next generation.

This analysis is designed to determine:

- strengths – that are working well and to be retained;
- weaknesses – defects that need to be corrected;
- opportunities – to be taken; and
- threats – to be eliminated or mitigated.

This involves assessing what the current deal has evolved to, what worked and did not, and what can be learnt from the earlier generation.

6. Determine the degree to which the original objectives for outsourcing were achieved.

This refers to the original business case, in particular, the strategic and tactical purposes the outsourcing arrangement was designed to achieve. This is not always easy, as the following case reveals.

Case: An educational institution cannot determine original objectives

Nearing the end of a five-year contract, the Chancellor of a university directed the Contract Manager to assess whether or not the benefits sought by outsourcing were achieved. This analysis was critical to forming part of the steering committee's strategic planning over whether further outsourcing should be considered. No documentation other than the original contract had been maintained and none of the decision makers or even personnel involved with the outsourcing process remained with the university. Although a valiant effort was made, the Contract Manager could not infer what benefits were intended let alone whether they were achieved.

Knowledge refreshment assessment

It is inevitable that the industry, and outsourcing practices in general, will have evolved since the original arrangement was put in place. The end of any contract offers the opportunity to investigate and adopt evolved practices, particularly if this had not been an ongoing process adopted by the organization's contract management function.

This assessment often includes:

1. Benchmarking performance levels and cost – against comparative industry standards to determine if KPIs should be upgraded and to determine future cost expectations.

   - Have new KPIs for the services emerged in the market?
   - Are the service levels in the current arrangement appropriate or have new industry standards emerged?
   - Have prices gone up or down for similar scope?

2. Updating knowledge of leading practice and new technologies – to ensure you will get the optimum price/performance

   - Is there new technology that offers better price/performance ratios?
   - Have new business processes been adopted that offer improved effectiveness or efficiency?

3. Updating knowledge of leading sourcing and contracting practices – to get best value for money and mitigate risks.

   - Are there better outsourcing practices that have emerged in other organizations?
   - Is there new best practice in outsourcing contracts and SLAs?

4. Determining the state of the market – the pool of potential suppliers, capability, and general market conditions.

   - What is the new degree of competitiveness in the industry?
   - Are there any new entrants to be considered?
   - What is the viability and organizational landscape for the 'known' providers?
   - Are there any windows of opportunities (i.e., a market slump, a new entrant)?
   - Are there windows of 'dis-opportunities' (i.e., competing tenders from other organizations)?

Sounds easy, but unfortunately is more difficult than you might expect as the following case, of a power company, brings to light.

Case: A utility experiences a lack of meaningful benchmarks

Here, the benchmarking yielded nothing but the desire not to go through it again. The utility's CIO had believed benchmarks were readily available and simple to apply; it was merely a matter of engaging the services of a benchmarking organization. Upon receipt of a voluminous report, the CIO struggled to find any meaningful information. When he queried attributes of source data (age, industry, location, etc) and the method of scope alignment, he was told all that was confidential. Having no way of knowing if the benchmarks represented current data in his industry for the scope in question, let alone whether any of the benchmarks were from international or local sources, he threw out the report. But, he still had to pay the $100,000 for it.

New requirements assessment

The end of any outsourcing contract offers the opportunity to determine new requirements and refresh original requirements, particularly if this had not been an ongoing inherent process adopted by your organization's contract management function.

This includes:

- forecasting business requirements and potential changes over the projected life of any new/revised arrangement;
- reconsidering the scope, potential bundling/unbundling of services, and services that should be discontinued and prepare the target services profiles;
- developing revised SLA(s), contract and price model in addition to the contract management function and the retained organization.

When faced with re-tendering or backsourcing as the preferred option, many organizations regretted the lack of knowledge they had over the detailed operations. Look at the following case, as an example.

Case: Knowledge shortfall leads to second generation failure

The first responsibility of the new IT manager for a port logistics company was to conduct a tender for the IT network management services, as the current five-year contract was expiring shortly. He awarded a contract to a new supplier that had offered a price that was extraordinarily less than any other bid. The contract was signed and sealed quickly to lock in that price. Unfortunately, he had poorly specified the nature of the services because he was unfamiliar with them, and did not have relevant technical expertise. The new supplier's bid was largely nonsense as it was grossly under-scoped compared to the actual nature of the services required. Furthermore, the new supplier did not have the expertise to conduct the required scope. After operations continuously fell over and court cases were threatened all around, the incumbent supplier was subcontracted back at premium prices by the new supplier.

Next generation options

Whichever way services are provided, internally or through the market, the choice should not be regarded as fixed. Both client organizations and supplier markets change over time in ways that may render an initial decision inappropriate in a current context. The degree of uncertainty may be diminished, market growth may support competitive (large number) supply relations, provider capabilities change, and information disparities between the parties may diminish. Thus, any organization should periodically reassess its sourcing decisions.

There are three fundamental options with regard to the 'go forward' decision for the next generation:

1. **Retain the incumbent** provider for all or part of the scope – renew the existing arrangement (rollover) or renegotiate the new/revised arrangement with the incumbent;
2. **Backsource** all or part of the scope – bring services back in-house; or
3. Put out all or part of the scope to competitive **negotiation or re-tender** – which may result in retaining the incumbent provider and/or employing other providers for all or part of the scope depending upon how the work is bundled and which provider is successful.

In practice, all options often take place in a single contract. Some services are backsourced, some the incumbent provider provides, and some a new provider supplies. To what extent this occurs varies widely. Figure 9.3 is based on limited evidence only, but shows that the most common end of contract process has been to extend the contract in some capacity rather than re-tender, negotiate directly with alternative providers, or bring back in-house.

The end result of the current 'next generation' Australian deals were that 70 percent of the total original scope stayed with the incumbent, a bit over a quarter of the scope went to a new supplier, and in two cases a portion was backsourced (brought back in-house) equating to 3 percent of the total scope (Figure 9.4). In broader, more global research, we found that only 10 percent of deals were backsourced in any significant way, and that nearly 66 percent of deals went with the existing supplier.[1] This is good news for incumbent suppliers. And even better news for incumbents to government contracts, if the Australian experience is replicated elsewhere. The entire scope of next-generation government contracts were given in their entirety to the incumbent, with one minor exception (a federal government gave 10 percent of the work to a new supplier). This was irrespective of whether a competitive tender or a direct negotiation was held – it made no difference. In practice, of course, government practices will vary from country to country – the UK and USA for example show more movement and competition than this across central and state/local governments.[2]

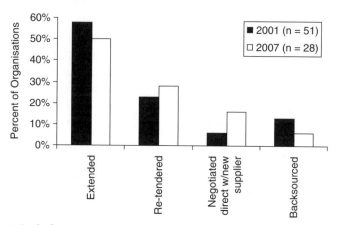

Figure 9.3 End of contract processes

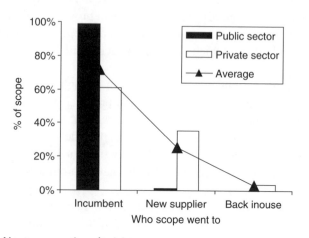

Figure 9.4 Next generation decisions

We now discuss each of the next-generation options in turn, and also the necessary contract clauses.

Keep the incumbent

As discussed, the most popular outcome of any end of contract process is to retain the incumbent provider. Ideally the incumbent provider is retained if:

- there is little change to scope,
- the provider provides at or below market prices and these can be demonstrated,
- the provider has performed at or better than the specified KPIs,
- both parties will save significant time and effort by not re-tendering, and
- both parties wish to continue the relationship.

But, more often than not, the extension is the result of the client running out of time to do anything else. A common notice period for extending the contract is three months prior to expiry. Unfortunately, this is often the first time the client gives any thought to it. The client soon realizes that it does not have time to go out to market since a re-tender process can take four to six months, let alone the months needed to handover to a new provider.

Given the odds that an organization will be extending the contract, it is useful to have some clauses in the contract that facilitate getting a better deal and not just rolling over. These include:

- having a short-term extension option, in case you do want to re-tender or have negotiations with alternative providers;
- having a performance-based extension clause – typically revolving around the achievement of KPIs over a specified period; and
- having a benchmarking clause to renegotiate KPIs and prices.

Examples of such clauses are given in Figure 9.5.

Backsource

Returning work in-house is thus an anomaly, not a trend. Once out – it tends to stay out! Not necessarily because outsourcing is the 'right answer', but because backsourcing is either too politically sensitive (e.g., calls into question the judgment of the people who made the initial outsourcing decision), or it is too uneconomical because the previous generation decisions did not leave a backsourcing option open (e.g., all assets, facilities, and people are gone).

---

1. **Extension options**
   1.1. (**Short-term extension**) Should the Client require a short-term extension of the Contract in order to ensure minimal disruption:
      a. the Client shall give no less than three (3) months notice of such a requirement; and
      b. the Contractor agrees to extend the Contract on a month-to-month basis under the terms of the Contract.
   1.2. (**Performance-based extension**) The Client will extend the Term of the Contract for a period of six (6) months for each twelve (12) month period in which there are no KPI Failure (as specified in the Service Level Agreement).
2. **Benchmarking as part of the extension**
   2.1. (**Exercises**) The Client may commission, or conduct itself, benchmarking exercises for all or part of the Services in order to establish market benchmarks in which to base an extension.
   2.2 (**Terms of reference**) The Client shall provide the Contractor with the terms of reference regarding the benchmarking exercise that shall include the scope of the exercise and the benchmarking sample to be used.
   2.3. (**Duty to assist**) The Contractor must comply with any request, and provide full cooperation, including access to relevant records and personnel, to the Client or its nominee in relation to any benchmarking exercised insofar as it pertains to the Services, this Contract, or the Client.
   2.4. (**Results**) The results, but not the underlying data, of the benchmarking exercise will be summarized and presented to the Contractor. If the Contract costs are above the benchmark costs, or Contract KPIs are lower than the benchmark KPIs, the Contractor shall:
      a. prepare an improvement plan to meet, or exceed, the benchmarks that meets the satisfaction of the Client within thirty (30) days of receiving the benchmarks; and
      b. specify an implementation deadline which shall be prior to the expiry of the current Term.
   2.5. (**Costs**) Each party shall bear its own costs with regard to any benchmarking exercises and implementation of the results. External fees in conjunction with benchmarking exercises shall be borne by the Client.

Figure 9.5 Example of clauses assisting retaining the incumbent

Nonetheless, the organizations that have backsourced either have done so because they wished to rebuild their competence in the area, to regain control over the resources and costs, or just to because the work was more effective if conducted inside because intimate knowledge of the organization was vital. As one high-profile example, in 2004 JP Morgan Chase cancelled the remaining portion of an IBM contract that was intended as a seven-year, $5 billion deal. Its July 2004 merger with Bank One Corp. led it to reconsider its IT strategy. The new firm had significantly greater capacity to manage its own technology infrastructure and decided to bring its IT support staff back in-house. In January JP Morgan began transferring back 4000 employees and contractors that were transferred to IBM when the deal was made in December 2002. The original contract called for IBM to take over significant IT functions for JP Morgan, including managing its data centers, help desks, distributed computing, data and voice networks. At that time, JP Morgan planned to retain some functions including application development and delivery and desktop support. Clearly backsourcing to this extent is not an easy undertaking. Depending on the degree of outsourcing that is being backsourced, infrastructures, work processes, and competencies all need to be re-built. To enable this to occur, it is common to find in contracts that leave the backsourcing option open the following clauses in their contracts:

- Transfer of resources – assets, software, third-party services via sale or assignment;
- Offers of employment – to the provider's staff;
- Transfer of knowledge – from the provider to the client; and
- Post-termination assistance – 'on call' support after the contract has ended.

Examples of such clauses are given in Figure 9.6.

---

1. **Resource transfers**

  1.1. (**Transaction obligations**) In conducting any of the assets, resource, license, agreements, or other transfers, the Contractor must:

    a. use best efforts to obtain any third party consents for any transfers of assets, licenses, or other agreements which the Client has directed the Contractor to obtain;

    b. prepare and execute any bills of sale or assignments; and

    c. do all other things necessary to transfer the ownership, or assign the lease, of equipment (as the case may be) as directed by the Client.

2. **Equipment/physical asset transfers**

  2.1. (**Notice**) The Contractor must give notice to the Client before removing any equipment, documents, or other material from the Client's sites.

  2.2. (**Relocation**) The Contractor must assist the Client as required to arrange for the physical de-installation, transportation, and relocation of equipment and physical assets.

  2.3. (**Removal**) As directed by the Client, the Contractor must arrange for the removal and delivery of any equipment or any physical assets owned or leased by the Client that is in the Contractor's possession or control.

  2.4. (**Sale**) On expiration or termination of this Contract, then the Contractor irrevocably and unconditionally offers to sell to the Client all equipment owned by the Contractor and used exclusively to perform the Removed Services. The Client may, at its option, purchase all or any part of that equipment for the written down book value.

  2.5. (**Lease assignment**) If requested by the Client, the Contractor must:

    a. assign to the Client effective from the Termination Date any lease from a third party for equipment used primarily to perform the Removed Services; or

    b. if entitled to do so exercise its option to purchase such equipment pursuant to the equipment lease and sell such equipment to the Client at the equipment lease option exercise price.

Figure 9.6 Example of clauses assisting backsourcing

3. **Software transfers**

 3.1. (**Assignment**) At the Client's request, the Contractor must, in relation to Software required to perform the Removed Services either by:
  a. assigning the Contractor's license (and obtaining the licensor's consent to assign if necessary and possible); or
  b. procuring a license for the Client.

 3.2. (**Consent**) If license terms do not include an automatic right to have the license assigned to the Client or a new license granted on the same terms, the Contractor must obtain the Client's consent before agreeing to have that license assigned or granted.

 3.3. (**Technical details**) The Contractor must provide the Client with appropriate interface information and other technical details to enable the Client to develop or replace any Software that is not commercially available.

4. **Contractor material**

 4.1. (**License**) At the **Client's request, the Contractor** must grant to the Client a free license to continue to use any material which is owned by the Contractor for a period no less than 12 months after the end of the Disengagement Period.

5. **Third party services transfers**

 5.1. (**Make available**) The Contractor must make available to the Client, on reasonable terms and conditions, any third party services used in providing the Removed Services, for a period no less than 12 months after the end of the Disengagement Period.

 5.2. (**Assignment**) The Contractor must then assign or terminate any agreements for third party services used solely to provide the Removed Services in accordance with the directions of the Client.

6. **Offers of employment**

 6.1. (**Employment offers**) The Client or its nominee may offer to employ any Contractor personnel, or contract with any subcontractors or third party suppliers of the Contractor who have been employed or used in providing the Removed Services. Accordingly, the Contractor:
  a. waives, and must ensure that its subcontractors waive, any contractual or other legal rights restricting the ability of the Contractor personnel to be recruited and employed by the Client or its nominee.
  b. must not, and must ensure that its subcontractors do not, hinder the Client or it nominee in offering employment to Contractor personnel.

 6.2. (**Duty to assist**) As directed by the Client, the Contractor must, and must ensure that its Subcontractors, give the Client or its nominee all reasonable assistance to employ Contractor personnel or employ substitute personnel, including by providing to the Client or its nominee:
  a. reasonable access to Contractor personnel for interviews and recruitment;
  b. an organizational chart showing the roles, responsibilities, authority, and salaries or resource values of all personnel employed in providing the Removed Services; and
  c. permanent or temporary personnel to fill vacancies as required by the Client.

Figure 9.6 *continued*

---

7. **Transfer of knowledge**

  7.1. (**Knowledge transfer**) As directed by the Client, the Contractor must provide for transfer of all knowledge to enable the Client to assume responsibility for continued performance of the Removed Services. This includes explanations, information, and documents pertaining to:

    a. standards and procedures to the Client's operations;

    b. copies of procedures and operations manuals;

    c. product information;

    d. agreements with third party suppliers of goods and services;

    e. details of physical and logical security processes and tools;

    f. documents and diagrams for information technology and communications infrastructure, networks, applications, and data/database schema; and

    g. all work in progress as commencement of the Disengagement Period.

  7.2. (**Training**) The Contractor must provide information and training to Client personnel as directed by the Client, to enable the Client to provide the Removed Services with minimum disruption and achieve the Service Levels. This training includes the Client assigning Client personnel to work with the Workforce to facilitate knowledge transfer from the Contractor to the Client.

8. **Post-termination assistance**

  8.1. (**Post-termination assistance**) period of six (6) months after to the Termination Date, the Contractor shall provide to the Client or its nominee the following services at no additional cost:

    a. answering questions regarding the Services on an 'as needed' basis;

    b. turning over of any remaining Client reports and documentation still in the Contractor's possession;

    c. providing the Client or its nominee with access to necessary information relevant to the ongoing provision Services;

    d. arranging or procuring the secondment of its Workforce as reasonably required by the Client subject to payment for those Workforce at agreed rates; and

    e. providing access to the Workforce, information, and records in connection in connection with any litigation to the Client is a party.

Figure 9.6 *continued*

The most common form of backsourcing is 'back tweaking' – taking back bits of scope over time as the need arises rather than a 'big bang' backsource of the entire contract. The area where this most frequently occurs is for systems development.

However, where an organization is considering a 'big bang' backsource, like JP Morgan above, it will need a detailed understanding of the work and what it will take to make it successful. Many problems with backsourcing stem from the client organization taking over activities that were not well understood by the client prior to disengaging the provider.

To gain this understanding, a profiling exercise is often required. Such profiling is necessary to provide an understanding of the services so that the organization can re-build the shop knowledgeably and minimize costly surprises, have a solid basis in which to facilitate future discussions, debates, and strategies with stakeholders, have a history in which to compare pre- and post-backsourcing baselines for the inevitable comparison with 'how it was before'; and 'what did we think we needed';

Profiling involves gaining an accurate understanding of seven aspects of the current state of the target services, as well as the desired or forecasted future state:

1. Services Profile – the nature and extent of the services including KPIs;
2. Cost Profile – the current and forecasted cost of delivering the work;
3. Balance Sheet Profile – the current and forecasted assets (including intellectual property) and liabilities (if any);
4. Staff Profile – the current and future staffing requirement including numbers, salaries, and skills;
5. Stakeholder Profile – the individuals and groups that care about the services and what they care about as these are the people that you will need make happy;
6. Commercial Relationships Profile – the existing contracts, agreements, and the like as well as desired future relationships with these parties and the former provider; and
7. Governance Profile – how service oversight currently occurs and how it will be done in the future.

Re-tender the contract

Many organizations have a policy on when a contract is required to be re-tendered, particularly in the government sector. However, if you have no such policy, consider a re-tender if:

- you wish to ensure the most competitive price is obtained;
- the scope has changed significantly and you believe other providers may have greater expertise; or
- the incumbent provider will not accept your revised contract/SLA at the desired price.

You will find that if you are considering a re-tender, you will need some (even a lot of) help from the incumbent, particularly with regards to operational information that you need to provide to potential bidders to enable them to quote. Such assistance is unlikely to be forthcoming if there is not a requirement to do so in the contract. There are not too many providers out there that will cheerfully help their competitors get the information they need to take over the contract. And most certainly, not for free.

---

1. **Re-tender assistance by the Contractor**

   1.1. **(Re-tender)** The Contractor agrees and acknowledges that the Client may re-tender this Contract, in whole or in part, at any time during the Term, in its absolute discretion.

   1.2. **(Duty to assist)** The Contractor must assist and cooperate with the Client in any market testing or tender process conducted. In particular, as requested by the Client, the Contractor must:

      a. provide, or assist in developing, the history over the Term of charges, Service and KPI performance, variations, and compliance;

      b. provide answers to any queries the Client may have during the course of the re-tender regarding Service operations, disengagement, and Contract performance; and

      c. provide access to the Contractor's site if deemed necessary for Service operations conducted at the Contractor's premises, for only the part of the premise so used.

Figure 9.7 Example re-tender assistance clauses

An example of a re-tender assistance clause is given in Figure 9.7.

There are two possible outcomes of a re-tender: (1) the incumbent will win, or (2) another provider will be chosen. The bulk of the next discussion covers the issues with handovers between incumbents and the new providers; however it is worth briefly discussing the long-term implications of choosing the incumbent.

Since past statistics regarding the likelihood of switching providers favors the incumbent, potential bidders to a re-tender are less likely to bid (or put in a high-quality effort). In fact, one of the bid/no bid criteria of most providers is whether or not an incumbent exists. If it does, and there does not appear to be a strong impetus for the client to switch, a potential bidder would have to give very serious thought as to investing its scarce resources to a higher probability opportunity. Once you have chosen the incumbent, the market of unsuccessful bidders (and those that chose not to bid and are watching the outcome) is likely to believe that you used them only to get a better price with your incumbent. If you choose to re-tender again one day, they will be even less likely to want to partake in gambling their resources once again. If they do bid, it may only be a half-hearted effort which again stacks the odds to the incumbent. When you are genuinely ready to switch, you will have to convince the market that their efforts will not be wasted yet again. The mere act of re-tendering will not be enough. Some organizations have paid potential suppliers to bid and others have not invited the incumbent to ensure that true competition occurs.

If you believe that a re-tender might yield a new provider, the hand-over process can be fraught with difficulties if not well planned far in advance. The handover process is loaded with inherent difficulties because there is often little incentive for the outgoing provider to ensure the process is thorough and comprehensive.

Many organizations assume that any new provider will have thorough hand-over procedures and do little in the way of due diligence to ensure that the procedures will be effective. Remember, however, that it is predominately in your own organization's best interest to ensure the hand-over is a smooth as possible, not necessarily in either provider's interests. Do not try to abdicate this to the new provider.

The former provider may have some motivation to retain goodwill, but this can be exhausted quickly. The new provider has motivation to create goodwill with the organization, but will have many opportunities to obtain out-of-scope charges if the former provider is not cooperative. Relying on the assumption that either provider will act in the customer's best interest is a high-risk strategy. Some of these difficulties can be readily seen in the following case.

Case: A water utility leaves it to the providers

A contract was awarded to a new provider for relatively complex services. The new provider did not have any handover procedures, nor were they asked to provide any by the utility. The handover meeting with the former provider took 15 minutes and comprised a brief conversation whereby the new provider asked what the former had prepared for them. The former provider just gave an overview of the configuration, although it had prepared other items quite at length in anticipation of an extensive handover process.

Over the course of the next six months, there were so many repeated operational failures that the systems were exceedingly unstable. Accordingly, the customer threatened to sue the new provider for breach of contract. The new provider, in turn, threatened to sue the former provider. The former provider was able to prove to the customer that it had left an effectively operating environment and through its comprehensive backup was able to restore the system as at the handover date. The new provider had to pick up the costs of the restoration and of the re-entry of six months company data, which were significant. It spent the remainder of the contract attempting to recoup those costs through out-of-scope charges.

Many of the problems associated with handovers between providers are because the client organization failed to:

- have explicit handover obligations in the former provider's contract, thus having to pay premium prices for assistance and intellectual property;

- require, as part of the re-tender bid response, the detailed handover approach by the new provider, thus having a faulty handover process and disrupted operations.

There are certain basic steps necessary to ensure a smooth transition between providers:

Electronic snapshots of departed operations – sealed, dated, and stored (potentially in escrow if desirable) to resolve the inevitable conflicts when the new provider blames current problems on the state in which the old one left it.

- comprehensive backup of all data and systems at handover date including at least one year of history;
- key documentation including network maps, configuration, systems software, etc; and
- photographs of onsite locations prior to the new provider taking over (if appropriate).

Detailed plan – agreed between all parties to ensure all parties know what needs to be done and who is to do it. This should contain a:

- comprehensive project plan and list of tasks;
- responsibility assignment matrix for all three parties;
- handover testing and acceptance procedures and approvals; and
- contingency and restoration plans.

Active Management – by all parties, including:

- a steering committee or oversight board comprising key personnel from all parties chaired by the client organization;
- a handover management team comprising all parties; and
- joint problem solving workshops and planning sessions.

Options analysis

Given that an organization is armed with the information and issues to consider for the next generation, the final activity is to assess the options and determine the right combination of options to employ in the next generation sourcing program.

The options business case analysis is designed to determine the viability and potential costs, benefits, and risks of transacting and managing each option along with the business case and strategy for the recommended option.

Identifying and defining options

The first task is to identify the options. In most cases, there will be also options within options. For example, a re-tender could be for all or part scope, as could backsourcing. The figure below (Figure 9.8) is an example of the three options and some sub-options within them.

Of course, when identifying the options, explicit assumptions will need to be made so that all the decision-makers are operating from the same understanding.

Below are the assumptions made in the example above (Figure 9.8) to trigger your development of the needed assumptions.

1. Rollover

- no modifications to current contract – same terms and conditions;
- no price change;
- if provider has right of refusal, they will not invoke it; and
- rollover will take one day.

2. Re-negotiate

- a slight price decrease will occur in some areas;
- scope will be better defined, but not substantially changed;

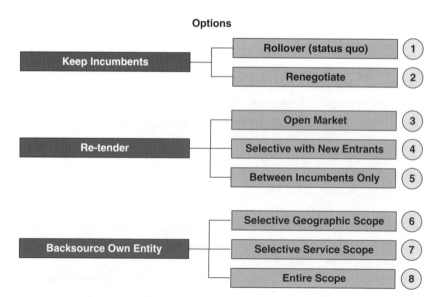

Figure 9.8 Example of end-of-term options

- KPIs will be better specified with a slight improvement; and
- re-negotiation will take one month.

3. Open market re-tender

- a 20 percent price decrease will occur;
- no progress payments, payments will only be made for final deliverables;
- significant improvements to KPIs;
- an expression of interest (EOI) and request for proposal (RFP) will be conducted;
- significant investment will need to be made to create a level playing field for new entrants due to the long history with the incumbents;
- seven bids will be received;
- at least one new entrant will be successful; and
- re-tender and possible handover will take 12 months.

5. Selective market re-tender

- a 10 percent price decrease will occur;
- no progress payments, payments will only be made for final deliverables;
- significant improvements to KPIs;
- five providers known to the client will be asked to bid;
- re-tender and possible handover will take nine months; and
- at least one new entrant will be successful.

6. Incumbent only re-tender

- only current providers will be asked to bid;
- significant improvements to KPIs;
- no progress payments, payments will only be made for final deliverables;
- one incumbent will lose their current contract; and
- re-tender and possible handover will take six months.

7. Backsource entire scope for a geographic region or a business unit

- the internal charge out rate will be 10 percent less than the current price;

- the same SLA will be put in place as that with external providers, as well as some of the contract conditions;
- the contract management area will manage the backsourced region identical to outsourced regions; and
- backsource will take six months.

8. Backsource entirety of selective scope

- the internal charge out rate will be 10 percent less than the current price;
- the same SLA for that scope will be put in place as that with the former providers, as well as some of the contract conditions;
- the contract management area will manage the SLA as if provided by a third party; and
- backsource will take three months.

9. Backsource entire scope

- the internal charge out rate will be 20 percent less than the current price;
- the same SLA will be put in place as that with the former providers, as well as some of the contract conditions;
- the contract management area will manage the SLA as if provided by a third party; and
- backsource will take nine months.

Elimination of options

The criteria in which to assess the best option for going forward will be a mix of strategic, risk, and financial criteria. What you are looking for is the optimum solution which balances all three – the best long-term financial estimated result with the strongest strategic fit at acceptable levels of risk.

Example criteria, to get you thinking include:

1. Strategic

- contribution to competitive position;
- improvements to operational excellence and reliability;
- flexibility to meet changing requirements and growth projections;
- innovation; and
- upgrading of aging equipment.

2. Risk

- disruption to operations;
- systems integration and interfaces;
- availability of internal resources to manage project; and
- ability of the contact center to undertake necessary changes.

3. Financial

- minimum savings of 10 percent off current price; and
- efficiency savings of at least five internal personnel conducting duplicate work in the supply chain.

What many organizations do is a first round elimination, getting rid of options that pose too great of risk without commensurate strategic benefit. The next diagram (Figure 9.9) is an example of this elimination whereby each option was 'scored' against three strategic criteria and five risk cri-teria, creating an options shortlist. The shortlist then progressed to the financial analysis (which takes considerably more time).

The final business case

The final business case then involves determining the net financial result:

1. **The net result of re-tendering:** the estimated savings that would result from a re-tender (typically derived from a brief benchmarking exercise

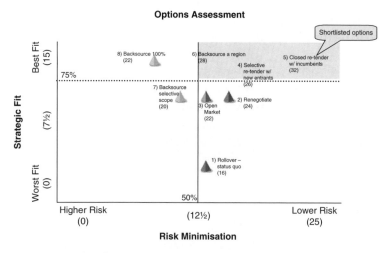

Figure 9.9 Example of options assessment and elimination

```
1.  Executive Summary
2.  Introduction and Background
    2.1.  The commercial imperative
    2.2.  The approach to the analysis
    2.3.  Past and budgeted expenditures
    2.4.  Scope
3.  Options
    3.1.  Options identified
    3.2.  Option modeling and assumptions
          3.2.1.  Extension
          3.2.2.  Re-tendering
          3.2.3.  Backsourcing
4.  Assessment
    4.1.  Key assessment assumptions
    4.2.  Strategic fit criteria
    4.3.  Risk criteria
    4.4.  Results
          4.4.1.  Comparative score
          4.4.2.  Strengths and weaknesses of each option
5.  Financial Estimation
    5.1.  Key financial assumptions
    5.2.  Savings goals and calculations
6.  Recommendation
    6.1.  Recommendation and rationale
    6.2.  Key impacts
    6.3.  Implementation and timeframe
    6.4.  Immediate next steps
```

Figure 9.10 An options analysis outline

or past realized savings experienced with re-tendering), less the cost of preparing the tender documents and the cost of switching providers (including any costs pertaining to the exit from the incumbent and the handover to the new provider).
2. **The net result of backsourcing**: projected savings less the estimated cost to rebuild and any costs pertaining to the exit from the incumbent as well as post-termination support.
3. **The net result of extending**: the estimated savings from the re-negotiation less the cost of the re-negotiation.

The entire analysis then needs to be documented so that someone not involved in the decision can readily ascertain how the decision was made (assuming the decision was made objectively, without any internal agenda!). Below (Figure 9.10) is an example of an outline of such a business case.

Conclusion

Preparing for termination, handover to another provider, or bringing an activity back in-house – all these can seem a very long way off when an organization is still at the highly promising stage of being about to sign what looks like a win–win contract. However, all contracts do terminate, and it is simply good management practice to ensure that there is as little 'devil in the detail' of termination, as there should be in the basic terms of the more active service arrangement with a provider.

Notes

1. See Willcocks, L. and Lacity, M. (2009) *The Practice of Outsourcing: From Information Systems to BPO and Offshoring.* Palgrave, London.
2. The best comparative reference on global government outsourcing patterns and buying behaviour is Dunleavy, P., Margetts, H. Bastow, S. and Tinkler, J. (2006) *Digital Era Governance: IT Corporations, the State, and e-Government.* Oxford University Press, Oxford.

Outsourcing into the Future

CHAPTER 10

Conclusion: Steering a course

Introduction

As this book has made clear, outsourcing is concerned with leveraging the distinctive and evolving capabilities provided by the external services market to achieve business advantage. This concept of outsourcing as a strategic sourcing tool applies in a downturn, and in recessionary times, as much as in periods of economic growth. This is an important point because during the 2007–10 global economic downturn, many organizations found themselves, initially at least, at a loss as to what to do. Many then decided to pass their pain on to incumbent or new suppliers. One lesson is that clients need to learn much better on how to shape and use outsourcing arrangements to ride business cycles, and deal with economic crises. Another lesson is that they should do this in ways that enable the parties to be prepared to take advantage of any economic upturn that then materializes.

In the 2000–03 downturn, outsourcing growth did not slow significantly. Corporates got lucky. Just as IT expenditures had to slow after the heady over-investing of the e-business bubble years, and as business slowed too in most sectors, the global services market produced two genuine safety valves to the downward pressure on costs in the form of increased offshoring (either as outsourced or captive) and the growth of business process outsourcing. And these standbys were still with us, though more matured, more globalized, and facing much more straightened circumstances in the 2007–10 period. Our view is that the wise executive will leverage offshoring and business process outsourcing vigorously in the next few years (through to 2015), not least as ways of managing through a recession that was likely to be with us until at least early 2011. On the positive side, most suppliers had spent 2004–10 driving down their cost base through standardization, and developing more efficient processes and technology platforms, whether on a national, regional, or global basis. Suppliers have also become more sophisticated in their ability to provide better and longer term financing, asset transfer, and lease-back possibilities, though the 2007–10 financial turmoil may have eroded some confidence around terms, stability, and future prospects here.

The big question is: how can client organizations manage their sourcing strategy to harness such service market strengths in ways that look after shorter term recessionary or any other exigencies, while positioning themselves advantageously for any sectoral, or larger, economic upturn? In this last chapter we comment first on initial corporate responses to current difficult times, and outsourcing's role in this, assess the implications of approaches adopted in the last downturn, then show how to steer a course through end-of-decade circumstances into the next five years.

This time it hurt

Between mid-2008 and mid-2010 our ongoing research projects uncovered a range of client behaviors, only some of which were exhibited in previous economic downturns. The shock of the credit crunch and its aftermath saw many clients first pausing – either for reflection, or just stunned – expressed in deferring project decisions, bringing more work in-house, and delaying decisions to commit to new contracts, for example. A strong cost reduction motif was also apparent, seen in deferring and reducing work in current contracts, negotiating down rates in current outsourcing arrangements, looking for dramatic cost cuts in new contracts; looking to reduce the number of independent contractors; reducing the number of suppliers; and looking to offshoring destinations for either cheaper captive or outsourced services.[1] Clients also looked for better and longer term financing, and asset transfer deals as part of their outsourcing arrangements. We saw a number of quick and relatively dirty outsourcing arrangements arrived at that needed to be unraveled at a later date. But sectors responded differently with the more hard-hit main-line banks, for example, pausing in 2008, then many looking to increase expenditure into 2009 and 2010 on banking-specific and finance and accounting BPO as well as applications outsourcing.[2] Our view was that once organizations had stabilized their financial positions and undertaken sourcing reviews, they would do more BPO – to cut costs, shift risks, secure more mature services from the developing services market, and get support for revenue generation. In other words in a recession, BPO would be useful in being able to address business needs that go much further than just cost reduction.[3] And indeed this seems to be, in part, what actually happened.

All this influenced some of the observed behaviors of suppliers. They needed to be sharper than ever on internal cost control, and many made strong pushes on standardization and financial planning (including for clients), and also on innovation that plays into client's short- and long-term challenges. Some offered cheap, even cost-free, transition phases to clients for signing contracts quicker. IT and BPO service companies have been hurrying to build and exploit global delivery resources that are cheap, scalable, and flexible. Many have offered finance options for projects, have been seeking to act as service aggregators, or be deep partners with IT leader firms, and emphasize these deep relationships to clients. Still others have moved to putting emphasis on demonstrating to clients the *business* impact of the IT or business service provided.

At the same time outsourcing is as likely to grow in a recession as it is in time of economic upturn, even though the terms of trade will be different, and the objectives pursued by the client may well have quite different emphases – that could themselves change quite quickly across the course of the deal. During 2008–10 clients showed in their outsourcing practices a strong focus on converting fixed to variable costs and avoiding the higher cost of money. Suppliers offered not just hardware financing but flexible billing and payment options for project work. Asset and software license transfers were seen as attractive ways of keeping cash, while rental extended to a range of services, including application services as sale and lease back programs, emerged. In this respect, the promising spectre of cloud computing had risen to considerable prominence by mid-2010.[4] One had also anticipated a quickening of mergers and acquisitions among suppliers – some of which has already happened. Also one saw clients accelerate the reduction of the number of relationships, together with a streamlining of internal headcount and processes for sourcing management and governance.

These were all pragmatic outsourcing responses to the problem of corporate survival in recessionary times. However, it is important that such practices are not isolated and short term, but form part of a more strategic sourcing approach to dealing with the next five years. What might this look like? We would suggest three key components – develop dynamic strategy; leverage relationships with suppliers; and harness the potential of offshoring and BPO. By way of rounding off this book, and preparing for the future, let us look at these more closely.

Learn from last time, and this – develop dynamic strategy

If we just focus on IT for the moment, the 2000–03 economic downturn saw IT managed in four main ways.[5] In their excellent paper on the subject Leidner et al. (2003) found each CIO tending to take one predominant approach. Nearly half retained their existing long-term IT plans, but stretched out the timeline for development and implementation. A quarter of the CIOs reconsidered the existing IT plan and focused on projects designed to 'bullet-proof' the infrastructure. The remaining CIOs had a more short-term perspective. Some suspended the existing IT plan, assuming continuation once the economy started to recover. Others used the downturn to radically re-evaluate existing and planned applications, and eliminated projects that were inconsistent with the firm's short-term business goals, thereby regaining control over application development and implementation.

One can see here those taking a longer term perspective *assuming,* while those taking a shorter term perspective merely *hoping* for a short period of decline. We can learn from these experiences, but have to accept first that this time it *is* different. The 2007–10 was deeper and would last longer than 2000–03. It also had different causes and proved more difficult to turn around. How then to steer a course? Building on Leidner et al. (2003), and using just IT as our example for the moment we would suggest four main responses (see Figure 10.1):

Short term

'Sweat the Assets' – Prolong life of legacy to survive recession. Shelve infrastructure investments. Cancel new applications portfolio. Large headcount reductions. IT and outsourcing focus on cost-efficiency and legacy alerts.

'Underpin Today's Business' – applications with quick business 'wins' sought. Support current, changeable business plans with IT. Reintroduce cost disciplines lost in growth period. Large cost savings from clear focus. Outsourcing focus on speed, cost, resources, applications development, and maintenance.

Long term

'Slow the (IT) Strategy' – Confidence in 3–5 year plans but slow the speed of delivery and review bi-annually. Maintain strategic investments.

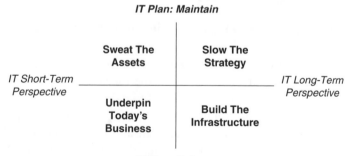

Figure 10.1 IT management in difficult times

Balance cost savings with investment for the upturn. Outsourcing focus on more efficient cost-service deals for commodity IT and services, applications development, and infrastructure build.

'Build the Infrastructure' – Create a foundation for integration so as to 'plug and play' independent and integrated applications. Focus on infrastructure which will be rewarded in the upturn. Regroup on architecture and IT discipline. Go for standardized and lower priced (in a recession) technology and packages. Outsourcing focus on infrastructure development, standardization, and package supply.

However, *this time* the use of these approaches had to dynamic, in combination, and had to depend on where a business was in the economic cycle. We studied 26 client organizations in early 2009 and found just over half had already anticipated the seriousness of the recession by moving to what was in fact a hybrid approach of 'sweating the assets' while 'underpinning today's business'. This reversed client's initial responses of 2000–03. Nevertheless, we did find firms that were in less trouble in their markets sticking with, if slowing their existing strategic IT plans, and some staying committed to existing plans to building their infrastructure. Unlike Leidner et al. (2003) however, this time we came across no organizations reframing their IT plans in order to start rebuilding their IT infrastructure during the recession.

The dilemmas inherent in dealing with difficult times while planning for the long -term come through when looking at the UK government's position in mid-2010 (see Figure 10.2). In early 2010 it launched an ambitious ICT strategy ('smarter, greener, cheaper') with 14 major components, including cloud computing (called the G-cloud), as well as major investments in infrastructure, information, and shared services. At the same time it was clear that major savings needed to be made in IT and back-office costs – estimated at some £36 billion per annum. A Government report of May 2009 suggested these could be reduced by some 30–50 percent by re-engineering, shared services, further or smarter outsourcing, and by offshoring. And these two documents largely frame the future agenda for the UK public sector. Though UK public sector outsourcing exceeded £12 billion in revenues in 2010, a lot more outsourcing was being considered.[6] In Figure 10.2 we try to capture the dilemmas on timing, investment, cuts, and the use of external suppliers faced across the UK public sector over the next five years.

The two short-term responses had to be to 'sweat the assets' and 'underpin todays business' (i.e., service to the public). This would involve extensive use of suppliers, shared services, and redirecting supplier activity in many existing or new contracts. Internal groups, with the help of external service suppliers would also need to embark on major re-engineering programs. On a long-term perspective it may well be that the ICT strategy would need to be slowed, but that a 'spend to save' philosophy would need

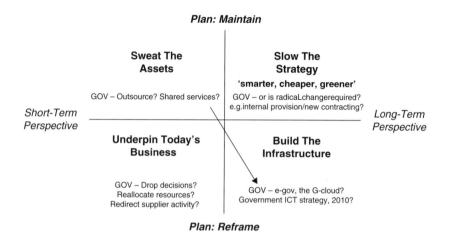

Figure 10.2 UK Government ICT Strategy 2010–15

to be adopted on building the very web-enabled future infrastructure. A part of the latter might well be to move to a variable cost, pay-as-you-go utility or rental model, assuming that cloud computing begins to delivers on its promise over the next five years. Many of the 14 strands have fundamental lower cost, efficiency goals, for example the government's data centre, common desktop, reliable project delivery, and supply management strategies. Others are long-term investments to achieve much more than these goals – for example the greening government, architecture and standards and Government Cloud strategies. There are also investments in the retained capabilities discussed in Chapter 4 – in professionalizing IT-enabled change and supply management. The dilemmas are what to invest in, what to cut, what to standardize, what to maintain as differentiating, and how to leverage the external services market, given that government agencies cannot deliver such an ambitious set of strands by themselves. The economic cycle and the level of government borrowing only raise further issues of timing and sequencing of the delivery of any decisions made. Given the huge budget cuts put in train by the incoming UK coalition government from May 2010, a number of additional twists were introduced. Firstly, the ICT strategy put forward by the previous government would be questioned closely, especially where it involved financial outlay. More seriously, outsourcing would be even more on the agenda, as both a cost and efficiency tactic. But the spend-to-save philosophy detailed in chapter 4 is very unlikely to be adopted. The result? The Achilles heel of large-scale public sector outsourcing is likely to be lack of investment in the key in-house management capabilities needed to shape procurement, strategy and service delivery.

Our own view is that over the next five years client organizations need to steer a dynamic course. Yes, they seriously do need to ensure they adopt the practices we detailed in Chapter 1 on strategy. But additionally they would need to see the four options in Figure 10.1 as a portfolio of possibilities. The preferred starting point in an economic downturn is to 'Slow the Strategy'. The objective here is to balance two major risks – on the one hand not cutting fast enough as revenues go away; and on the other abandoning IT initiatives so quickly that the future is mortgaged. But even in a recession some IT can be cut, using a 'sweat the assets' lens, while other IT needs to be still invested in, including that which 'underpins today's business'. Moreover, after a hard look, organizations will find some strategic investments must still be made, including in infrastructure, even if from 2010, when the recession began to ease. From then, assuming a period of economic growth, it may be that organizations can then focus on 'speed (or refocus) the strategy', changing objectives and investment for different sectoral and global conditions. Staying alive to the issues, including the possibility of IT supporting IT operational, business process, or even business innovation, is also a way of staying alive as a business.

Leverage suppliers: Deeper collaboration, more innovation

Such dynamic strategy must embrace every resource, including leveraging the external services market. All the organizations we have been researching during 2009–10 were planning, or already doing this, and all had several major outsourcing contracts. However, *how* suppliers are leveraged, and *for what*, matters a great deal.

In several chapters in this book we have pointed to the trend of relationships being increasingly leveraged as strategic assets – with more contracting based on values and behaviors, relationship planning becoming more rigorous, and suppliers becoming more entrenched in their client's business. We have noted in our research that suppliers were increasingly being expected to support clients' mainline services, for example identifying new sales and cross-selling opportunities, and becoming a client of the client.[7] We also noted that 'relationship engineering' was becoming more sophisticated. Techniques such as relationship health diagnostics, contract scorecards, team building, developing people and skills for more relationship-orientated roles, were becoming more common (see Chapter 2).

The recessionary climate has provided a strong test for the power of existing relationships. Many organizations looked to reduce and consolidate the number of suppliers, focusing on a model that sees several preferred suppliers, each with distinctive capabilities, for example infrastructure, telecoms, application development and support, help-desk, data processing, accounting and finance, or human resource BPO. Other suppliers would be pulled in as needed, but the relationship would be on a much more transactional basis.

In all this a note of caution is necessary. As we discussed in Chapters 2 and 5, the power-based transactional type of contract and relationship – which many organizations have got sucked into during the 2007–10 economic downturn – can only get you so far. So does screwing supplier margins down to a threadbare level. The 'Winner's Curse' can then arise for a supplier, with the likely consequences as described in Chapter 3. Conversely, for the organizations we studied for Chapter 5, where they have made long-term prior investments in supplier relationships, these seem to have paid off into 2010. Note that these organizations tend to be quite mature in their ability to manage outsourcing, being in their second or third generation, and had undergone hard learning from the 1990s onwards. Relationships with their strategic suppliers tend to be much more collaborative, reflected in the 'partnering-based' practices detailed in Chapter 5. However, it should also be emphasized that in recessionary times, these were being conducted by both client and supplier as hard-nosed, commercial relationships. In Chapter 5 we also noted the more mature clients leveraging what we might call this 'collaborative capital' to go for IT operational, business process and, in some cases market innovation. Examples included Statoil Hydro, Michelin, Vodafone, and KPN. And their executives believed that tough times needed more innovation, not less.

All this becomes possible provided that suppliers have the requisite capabilities. In Chapter 3 we argued that it is fundamental to sourcing strategy for a client to understand both the *capabilities and incapabilities* of suppliers, because this shapes expectations and renders decisions on supplier utilization realistic. What is likely over the next five years is that increasing number of clients will look beyond the delivery competency of supplier – suppliers unable to deliver will not appear on short-lists – and focus much more on suppliers' *Relationship competency* and their ability to help the client to deliver a *transformation agenda*, that is, to deliver radically improved services, or change an entire function, whether it be for example IT, HR, Procurement, Accounting etc. In this respect the next few years may see suppliers focusing, certainly needing to focus, much more on acquiring the requisite capabilities for Relationship and Transformation, as delineated in Chapter 3.

Release the pressure with BPO and offshoring

In some ways, business process outsourcing has had a false start. The potential for radically improving back-office functions has been massive, but a combination of customer reluctance, internal politics, and immature capabilities on the supply side slowed take-up between 1999 and 2005. However, greater competition and maturity in the supply market together with improved buying capabilities in more organizations, and economic disciplines imposed by recession have combined to make BPO a strong candidate for growth over the next five years, if clients only grasp the opportunity. Certainly, as we saw in Chapter 1, the predictions are that this is what is going to happen. BPO expenditure will be in areas such as the human resource function, procurement, back-office administration, call centers, legal, finance and accounting, customer facing operations, and asset management. BPO is outpacing ITO because many executives recognize that they under-manage their back-offices, and do not wish to invest in back-office innovations. Suppliers are rapidly building capabilities to reap the benefits from improving inefficient processes and functions. IT provides major underpinning for, and payoff from, reformed business processes. Thus, many of the BPO deals will swallow much of the back-office IT systems. This is also evidenced by the shift in strategy of traditional IT suppliers like IBM, HP, and EDS to provide more business process services. Suppliers will increasingly replace clients' disparate back-office IT systems with web-enabled, self-serve portals.

The other lever there to be pulled in both difficult and better times is offshoring (either in captive or outsourcing form). And indeed the majority of organizations we have been studying to see more offshoring as very much on their agendas over the next five years – including in the public sectors of an increasing number of countries. The global offshore outsourcing market for IT and business services exceeded $US55 billion in 2008 and some estimates posit an annual growth rate of 20 percent over the next five years, indicating a continuing take-up through the recession. It is common to talk of Brazil, Russia, India, and China as the BRIC inheritors of globalization, with India in particular posting some 65 percent of the ITO and 43 percent of the BPO market in 2008.[8] However, the BRIC countries are not without their problems with Brazil, and China hardly leveraging their potential. Russia lacks government support and is being led into high-value but niche work, while India and China may even be seen turning to non-BRIC locations for some of the solutions, for example to secure low cost and labor availability.

Our recent study[9] suggested a range of second and third tier offshoring venues preparing for business expansion that the recession may well accelerate rather than retard. Recession-bound organizations keen on new sources of value on cost and service may well look here. Where they do so, 'nearshoring' is likely to figure strongly. Nearshoring is defined as outsourcing work to a supplier located in a lower wage foreign country close in distance and/or time zone. Compared to offshore outsourcing, the benefits of nearshoring include less travel costs, less time zone differences, and closer cultural compatibility. In their study of nearshoring Carmel and

Abbott argue convincingly that distance still matters, and point to customers choosing the nearshore option to gain benefit from one or more of the following constructs of proximity: geographic, temporal, cultural, linguistic, economic, political, and historical linkages.[10] They identify three major global 'nearshore clusters' based around clients in (a) North America, (b) Western Europe and (c) a smaller cluster in East Asia.

Many US clients already use Central American suppliers for Spanish-speaking business processes like help desks, patient scheduling, and data entry. In Western Europe, organizations are increasingly sourcing IT and businesses services to providers located in Eastern Europe. For example, the Visegrad-Four Countries (Czech Republic, Hungary, Poland, and Slovakia) offer Western European firms closer proximity, less time zone differences, and lower transaction costs than Asian alternatives. Within these countries there is some movement of outsourcing work to lower cost cities (a trend noticeable in many countries including for example India, China, and rural sourcing in the USA). In sub-Saharan Africa, several countries are actively seeking to become players in the global ITO and BPO markets and building their economies partly on IT. Mediterranean North Africa already exports IT services to Europe and the Middle East. In our study of 14 non-BRIC countries Egypt particularly emerged as top on cost, skills, and market potential.

If the offshoring option is available, it also needs to be approached with care. Clearly the supplier capability analysis outlined above needs to be carried out. But a client can also apply a sixfold framework we have defined to assess location attractiveness, and it has proven very useful:

Cost – labor, infrastructure, taxes

Skills – skill pool, vendor landscape

Environment – government support, business environment, living environment, accessibility

Quality of infrastructure – telecomms and IT, real estate, transportation

Risk profile – security, disruptive events, macroeconomic risks, intellectual property risk

Market potential – captive using local resources, outsourced to local supplier, or as outsourcing supplier to local/regional market.

Our own analysis of non-BRIC countries looking to break free from the pack shows many creating new and profitable outsourcing and offshoring opportunities, capable of development and exploitation even in recessionary times.[11] Their ability to deliver on the opportunities and deal with the related challenges will serve as a foundation for moving further up the value chain, for example in some cases from mainly call centre work to software development and effective R&D. IT and skilled labor shortages in client and supplier companies in Western Europe, North America, and BRIC countries, represent both real opportunities and a set of strong challenges to non-BRIC countries. They point to the need for long-term strategy and investment in education and training, together with attractive employment conditions to draw in and retain skilled labor. The larger issues of environment, risk and legal conformity are driven and policed by governments and this determines the levels of confidence that businesses have to invest. The non-BRIC countries that have provided these are attracting more complex and longer term offshoring and outsourcing contracts.

Retaining core capabilities

Finally, in uncertain, pressured times, a major danger has been erosion of the key in-house capabilities that allow an organization to keep control of its IT and BPO sourcing destiny, while ensuring flexibility and responsiveness in the face of inevitably changing conditions and requirements. In late 2008 we saw organizations cut their workforces by 10–20 percent, with little consideration for the specifics of the skills and capabilities going out of the door. The desire to cut the headcount budget was understandable, but this should never be at the expense of hollowing out an organization's capability to operate on core tasks. We have seen some organizations then declare recruitment freezes, and shift spending into the outsourcing budget to render a fixed labor cost more flexible. As Chapter 4 detailed, our strong finding over 20 years of monitoring, and working in, the outsourcing field, is that retaining key capabilities staffed with high performers with distinctive, specific skills sets, is the single biggest influence on the levels of success achieved. We have also found, historically, that retaining such capabilities has been the single most neglected area in sourcing practice. There has been much progress in this area, as we indicated in our recent study. The worry is that recessionary conditions have caused organizations to regress, and so lose control of their outsourcing arrangements precisely when this can do them most damage, and not put them in a pro-active position for managing possible better times.

Conclusion

Writing in mid-2010, it seemed likely that the global economic recession would only start easing significantly from around early 2011. The key question for clients remained the same as it ever was, namely how to leverage the ever expanding services market for significant business advantage. We have researched and participated in the outsourcing phenomenon since 1989. The common denominator in our own findings is that there is no quick fix; not in periods of growth nor in periods of economic decline. Outsourcing itself is not a quick fix but represents a different way of managing. Much depends on experiential learning and sheer hard work. Back office executives must conquer a significant learning curve and build key in-house capabilities in order to successfully exploit outsourcing opportunities. They need to accept that outsourcing is not about giving up management but managing in a different way.

Getting the perennials right is an essential part of surviving, even thriving, in difficult times. Our first five chapters discussed in detail the management foundations for effective outsourcing. And we also provided four chapters describing key practices. In this chapter we offered an additional framework ideas for steering a course through difficult times while preparing strategically for the next five years. ITO and BPO have grown in the economic downturn, and will continue to grow apace thereafter. Maturing capability among both client and suppliers make outsourcing an important strategic tool for coping with the recession's challenges and uncertainties, and the likely subsequent period of economic growth. It is too early to tell whether cloud computing, or something else altogether, is the 'next big thing' in the outsourcing space. We have written at length elsewhere[12] on the likely trends in global outsourcing over the next five years.[13] But the next big thing is not going to shift the importance of four parts of the recipe for success over the next five years for most organizations. For executives these are:

- Develop a dynamic strategy with business, sourcing and IT objectives and actions closely linked.
- Leverage suppliers through collaboration and look for innovation as well as cost reduction opportunities.
- Reduce the pressure through more BPO and offshoring.

But above all, executives must not lose control of their outsourcing arrangements. Following Machiavelli, that would be steering a course to the wrong place altogether.

Notes

1. See Oshri, I., Kotlarsky, J. and Willcocks, L. (2008) *Outsourcing Global Services*. Palgrave, London.
2. Willmott, J. (2008) *BPO Opportunities in Banking During 2009*. Nelson Hall, London.

3. Willmott, J. (2008) BPO Perspective October 2008. Nelson Hall, London. Also Willcocks, L. and Lacity, M. (2009) *The Practice of Outsourcing: From IT to BPO and Offshoring.* Palgrave, London especially chapter 1.
4. Cloud computing is only touched upon here, though it may represent the early part of a much large transformation in the sourcing landscape over the next decade. Cloud computing is the subject of a major research project being conducted at LSE's Outsourcing Unit during 2010–11, and will be reported on in later publications.
5. Leidner, D., Beatty, R. and Mackay, J. (2003) 'How CIOs manage IT during economic decline: surviving and thriving amid uncertainty', *MISQ Executive*, 2, 1, pp. 1–14.
6. See HM Government (2010) Government ICT Strategy, HMSOs, London.
7. See for example See Willcocks, L. and Cullen, S. (2006) *The Outsourcing Enterprise 2 – The Power of Relationships.* Logica, London
8. Willcocks and Lacity (2009) *The Practice of Outsourcing: From ITO to BPO and Offshoring.* Palgrave, London. The figure is based on various sources, and reflects the more conservative of the estimates given. See also chapter 1 for additional estimates.
9. Willcocks, L., Griffiiths, C. and Kotlarsky, J. (2009) *Beyond BRIC – Offshoring in Non-BRIC Countries: Egypt a New Growth Market.* Hill and Knowlton/LSE, London March.
10. Carmel and Abbott (2007) 'Why 'Nearshore' means that distance still matters', *Communications of the ACM*, 50, 10, pp. 40–6.
11. Details of the framework and examples of its application appear in Willcocks, Griffiths and Kotlarsky (2009) op. cit.
12. See Willcocks, L. and Lacity, M. (2009) *The Practice of Outsourcing: From Information Systems, to BPO and Offshoring.* Palgrave, London.
13. See for example Willcocks and Lacity (2009) op. cit chapter 1, which suggests 12 major trends over the 2009–14 period.

INDEX

Aase, Rune, 142–3
ABNAmro bank, 83, 107
absolute financial scale, 22
Accenture, 152
adaptive work/challenges, 116–19, 124–5,
    147–8, 153–4
adversarial relationships, 110
Africa, 276
agenda perspective, 220
alignment with corporate initiatives/goals, 230
analysis strategy, 35
applications coding, 83
Architect Phase, of outsourcing lifecycle, 8, 31,
    32–6, 233–4
architecture planning and design, 104, 105–6
arms-length relationship, 24, 26
assessments, 239–47
    contract assessment, 239–41
    knowledge refreshment assessment, 239, 244–6
    new requirements assessment, 239, 246–7
    whole-of-life arrangement assessments, 239,
    241–4
asset transfer clause, 241
audit compliance, 242, 243
audits, 173, 202–7

back tweaking, 253
back-office functions
    core retained capabilities for, 101–2, 123
    outsourcing, 274–7
back-office innovation, 150–1
backsourcing, 247, 249–54, 259–60, 262
BAE Systems, 117–18, 134, 149
balance sheet, 60
balanced scorecard, 70–3, 218–19
bank financial guarantees, 205
bargaining power, 7, 9, 10, 76
baseline costs, 60
behavior
    change, 155–7
    drivers of, 54
    management, 77
benchmarking, 224–5, 245–6
best alternative to a negotiated agreement
    (BATNA), 39

best and final offer (BAFO), 38
best-of-breed supplier approach, 21, 81, 82
bestshoring, 83
BH Billiton, 104, 115
bidding
    competitive, 37–8
    evaluation techniques, 96
    facilitation techniques, 94–5
    process, 94–5
    winner's curse and, 91–7
BP, 11–12, 111, 126n7, 149
Brazil, 275
BRIC (Brazil, Russia, India, China) countries,
    83, 275
British Aerospace, 111
British Airport Authority (BAA), 138–41
British Airways, 14
broad suppliers, 83, 84
Browne, John, 11
budget/target measurements, 224
Bunyan, Damian, 157
business activities
    identifying, for outsourcing, 34
    strategic sourcing by, 13, 14–16
business contribution, 230
business innovation, 7, 53
    see also innovation
business management, 77
business process innovation, 134–5
business process outsourcing, 274–7
business processes, 83, 230, 232
business requirements, eliciting and delivering on, 103
business systems thinking, 104, 105

calculation of charges, 206–7
call centers, 16, 83, 276
Capital One, 10
CBA, 115, 122
Central America, 276
chief executive officer (CEO)
    bargaining power of, 7, 9
    challenges for, 46–7
    importance of outsourcing to agenda of, 3–10
    leadership by, 149
    supplier selection process and, 75–6

Index